"The writings of J. I. Packer have been ~~a great help to many~~ believers in many ways. It is therefore most welcome that Sam Storms has synthesized insights from those writings in this helpful, accessible book. I'm sure Pastor Storms agrees that the very best thing about his book would be if it encouraged readers to dive into Packer's works themselves."

Mark A. Noll, Francis A. McAnaney Professor of History,
University of Notre Dame; author, *Protestantism: A Very Short Introduction*

"This is one of the best books on J. I. Packer I have read. It gets to the heart of this great theologian's central concern, what Henry Scougal called 'the life of God in the soul of man.' For those of us who have sat at Packer's feet for many years, this is a delightful reprise and refresher. For new Christians just getting to know Packer, fasten your seat belts!"

Timothy George, Founding Dean, Beeson Divinity School;
General Editor, Reformation Commentary on Scripture

"The most noteworthy feature of this book is the author's ability to assimilate vast quantities of data, condense it, and put it into a systematic format. This begins with a wonderful biographical chapter and then proceeds to Packer's theology. A brief version of the systematic theology that Packer has long promised the world, this book is a triumph of scholarship."

Leland Ryken, Emeritus Professor of English, Wheaton College;
author, *J. I. Packer: An Evangelical Life*

PACKER

on the Christian Life

THEOLOGIANS ON THE CHRISTIAN LIFE

EDITED BY STEPHEN J. NICHOLS AND JUSTIN TAYLOR

Bonhoeffer on the Christian Life:
From the Cross, for the World,
Stephen J. Nichols

Calvin on the Christian Life:
Glorifying and Enjoying God Forever,
Michael Horton

Edwards on the Christian Life:
Alive to the Beauty of God,
Dane C. Ortlund

Luther on the Christian Life:
Cross and Freedom,
Carl R. Trueman

Newton on the Christian Life:
To Live Is Christ,
Tony Reinke

Packer on the Christian Life:
Knowing God in Christ, Walking by the Spirit,
Sam Storms

Schaeffer on the Christian Life:
Countercultural Spirituality,
William Edgar

Warfield on the Christian Life:
Living in Light of the Gospel,
Fred G. Zaspel

Wesley on the Christian Life:
The Heart Renewed in Love,
Fred Sanders

PACKER

on the Christian Life

KNOWING GOD IN CHRIST, WALKING BY THE SPIRIT

SAM STORMS

CROSSWAY

WHEATON, ILLINOIS

Packer on the Christian Life: Knowing God in Christ, Walking by the Spirit

Copyright © 2015 by C. Samuel Storms

Published by Crossway
1300 Crescent Street
Wheaton, Illinois 60187

Cover design: Josh Dennis

Cover image: Richard Solomon Artists, Mark Summers

First printing 2015

Printed in the United States of America

Trade paperback ISBN: 978-1-4335-3952-7
ePub ISBN: 978-1-4335-3955-8
PDF ISBN: 978-1-4335-3953-4
Mobipocket ISBN: 978-1-4335-3954-1

Library of Congress Cataloging-in-Publication Data

Storms, C. Samuel, 1951–
    Packer on the Christian life : knowing God in Christ,
walking by the Spirit / Sam Storms.
        pages cm. — (Theologians on the Christian life)
    Includes bibliographical references and index.
    ISBN 978-1-4335-3952-7 (tp)
    1. Christian life. 2. Packer, J. I. (James Innell)—Teachings.
3. Spirituality. 4. Anglicans—England—Biography.
5. Anglicans—Canada—Biography. I. Title.
BV4501.3.S76283   2015
248.4092—dc23   2014042099

Crossway is a publishing ministry of Good News Publishers.

VP		25	24	23	22	21	20	19	18	17	16	15
15	14	13	12	11	10	9	8	7	6	5	4	3	2	1

To
James Innell Packer

with deep affection and appreciation for a
lifetime of devotion to the glory of God

The older I get, the more I want to sing my faith and get others singing it with me. Theology, as I constantly tell my students is for doxology: the first thing to do with it is to turn it into praise and thus honour the God who is its subject, the God in whose presence and by whose help it was worked out. Paul's summons to sing and make music in one's heart to the Lord is a word for theologians no less than for other people (Eph. 5:19). Theologies that cannot be sung (or prayed for that matter) are certainly wrong at a deep level, and such theologies leave me, in both senses, cold: cold-hearted and uninterested.

J. I. PACKER, *GOD HAS SPOKEN*, 7

CONTENTS

SERIES PREFACE

Some might call us spoiled. We live in an era of significant and substantial resources for Christians on living the Christian life. We have ready access to books, DVD series, online material, seminars—all in the interest of encouraging us in our daily walk with Christ. The laity, the people in the pew, have access to more information than scholars dreamed of having in previous centuries.

Yet for all our abundance of resources, we also lack something. We tend to lack the perspectives from the past, perspectives from a different time and place than our own. To put the matter differently, we have so many riches in our current horizon that we tend not to look to the horizons of the past.

That is unfortunate, especially when it comes to learning about and practicing discipleship. It's like owning a mansion and choosing to live in only one room. This series invites you to explore the other rooms.

As we go exploring, we will visit places and times different from our own. We will see different models, approaches, and emphases. This series does not intend for these models to be copied uncritically, and it certainly does not intend to put these figures from the past high upon a pedestal like some race of super-Christians. This series intends, however, to help us in the present listen to the past. We believe there is wisdom in the past twenty centuries of the church, wisdom for living the Christian life.

Stephen J. Nichols and Justin Taylor

CHAPTER I

PACKER THE PERSON

A Puritan, Theological Exegete, and Latter-Day Catechist

I don't think it an exaggeration to say that I owe much of what I am as a pastor and theologian to the combined influence of a school-yard bully and an inattentive bread-truck driver. Such are the mysteries of divine providence that largely account for the remarkable spiritual influence, not only on me personally but on the whole of the evangelical world, of one James Innell Packer. I'm not alone in this assessment of Packer's impact. The readers of *Christianity Today* identified him as second only to C. S. Lewis when it came to the most influential theological writers of the twentieth century. But how did the bully and the bread-truck driver enter the picture?

For the answer to this question we must go back to September 19, 1933, and the city of Gloucester, England. J. I. Packer was only seven at the time, having been born on July 22, 1926, the son of a clerk for the Great Western Railway. It was from the grounds of the National School in Gloucester that the young Packer was chased by the bully, himself an obviously unwitting piece of the providential puzzle that would ultimately make Packer into the man we know and love him to be. Who knows what was passing through the mind of that bread-truck driver. Were his eyes momentarily distracted by some random event? Was he daydreaming? Or was he fully engaged so that the blame must be laid at the feet of young Packer himself? Regardless, the force of the collision thrust the seven-year-old to the ground, inflicting on him a serious head injury.

Packer was immediately rushed into surgery, where he was treated for "a depressed compound fracture of the frontal bone on the right-hand side of his forehead, with injury to the frontal lobe of the brain."[1] It left him with an indentation on the right side of his forehead, still quite visible today. The accident was "thought to have damaged my brain," wrote Packer.[2] More than eighty years later one can only conclude that, if anything, it served rather to stimulate what we have come to know and appreciate as one of the great Christian minds not merely of the past century but in the history of the church these past two thousand years.

The recovery was not without its inconveniences, as the young Packer was forced to withdraw from school for a period of six months. From that time until he went to university, Packer wore a protective aluminum plate over the injury. Needless to say, this was not the sort of thing that would contribute to a young man's participation in athletics or widespread acceptance among his peers. This only reinforced his tendency to keep unto himself and thrust him into a more secluded life of reading and writing.

When he turned eleven, like most boys his age Packer anticipated a bicycle for a birthday present. But given his parents' lingering and well-justified concerns about their son's head injury, sending him into the streets once again did not strike them as the wisest course of action. Instead, he received an old Oliver typewriter. Once he had overcome his initial disappointment, Packer took to typing with fervor. To this day, notwithstanding the many technological advances we all now enjoy, Packer still writes all his books on an old-fashioned typewriter! I doubt that any of us who have been so richly blessed by his ministry are inclined to protest.

The Packer home was nominally Anglican, and his church attendance, though regular, was spiritually uneventful. On reaching the age of fourteen, Packer consented to his mother's request that he be confirmed in their local church. "Confirmation, as the Church of England understands it, marks the point at which an individual chooses to affirm his or her faith on their own behalf, rather than simply rely on promises made on their behalf at their baptism by their parents and godparents."[3]

The journey to genuine conversion was soon to take several interesting turns, the first of which came in conversations with the son of a Unitarian minister between their regular chess games. Packer, fifteen at the time, was

[1] Alister McGrath, *J. I. Packer: A Biography* (Grand Rapids: Baker, 1997), 1.
[2] J. I. Packer, *Rediscovering Holiness* (Ann Arbor, MI: Servant, 1992), 40.
[3] McGrath, *J. I. Packer*, 7.

not persuaded by his friend's arguments. The notion that Jesus was little more than an ethical model simply made no sense to him. "If you are going to deny the divinity of Christ," said Packer," "which is so central to the New Testament, you also deny all the rest of it. If you are going to affirm that the ethic of Jesus is the best thing since fried bread, well then you ought to take seriously what the New Testament says about who He is. That got me going."[4]

His newly awakened interest in Christianity was deepened upon the discovery of the early works of an increasingly popular author, C. S. Lewis. *The Screwtape Letters* (1943), followed by Lewis's best-selling classic *Mere Christianity* (1944), proved stimulating to Packer. So too were conversations with his friend Eric Taylor, whose own conversion experience left Packer wondering what he himself lacked and how it might be attained.

Upon his arrival at Oxford University in 1944, Packer fulfilled his promise to young Taylor that he would pay a visit to the Oxford Inter-Collegiate Christian Union (the OICCU). On Sunday evening, October 22, 1944, the Reverend Earl Langston was preaching—boringly, according to Packer. But halfway through the sermon something changed. Langston

> started telling at length the story of his own conversion and suddenly everything became clear. I am not a person who gets much in the way of visions or visuals, but the concept called up a picture which was there in my mind . . . that here I am outside of the house and looking through the window and I understand what they are doing. I recognize the games they are playing. Clearly they are enjoying themselves, but I am outside. Why am I outside? Because I have been evading the Lord Jesus and His call.[5]

At the conclusion, as was customary at such meetings, they sang Charlotte Elliot's famous hymn, "Just As I Am." And so, "about 100 feet from where the great evangelist George Whitefield committed himself to Christ in 1735, James I. Packer made his own personal commitment."[6]

Though he was truly born again by the Spirit of God, the struggle for Packer had, in a sense, only begun. The OICCU at that time was under the influence of what has come to be known as Keswick theology, a perspective that we will examine in some depth in subsequent chapters.[7] Suffice

---

[4] J. I. Packer, "The Lost Interview," by Joel Belz, www.worldmag.org, December 7, 2013.
[5] Ibid.
[6] McGrath, *J. I. Packer*, 18.
[7] For an excellent history and critique of this movement, see Andrew David Naselli, *Let Go and Let God? A Survey and Analysis of Keswick Theology* (Bellingham, WA: Lexham, 2010).

it to say for now that this view promised a victorious Christian life solely through an act of faith that leads to total surrender. This decisive moment, in which one wholly yields and trusts the work of Christ within the heart rather than making any effort to overcome the power of sin, was considered the key to Christianity. As Packer's biographer, Alister McGrath, has explained, "The notion of 'active energetic obedience' was thus criticized as representing a lapse into legalism, and a dangerous reliance on one's own abilities."[8]

This not only proved unhelpful to Packer; it was deeply damaging to his spiritual growth. His increasing frustration over the inability to get past daily sins into that promised victory robbed him of the joy of his salvation. He was told that he simply needed to reconsecrate himself, over and over again, until such time that he could identify whatever obstacle stood in the way of the fullness of moral victory.

No less providential than his encounter with the bread truck in 1933 was Packer's discovery of the Puritans in 1944. We today take for granted the availability of Puritan books, largely, and at least initially, due to the publishing efforts of the Banner of Truth Trust. But such was not the case in the 1940s. C. Owen Pickard-Cambridge, an Anglican clergyman, donated his considerable collection of books to the OICCU, over which Packer was given authority as the junior librarian. Packer began the arduous task of sorting through the dusty piles of books in the basement of a meeting hall on St. Michael's Street in central Oxford. There he came upon an uncut set of the works of the great Puritan pastor and theologian John Owen (1616–1683). Two of the titles in volume 6 caught his attention: *On Indwelling Sin in Believers* and *On the Mortification of Sin in Believers*. We will have occasion to explore in some depth the effect of these treatises on Packer's life. For now, it is enough to observe that a major watershed in his spiritual development was this providential discovery. Owen's realistic and thoroughly biblical grasp on the nature of indwelling sin and the believer's Spirit-empowered battle throughout one's earthly existence set Packer free from the Keswick-induced discouragement of soul under which he had been laboring. We will return to this later.

I will not describe much of Packer's academic career, as this has been done in considerable detail by McGrath. Suffice it to say that upon completion of his work at Oxford he took a one-year teaching post at Oak Hill Theo-

---

[8] McGrath, *J. I. Packer*, 23.

logical College in London (1948–1949). His primary responsibility was as an instructor in both Greek and Latin, although he ended up teaching philosophy as well. It was at Oak Hill that Packer discovered his gift for teaching. He was somewhat "shy and withdrawn, lacking in self-confidence; [but] as a teacher, he was seen as caring, competent and considerate."[9]

Of greatest importance during this one-year tenure at Oak Hill was the establishment of the Puritan conferences that ultimately bore considerable impact not only on British evangelicalism during the 1950s and 1960s but also on a more global scale in the West. Together with his friend Raymond Johnston, they made contact with Dr. Martyn Lloyd-Jones, minister at Westminster Chapel in London. During this year Packer was often found listening to John R. W. Stott at All Souls, Langham Place, on Sunday morning, and to Lloyd-Jones at Westminster Chapel on Sunday nights, enough to make even the most privileged of Reformed Christians salivate with envy! The relationship that developed between Packer and Lloyd-Jones, together with the formation of the Puritan conferences, was of massive significance in Packer's personal and professional development. The first conference convened in June 1950 and met annually until the conferences terminated in 1969. Their importance cannot be overestimated. Through them, notes McGrath,

> a rising generation of theological students and younger ministers were being offered a powerful and persuasive vision of the Christian life, in which theology, biblical exposition, spirituality and preaching were shown to be mutually indispensable and interrelated. It was a vision of the Christian life which possessed both intellectual rigour and pastoral relevance. It was a powerful antidote to the anti-intellectualism which had been rampant within British evangelical circles in the immediate post-war period.[10]

Packer then enrolled at Wycliffe Hall, Oxford, with a view toward ordination in the Church of England. There he studied theology from 1949 to 1952, eventually being awarded the degree of Doctor of Philosophy. In December 1952 Packer was ordained a deacon in the Church of England and a year later was ordained a priest at Birmingham Cathedral. He served as a curate at St. John's, Harborne, a suburb of Birmingham, from 1952 until 1954.

[9] Ibid., 36.
[10] Ibid., 53.

There was yet another event of great import that came about, again, by a twist of God's gracious providence. In the late spring of 1952, Packer was asked to fill in at a weekend conference near Surrey. Evidently the original speaker had been inadvertently double-booked. Following his first talk on Friday night, a young nurse approached Packer and informed him that his style of preaching was somewhat similar to another that she greatly admired: Dr. Martyn Lloyd-Jones. Her name was Kit Mullett.

At the Puritan conference in 1952, Kit was present to hear Packer speak. McGrath explains what happened next:

> Noticing Kit and one other woman in the audience, Lloyd-Jones complained of their presence to Packer [the attendance of females at such conferences was unexpected, though not forbidden]. At the time, they were enjoying a cup of tea in the chapel vestry, and planning the next year's conference. "They don't come here to study the Puritans!" he remarked. "They're only here for the men! I know one of them [Kit, of course], she's a member of my church." "Well, Doctor," Packer replied, "as a matter of fact, I'm going to marry her." Packer recalls that Lloyd-Jones's reply was: "Well, I was right about one of them. Now what about the other?"[11]

Following his marriage to Kit in the summer of 1954, Packer served as lecturer at Tyndale Hall, Bristol, from 1955 to 1961, and as librarian and then principal at Latimer House, Oxford, from 1961 to 1970. In 1970 he was appointed principal of Tyndale Hall and became associate principal of Trinity College, Bristol, from 1971 until 1979. After that he moved permanently to Regent College, Vancouver, British Columbia, where he remains at the time of this writing.

The Crisis of 1966 and Packer's Break with Martyn Lloyd-Jones

A defining moment in Packer's relationship with Lloyd-Jones as well as how he was henceforth perceived in the broader evangelical world occurred in 1966. The event has been retold countless times, often with vastly divergent interpretations of what occurred and, more importantly, what it meant.[12] It was October 18, and the occasion was the Second National As-

---

[11] Ibid., 68.
[12] To gain a sense for Packer's own perspective on what occurred, as well as its aftermath, see J. I. Packer, "D. Martyn Lloyd-Jones: A Kind of Puritan" (61–76), and "David Martyn Lloyd-Jones" (77–87), both in *Honouring the People of God*, vol. 4 of *The Collected Shorter Writings of J. I. Packer* (Carlisle, UK: Paternoster, 1999). See also the account provided by his biographer, Alister McGrath, *J. I. Packer*, 116–28.

sembly of Evangelicals, organized by the Evangelical Alliance. At its core was the question "Should evangelicals concerned with doctrinal orthodoxy withdraw from denominations which publicly fail to maintain such orthodoxy, or should they try to reform them from within?"[13]

Lloyd-Jones had become increasingly concerned with the theological liberalism espoused by the World Council of Churches and its ever-increasing presence among certain denominations in the United Kingdom, especially the Church of England. He let it be known that the time had come for the theologically orthodox to "come out" of such denominations. In the absence of agreement on the fundamental issues of the gospel there simply can be no meaningful spiritual fellowship. In his opening address at the assembly Lloyd-Jones issued what many, if not most, understood as an appeal for evangelicals to withdraw from their mixed denominations to form a "pure church" that could unite around orthodox doctrine. Packer was not even present that night, but received the news of this event by telephone at his home in Oxford. John Stott, on the other hand, was obviously concerned that many impressionable younger evangelicals might heed the call and pull out. Immediate intervention was required, he believed, to defuse an otherwise volatile situation. McGrath summarizes Stott's view: the "rightful and proper place of evangelicals was *within* those mainstream denominations, which they could renew from within." McGrath adds, "It is entirely possible that Stott's intervention was improper; he himself apologized to Lloyd-Jones subsequently."[14] In any case, Stott's action "prompted a crisis in itself, in that it exposed a major division within evangelicalism on the opening day of a conference which was intended to foster evangelical unity; nevertheless, Stott reckoned that it had to be done."[15]

Packer sided with Stott, a decision that served to damage not only his friendship with Lloyd-Jones but also his reputation among many in

---

Iain H. Murray has provided insight into the point of view of Lloyd-Jones in *The Life of D. Martyn Lloyd-Jones: 1899–1981* (Carlisle, PA: Banner of Truth, 2013), 375–408. For a helpful analysis of things from Stott's perspective, see Alister Chapman, *Godly Ambition: John Stott and the Evangelical Movement* (New York: Oxford University Press, 2012), 90–111, as well as Timothy Dudley-Smith, *John Stott: A Global Ministry: A Biography, the Later Years* (Downers Grove, IL: InterVarsity, 2001), 65–71. See also the helpful portrayal of this event by Andrew Grills in his article "Forty Years On: An Evangelical Divide Revisited," *Churchman* 120, no. 3 (Autumn 2006): 231–46, http://www.churchsociety.org/churchman/documents /Cman_120_3_Grills.pdf. For more details on the background and the aftermath, see Andrew Atherstone, "Lloyd-Jones and the Anglican Succession Crisis," in *Engaging with Martyn Lloyd-Jones: The Life and Legacy of 'the Doctor'*, ed. Andrew Atherstone and David Ceri Jones (Nottingham, UK: Apollos, 2011).
[13] McGrath, *J. I. Packer*, 119.
[14] Ibid., 124–25.
[15] Ibid., 125.

Britain's evangelical community. His interpretation of the event is best summarized in his own words:

> The Doctor [i.e., Lloyd-Jones] believed that his summons to separation was a call for evangelical unity as such, and that he was not a denominationalist in any sense. In continuing to combat error, commend truth, and strengthen evangelical ministry as best I could in the Church of England, he thought I was showing myself a denominationalist and obstructing evangelical unity, besides being caught in a hopelessly compromised position. By contrast, I believed that the claims of evangelical unity do not require ecclesiastical separation where the faith is not actually being denied and renewal remains possible; that the action for which the Doctor called would be, in effect, the founding of a new, loose-knit, professedly undenominational denomination; and that he, rather than I, was the denominationalist for insisting that evangelicals must all belong to this grouping and no other.[16]

Some believe that Lloyd-Jones destroyed evangelical unity and that Packer and Stott together followed the pathway of compromise. These judgments are almost certainly wrong. In any case, the long-standing friendship between Lloyd-Jones and Packer suffered serious damage. Whatever else may be said of the matter, Packer did not hesitate to continue to speak highly and in virtually reverential terms of the Doctor. "He was the greatest man I have ever known," said Packer, "and I am sure that there is more of him under my skin than there is of any other of my human teachers."[17]

Although Packer remained in England for another thirteen years, Carl Trueman believes the events of 1966 and his break from Lloyd-Jones, together with its aftermath, had much to do with his eventual move to Canada: "In short, he had nowhere to call home: the nonconformists despised him as a traitor; the Anglicans distrusted him. The result: his move to Canada must surely be seen as much as indicating the theological and ecclesiastical poverty of Britain as any positive commentary on North America."[18]

Whatever else may be said of Packer, it seems highly unlikely (at least to this author) that his choice to side with Stott was due to some latent overly

---

[16] Packer, "David Martyn Lloyd-Jones," 79.
[17] Ibid., 77.
[18] Carl R. Trueman, "J. I. Packer: An English Nonconformist Perspective," in *J. I. Packer and the Evangelical Future: The Impact of His Life and Thought*, ed. Timothy George (Grand Rapids: Baker Academic, 2009), 125.

ecumenical impulse. Packer has made it clear on repeated occasions that "compromise of convictions is not the way to godly union; church union is not an altar on which biblical essentials, as we apprehend them, may be sacrificed. Union of churches must rest upon manifest unity of faith."[19]

"A Modest, Christian Gentleman"

I can't recall the first time I met Jim Packer, but each time I was in his presence, I came away sensing that there was something of greatness in him. Of course, Packer himself would bristle at such language. He is, as Trueman aptly describes, "the classic example of a modest, Christian gentleman."[20] Whatever greatness there is in him (and it is there), whatever constructive influence he has exerted on the Christian church (and it has been incalculable), he himself would attribute to the sovereign grace of God working through yet another "clay jar" (2 Cor. 4:7). In our age of Christian celebrity, Jim Packer feels oddly out of place. He is, as best I can tell, entirely devoid of self-promotion. I echo Timothy George's assessment:

> I have seen him buffeted by adversity and criticized unfairly, but I have never seen him sag. His smile is irrepressible and his laughter can bring light to the most somber of meetings. His love for all things human and humane shines through. His mastery of ideas and the most fitting words in which to express them is peerless. Ever impatient with shams of all kinds, his saintly character and spirituality run deep.[21]

Our concern in this book, of course, is with his theology of the Christian life. For those not familiar with Packer, perhaps the most helpful portrayal of his broader theological orientation comes from his own pen. The problem is that he rarely speaks of himself except when pressed to do so. In one place he writes, "I theologize out of what I see as the authentic biblical and creedal mainstream of Christian identity, the confessional and liturgical 'great tradition' that the church on earth has characteristically maintained from the start."[22] But this is somewhat broad and fails to capture the essence of the man. From other statements we may think of him

---

[19] J. I. Packer, "Anglican-Methodist Unity," in *Fellowship in the Gospel: Evangelical Comment on Anglican-Methodist Unity and Intercommunion Today* (Abingdon, UK: Marcham Manor, 1968), 26.
[20] Trueman, "J. I. Packer: An English Nonconformist Perspective," 129.
[21] Timothy George, "Preface," in George, *J. I. Packer and the Evangelical Future*, 11.
[22] J. I. Packer, "On from Orr: Cultural Crisis, Rational Realism and Incarnational Ontology," *Crux* 32, no. 3 (September 1996): 12. For an example of this, see the book on which he collaborated with Thomas Oden, *One Faith: The Evangelical Consensus* (Downers Grove, IL: InterVarsity, 2004).

as a Puritan, a theological exegete, and a latter-day catechist. Here is how he himself put it:

> Rather than identify myself as a fundamentalist, however, I would ask you to think of me as a *Puritan*: by which I mean, think of me as one who, like those great seventeenth-century leaders on both sides of the Atlantic, seeks to combine in himself the roles of scholar, preacher, and pastor, and speaks to you out of that purpose.[23]

Elsewhere he explains:

> My goal [as a Christian theologian] is not adequately expressed by saying that I am to uphold an evangelical conservatism of generically Reformed or specifically Anglican or neo-Puritan or interdenominational pietist type, though I have been both applauded and booed on occasion for doing all these things, and I hope under God to continue to do them. But if I know myself I am first and foremost a *theological exegete*.[24]

Finally, he believes the best way to describe himself is

> as a *latter-day catechist*—not, indeed, a children's catechist (I am not good with children), but what may be called an adult or higher catechist, one who builds on what children are supposed to be taught in order to spell out at adult level the truths we must live by and how we are to live by them.[25]

Of course, no one who exerts such widespread influence emerges in a historical vacuum. Packer is quick to acknowledge the rich heritage that most powerfully shaped his own mind:

> I am the product of a fairly steady theological growth. Starting with the sovereign-grace, pastorally developed theology of Martin Luther, John Calvin, the English reformers, and the evangelical tradition from Puritans Owen and Baxter through Whitefield, Spurgeon, and J. C. Ryle to Pink and Lloyd-Jones, and holding to this as the Western Bible-believer's basic heritage, I have come within this frame increasingly to appreci-

[23] J. I. Packer, "Inerrancy and the Divinity and Humanity of the Bible," in *Honouring the Written Word of God*, vol. 3 of *The Collected Shorter Writings of J. I. Packer* (Carlisle, UK: Paternoster, 1999), 162 (emphasis mine).
[24] J. I. Packer, "In Quest of Canonical Interpretation," in *Honouring the Written Word of God*, 223 (emphasis mine).
[25] J. I. Packer, "Reflection and Response," in George, *J. I. Packer and the Evangelical Future*, 174 (emphasis mine).

ate the patristic fathers, most of all Tertullian, the Cappadocians, and Augustine, and with them Anselm, Thomas Aquinas, and the Oxford Ink- lings. As a result, my discernment of orthodoxy and heresy, my insight into Christ-centered communion with God and obedience to God, and my understanding of transformation by God into the image and likeness of Christ, seem to me to have deepened. Twenty years after my conversion, I remember telling the man who at that time counseled me that honoring and magnifying Christ had become the central concern of my ministry, and forty years further on so it remains. My pneumatology, enriched to be sure by Edwards on revivals and by interaction with charismatics, is still essentially that of John Owen, and though current needs have led me to say much about the Holy Spirit, Jesus Christ—crucified and risen, who is my Lord and Savior, my life and my hope—still stands at the center of my horizon—which surely is how it should always be, for all of us. My overall theological outlook has seen small adjustments but no major changes, and I thank God for the gift of consistency in holding to the things I first embraced, and embrace today, as his revealed truth.[26]

Packer's primary impact has come in the classroom through his train- ing of a multitude of this generation's pastors and theologians, and espe- cially in his voluminous writings. Indeed, as Timothy George has noted, his writings are so extensive, "it is hard to imagine that they have come from the pen of one person."[27] I concur with Trueman that "his writings are among the clearest and most lucid statements of orthodoxy available, lacking both pomposity and that dusty piety that so often weighs down other writers of the neo-Puritan revival."[28] Indeed, this has presented me with something of a challenge insofar as I find Packer's prose to be so lucid and persuasive that I often hesitate to cast myself in the role of interpreter. I have repeatedly found myself reluctant to explain Packer's points and would have preferred simply to quote him extensively. His words, more

---

[26] Ibid., 173. In personal correspondence to Don Payne, Packer wrote, "My theology has no doubt broad- ened its base since 1947 but apart from getting clear on particular redemption in 1953 or 1954 [by read- ing Owen's treatise *The Death of Death in the Death of Christ*] I don't think there has been any change in its structure, method or conclusions. Like Calvin, I was blessed in getting things basically right from the start" (cited in Payne, *The Theology of the Christian Life in J. I. Packer's Thought: Theological Anthropol- ogy, Theological Method, and the Doctrine of Sanctification* (Colorado Springs: Paternoster, 2006), 73. For Payne's excellent portrayal of the historical and theological context of Packer's life and ministry, see 15–49, where Packer's self-identification as an evangelical is rooted in the events of the past 150 years.
[27] George, "Preface," 10. One also thinks of the countless books to which Packer has contributed a fore- word. One could easily compile an entire volume of theological and pastoral reflections based solely on these often overlooked gems. Packer's first publication came in the year after I was born, 1952: "The Puritan Treatment of Justification by Faith," *Evangelical Quarterly* 24, no. 3 (1952): 131–43.
[28] Trueman, "J. I. Packer: An English Non-Conformist Perspective," 128.

than any other contemporary theologian's, speak for themselves and hardly need explanation!

In this biographical sketch I've made much of the obvious role of divine providence in shaping this man whom so many of us have come to admire and love. I can do no better than to cite the observations of Packer's close friend Timothy George. He wonders:

> Peradventure? What would have happened had that seven-year old J. I. Packer not been hit by the bread truck in 1933? Would humanity have gained a champion cricket player and lost a world class theologian? Peradventure. What would have happened had Packer, as a young Christian at Oxford, still seeking his theological bearings, reached into that bin of dusty old books and pulled out not John Owen, but a volume, say, by Jeremy Taylor or Lancelot Andrewes? Would that have lit a fire in his soul for the things of God? Or what would have happened had a beautiful young nurse named Kit Mullet not seen the visiting bachelor curate sitting alone at the lunch table after his presentation at church? What if Mullet had not struck up a conversation with that lonely fellow, a relationship that has led now to more than fifty years of marriage and three children? Did God meet J. I. Packer at the crossroads and direct him in ways that he could not have foreseen at the time? Peradventure. For Philemon 15 must be matched with Proverbs 16:33, which in none of our modern translations quite matches the beauty of the Authorized Version, "The lot is cast into the lap; but the whole disposing thereof is of the Lord." Antinomies everywhere.[29]

Packer's Theological Framework for Christian Living

For J. I. Packer, all theological reflection, to be of value, must issue in holiness of life in which the love of God and his glory are preeminent. Put another way, theology and spirituality are inseparable. This isn't because Packer and other theologians have artificially forged a connection between the two, "but because theology, when rightly understood, leads into spirituality. Theology is to be understood, [Packer] writes, as 'a devotional discipline, a verifying in experience of Aquinas' beautiful remark that theology is taught by God, teaches God, and takes us to God.'"[30] For Packer, theology

---

[29] Timothy George, "Unde, Quonam, et Quemadmodum? Learning Latin (and Other Things) from J. I. Packer," in George, *J. I. Packer and the Evangelical Future*, 164.
[30] Alister McGrath, "The Great Tradition: J. I. Packer on Engaging with the Past to Enrich the Present," in George, *J. I. Packer and the Evangelical Future*, 22–23.

"cannot, and should not, be detached or dissociated from the relational activity of trusting, loving, worshiping, obeying, serving, and glorifying God."[31] "One way of judging the quality of theologies," he explains, "is to see what sort of devotion they produce."[32]

The overall sense Packer has for the nature of Christian living is captured beautifully, and humorously, in his book *Hot Tub Religion*. When searching for an image or metaphor or analogy to summarize the approach of many to Christian living today, Packer landed on the experience one has in a hot tub! Set aside for a moment your struggle with the image of J. I. Packer in a hot tub and let him make his point. As he sat in a hot tub for the first time, it struck him that the experience

> is the perfect symbol of the modern route in religion. The hot tub experience is sensuous, relaxing, floppy, laid-back: not in any way demanding, whether intellectually or otherwise, but very, very nice, even to the point of being great fun. . . . Many today want Christianity to be like that, and labor to make it so. . . . [To this end many] are already offering occasions which we are meant to feel are the next best thing to a hot tub—namely, happy gatherings free from care, real fun times for all. . . . [Thus] when modern Western man turns to religion (if he does—most don't), what he wants is total tickling relaxation, the sense of being at once soothed, supported and effortlessly invigorated: in short, hot tub religion.[33]

He goes on to say that the feelings generated by a hot tub are okay; in fact, they are great! And relaxation and soothing emotions and exuberant celebrations are all permissible within biblical Christian experience.

> But if there were no more to our Christianity than hot tub factors—if, that is, we embraced a self-absorbed hedonism of relaxation and happy feelings, while dodging tough tasks, unpopular stances and exhausting relationships—we should fall short of biblical God-centeredness and of the cross-bearing life to which Jesus calls us, and advertise to the world nothing better than our own decadence. Please God, however, we shall not settle for that.[34]

---

[31] Ibid., 23.
[32] J. I. Packer, "On Covenant Theology," in *Celebrating the Saving Work of God*, vol. 1 of *The Collected Shorter Writings of J. I. Packer* (Carlisle, UK: Paternoster, 1998), 19.
[33] J. I. Packer, *Hot Tub Religion* (Wheaton, IL: Tyndale House, 1987), 68–69.
[34] Ibid., 70.

But Packer is no killjoy! He repeatedly insists that happiness plays an essential role in Christian experience; indeed, he asserts that "real enjoyment is integral to real godliness."[35] But it "comes from basking in the knowledge of the redeeming love of the Father and the Son, and showing actively loyal gratitude for it. You love God and find yourself happy. Your active attempts to please God funnel the pleasures of his peace into your heart."[36] Thus, what Packer advocates is genuine "joy" and not hot tub pleasures. We desperately need to hear his point that joy is always deeper than and never dependent on physical, financial, and emotional pleasure, and how damaging it is ever to equate the two.

Clearly, then, he resists the sort of happiness or pleasure or even joy that comes from egocentricity, which he defines as "unwillingness to see oneself as existing for the Creator's pleasure and instead establishing oneself as the center of everything. The quest for one's own pleasure in some shape or form is the rule and driving force of the egocentric life."[37] Jesus, on the other hand,

> demands self-denial, that is, self-negation (Matt. 16:24; Mark 8:34; Luke 9:23), as a necessary condition of discipleship. Self-denial is a summons to submit to the authority of God as Father and of Jesus as Lord and to declare lifelong war on one's instinctive egoism. What is to be negated is not personal self or one's existence as a rational and responsible human being. Jesus does not plan to turn us into zombies, nor does he ask us to volunteer for a robot role. The required denial is of carnal self, the egocentric, self-deifying urge with which we were born, and which dominates us so ruinously in our natural state.[38]

Packer's Reformed orientation comes to light when he insists that God's ultimate end in his dealings with his children is not simply their happiness but his own glory. The purpose of the Christian life is God's glory, not ours. "He does not exist for our sake, but we for his."[39] Some object to this. Such folk, he acknowledges,

> are sensitive to the sinfulness of continual self-seeking. They know that the desire to gratify self is at the root of moral weaknesses and shortcom-

---

[35] Ibid., 71.
[36] Ibid., 70–71.
[37] Ibid., 76.
[38] Ibid., 77.
[39] Ibid., 36.

ings. They are themselves trying as best they can to face and fight this desire. Hence they conclude that for God to be self-centered would be equally wrong.[40]

Is their conclusion valid? No, says Packer. His explanation deserves careful consideration:

> If it is right for man to have the glory of God as his goal, can it be wrong for God to have the same goal? If man can have no higher purpose than God's glory, how can God? If it is wrong for man to seek a lesser end than this, it would be wrong for God, too. The reason it cannot be right for man to live for himself, as if he were God, is because he is not God. However, it cannot be wrong for God to seek his own glory, simply because he is God. Those who insist that God should not seek his glory in all things are really asking that he cease to be God. And there is no greater blasphemy than to will God out of existence.[41]

In other words, "for us to glorify him is a duty; for him to bless us is grace. The only thing that God is bound to do is the very thing that he requires of us—to glorify himself."[42] This is why "the only answer that the Bible gives to questions that begin: 'Why did God . . . ?' is: 'For his own glory.' It was for this that God decreed to create, and for this he willed to permit sin."[43]

If God's glory is the ultimate aim of all Christian living, God's love for sinners in Christ is its sustaining power. It is this redemptive love that

> generates and sustains the love to God and neighbor that Christ's two great commandments require (Matt. 22:35–40). Our love is to express our gratitude for God's gracious love to us, and to be modeled on it (Eph. 4:32–5:2; 1 John 3:16). The hallmark of Christian life is thus Christian love. The measure and test of love to God is wholehearted and unqualified obedience (1 John 5:3; John 14:15, 21, 23); the measure and test of love to our neighbor is laying down our lives for them (1 John 3:16; cf. John 15:12–13).[44]

---

[40] Ibid., 37.
[41] Ibid., 38.
[42] Ibid., 39.
[43] Ibid., 42.
[44] J. I. Packer, *Concise Theology: A Guide to Historic Christian Beliefs* (Carol Stream, IL: Tyndale House, 1993), 181–82.

The Christian life for Packer can largely be summed up in the single word, *piety*, which in his writings is typically used as a synonym for godliness and holiness. Today the word *spirituality* is more commonly seen, and Packer himself is often found using the two interchangeably. Whereas *spirituality* may encompass virtually all forms of religious devotion, including those not governed by biblical standards, he yet defines it as "the study of godliness in its root and in its fruit."[45] That will be the focus of our attention in the remaining pages of this book.

---

[45] Cited by Payne, *The Theology of the Christian Life in J. I. Packer's Thought*, 11.

CHAPTER 2

THE CENTRAL REFERENCE POINT FOR CHRISTIAN LIVING

Atonement

Why this chapter here? Why atonement first? Why not some other feature of Packer's theology? What relationship does the atoning sacrifice of Christ sustain to the idea and practice of Christian living? Should we not first examine Packer's affirmation of biblical authority as the first principle of Christian living, the inspired resource that governs all of life and thought? Be assured, that is precisely how Scripture functions in Packer's view of the Christian life. And it is only in Scripture that we discover anything of the meaning and saving efficacy of Christ's atoning death. So, am I not guilty of putting the cart before the horse by taking up the issue of atonement before that of biblical authority?

I'm not oblivious to this objection, nor would I be opposed to reversing the order in which these two topics are addressed. But my reason for retaining this sequence is found in Packer himself. Indeed, I would argue that atonement must come first because Packer demands it—not by direct assertion but in the way he conceives of Christ's atoning sacrifice as the foundation and source of everything in one's Christian experience. As far as Packer is concerned, there is but one explanation for why there *is* such a thing as Christian living. It is found in this singular truth: Jesus Christ died for sinners! Nothing in this book or in the theology of J. I. Packer makes sense apart from the fact that God the Son endured and satisfied the wrath of God the Father in the place of sinners who otherwise merit eternal damnation.

We see this, for example, where Packer addresses the very notion of what the words *Christian life* mean and entail. When we speak of the Christian life,

> the noun covers all of our existence—rational and relational, active, reactive, and passive—with all its aims, hopes, fears, joys, dreams, plans, powers, bonds and problems; and the adjective is saying that each part of it, always and everywhere, morning, noon and night, should be shaped by the realities of Christianity.[1]

Packer then repeatedly insists that "the central reference point" (hence the title of this chapter) for everything entailed in Christian living (love, gratitude, adoration, and obedience to God; love, goodwill, care, and service to others; self-denial and self-discipline in vivifying virtues, mortifying vices, and cultivating Christlikeness; etc.) is "Christ's self-offering, bloodshedding, ransom, peacemaking, propitiation and penal substitution, on behalf of us sinners. This cross-centeredness, with its resultant cruciform perception of everything else, is modeled for us in Scripture and then confirmed to us by centuries of Christian life."[2] Penal substitution, the model of Christ's saving death that Packer will vigorously defend, is, in his words, "the mainspring of all their [believers'] joy, peace, and praise both now and for eternity."[3]

The atonement as the central reference point for all Christian living is supported by several statements in Paul's letter to the Galatian church. For example, in Galatians 1:4 the apostle Paul portrays Jesus as the one "who gave himself for our sins to deliver us from the present evil age." In other words, as Packer declares, the atoning death of Christ is "foundational for entry into the new order."[4] He also points to Galatians 2:19–20

---

[1] J. I. Packer, "The Atonement in the Life of the Christian," in *The Glory of the Atonement: Biblical, Historical, and Practical Perspectives: Essays in Honor of Roger Nicole*, ed. Charles E. Hill and Frank A. James III (Downers Grove, IL: InterVarsity, 2004), 409.
[2] Ibid., 410.
[3] J. I. Packer, "What Did the Cross Achieve? The Logic of Penal Substitution," in Mark Dever and J. I. Packer, *In My Place Condemned He Stood: Celebrating the Glory of the Atonement* (Wheaton, IL: Crossway, 2007), 77.
[4] Packer, "The Atonement in the Life of the Christian," 411.

and Paul's statement that "through the law I died to the law, so that I might live to God. I have been crucified with Christ. It is no longer I who live, but Christ who lives in me. And the life I now live in the flesh I live by faith in the Son of God, who loved me and gave himself for me." From this we see that God

> exchanges our sin-serving existence for a Spirit-led existence by incor-porating us, invisibly and intangibly, yet really and truly, into the space-time, trans-historical death and resurrection of our Savior, who now through his indwelling Spirit can truly be said to live in us and shape us as we live our new life in faith-fellowship with him. Atonement—Christ's dying for us—is thus foundational, says Paul, for entry upon the new life—Christ living in us—which is a life totally free from sin's penalty and significantly free from sin's power and ruling over us also.[5]

These few texts alone more than substantiate Packer's argument that atonement is the central reference point for all Christian living. But Packer doesn't stop there. He notes that Paul also links Christ's death to personal holiness, for according to Galatians 5:24, "those who belong to Christ Jesus have crucified the flesh with its passions and desires." This graphic metaphor is designed "to link the crucifying of our 'flesh' with the crucifixion suffered for us by our Savior. Paul is telling his readers that being Christ's by faith through the atonement entails repudiating all forms and fancies of future sinning."[6] Again, "knowing that Christ was crucified as sin-bearer for us, we crucify sin in our personal moral system for him. Atonement, says Paul, is thus foundational to Christian holiness."[7]

Finally, Packer appeals to Galatians 6:14, where Paul declares, "But far be it from me to boast except in the cross of our Lord Jesus Christ, by which the world has been crucified to me, and I to the world." What Paul means is "that because of Christ and the atonement he now repudiates the world's value system as a delusive cheat, while the world repudiates him as a de-luded freak. Atonement, he says, has thus changed his life, and, he implies, should change others' lives in the same way."[8] Without knowledge of the atonement as Paul portrays it, life is not Christian at all. So the atonement,

---

[5] Ibid.
[6] Ibid., 413.
[7] Ibid., 414.
[8] Ibid.

which as we have already seen is for the believer the foundation of faith, the source of freedom, the ground of justification, the spur for sanctification, the theme of witness, the trigger for worship, the warrant for hope and the model for love—is also the litmus test for reality: should we lose sight of the atonement, our Christianity would reduce to hollow externalism, a mere copy of the real thing. This is perhaps the first truth to establish in any systematic reflection on the Christian life.[9]

This is why I do not think it a stretch to say that Packer *demands* this chapter come before all the rest. If we are to *reflect systematically on the Christian life*, to use Packer's own words, this is the first truth to establish. So, I trust that this brief introduction is sufficient warrant for beginning our study of Packer's theology of the Christian life with the loving, sacrificial, atoning death of Jesus Christ for sinners. So we proceed.

The Necessity of Atonement

Why is atonement even necessary? Have we not made too much of sin and wrath? Might we not expect a God who is genuinely loving and compassionate to simply dismiss the charges against us and usher every sinner freely and fully into his kingdom? Why blood sacrifice? Why such suffering? Packer's answer is grounded in his understanding of divine justice, wrath, and the principle of retribution, all of which are essential expressions of the nature of God as God. They are not tangential or secondary realities to be viewed as optional. They are intrinsic to the divine nature and can be set aside only to the detriment of the biblical portrait of who God is. Thus, when we read in Scripture or speak theologically of divine wrath, we do not have in mind "a fitful, petulant, childish thing in God. Wrath is the attribute expressed in righteous judgment. It is holiness rejecting sin."[10] That is to say, wrath is as much a personal dimension of God's character as is his love. It cannot be casually dismissed because some find it offensive, or trumped by another attribute considered more essential. Wrath and justice are not impersonal forces independent of God, but they define the nature of deity itself, no less than do God's power and holiness and compassion and authority, just to mention a few.

---

[9] Ibid., 415.
[10] J. I. Packer, "Sacrifice and Satisfaction," in *Celebrating the Saving Work of God*, vol. 1 of *The Collected Shorter Writings of J. I. Packer* (Carlisle, UK: Paternoster, 1998), 125.

Most modern people, if they care to think about their relationship with God in the least, envision themselves as children of God by creation, by the mere fact that they exist, those who by nature alone are born into God's family and are objects of his affection. They do not realize that we are all, says Paul, "by nature children of wrath" (Eph. 2:3). In other words, people outside the community of faith

> are commonly unwilling to believe that there is in God a holy antipa-
> thy against sin, a righteous hatred of evil, which prompts him to exact
> just retribution when his law is broken. They are not, therefore, prepared
> to take seriously the biblical witness that humanity in sin stands under
> the wrath of God. . . . Some dismiss the wrath of God as another of Paul's
> lapses; others reduce it to an impersonal principle of evil coming home
> (sometimes) to roost: few will allow that wrath is God's personal reaction
> to sin, so that by sinning we make God our enemy.[11]

Therefore, we cannot expect to understand the atonement until we have properly embraced the biblical view of God's justice "as one facet of his holiness and of human willfulness as the root of our racial, communal, and personal sinfulness and guilt."[12]

This truth is so central to Packer's theology as a whole that we should devote some time to its explication. When Packer speaks about the justice of God, he has in mind the idea that God always acts and speaks in perfect conformity and harmony with his own character. To say that God is just is to say that whatever he does is perfectly consistent with whatever his righteous nature requires.

In his reflections on the atonement Packer speaks often of what has been called the *retributive* justice of God, or that which God's nature requires him to require of his creatures. Retributive justice is in view when God gives each of us what we deserve. It is God's treating us according to our deserts. Retributive justice is thus somewhat synonymous with punishment. This is a *necessary* expression of God's reaction to sin and evil. Retributive justice is not something God may or may not exercise, as is the case with mercy, love, and grace. Retributive justice, that is, punishment for sin, is a matter of debt. It is something God cannot refrain from doing lest he violate the rectitude and righteousness of his nature and will. Sin

---

[11] J. I. Packer, "Justification: Introductory Essay," in *Celebrating the Saving Work of God*, 141.
[12] J. I. Packer, "Penal Substitution Revisited," in Dever and Packer, *In My Place Condemned He Stood*, 23.

must be punished. It is a serious misunderstanding of Christianity and the nature of forgiveness to say that believers are those whose guilt is rescinded and whose sins are not punished. Our guilt and sin were fully imputed to our substitute, Jesus, who suffered the retributive justice in our stead. Packer pushes the point:

> Would a God who did not care about the difference between right and wrong be a good and admirable Being? Would a God who put no distinction between the beasts of history, the Hitlers and Stalins (if we dare use names), and his own saints, be morally praiseworthy and perfect? Moral indifference would be an imperfection in God, not a perfection. But not to judge the world would be to show moral indifference. The final proof that God is a perfect moral Being, not indifferent to questions of right and wrong, is the fact that he has committed himself to judge the world.[13]

An excellent illustration of this principle is found in Psalm 103:10. As noted, Packer would define retributive justice as that in God's nature which requires him to deal with us according to our sins and repay us according to our iniquities. But in Psalm 103:10 we are told that God has *not* dealt "with us according to our sins," *nor* has he repaid "us according to our iniquities." Indeed, according to verse 12, we are told that

> as far as the east is from the west,
>   so far does he remove our transgressions from us.

Does this mean, then, that God has simply ignored the righteous requirements of his nature, that he has dismissed or set aside the dictates of divine justice? Certainly not. All sin is punished, says Packer, either in the person of the sinner or in the person of his or her substitute. The only reason why God does not deal with us according to our sins and repay us accordingly is that he dealt with *Christ* and repaid *him* for our transgressions. God's retributive justice was satisfied for us in the person of Christ, who endured the full measure of punishment that the justice and righteousness of God required. This is the core truth in what is known as penal substitution (on which more below).

That attribute in God's character that expresses itself in retributive justice is also called wrath. As noted earlier, some contend that the notion

---

[13] J. I. Packer, *Knowing God* (Downers Grove, IL: InterVarsity, 1973), 143.

of wrath is beneath God's dignity and wholly out of character with what we know him to be. Packer cites the work of C. H. Dodd (1884–1973) in this regard. Dodd envisioned wrath as no more than an inevitable process of cause and effect in a moral universe. Wrath may well be ordained and controlled by God, concedes Dodd, but is clearly no part of him, as are love, mercy, kindness, and so forth.

Clearly, Dodd and others misunderstand divine wrath. It is not the loss of self-control or a celestial bad temper or as Packer says, "an outburst of 'seeing red' which is partly if not wholly irrational."[14] Divine wrath is righteous antagonism toward all that is unholy. It is the revulsion of God's character to what violates God's will. Indeed, one may speak of divine wrath as a function of divine love. For God's wrath is his love for holiness and truth and justice. It is because God passionately loves purity and peace and perfection that he reacts angrily toward anything and anyone who defile them. Packer explains:

> Would a God who took as much pleasure in evil as he did in good be a good God? Would a God who did not react adversely to evil in his world be morally perfect? Surely not. But it is precisely this adverse reaction to evil, which is a necessary part of moral perfection, that the Bible has in view when it speaks of God's wrath.[15]

Leon Morris (1914–2006), to whose defense of penal substitutionary atonement Packer frequently appeals, agrees:

> Then, too, unless we give a real content to the wrath of God, unless we hold that men really deserve to have God visit upon them the painful consequences of their wrongdoing, we empty God's forgiveness of its meaning. For if there is no ill desert, God ought to overlook sin. We can think of forgiveness as something real only when we hold that sin has betrayed us into a situation where we deserve to have God inflict upon us the most serious consequences, and that it is upon such a situation that God's grace supervenes. When the logic of the situation demands that He should take action against the sinner, and He yet takes action for him, then and then alone can we speak of grace. But there is no room for grace if there is no suggestion of dire consequences merited by sin.[16]

---

[14] Ibid., 150.
[15] Ibid., 151.
[16] Leon Morris, *The Apostolic Preaching of the Cross* (Grand Rapids: Eerdmans, 1972), 185.

And, as Packer will argue with relentless appeal to both the biblical text and sound reasoning, the blood shedding of the Lord Jesus Christ was simultaneously the highest expression of God's love and the only way by which the Father's wrath against us might be averted.

Atonement by Substitution

When Packer and others use the word *substitution* to describe the essence of what Christ did on the cross, they mean that one person (Jesus) took action to supply another's (the sinner's) need by discharging her obligation so that she no longer is required to fulfill it by her own effort. But why use the term *substitution* to describe what happened at Calvary? Packer finds help from James Denney (1856–1917) in answering this question. Denney said, "If Christ died the death in which sin had involved us—if in His death He took the responsibility of our sins on Himself—no word is equal to this which falls short of what is meant by calling Him our substitute."[17]

Others have argued that we are served equally well by the word *representative* and thereby avoid the negative implications of referring to Jesus as our substitute. But Packer sees no fundamental difference between the two.

> We identify with Christ against the practice of sin because we have already identified him as the one who took our place under sentence for sin. We enter upon the life of repentance because we have learned that he first endured for us the death of reparation. The Christ into whom we now accept incorporation is the Christ who previously on the cross became our propitiation—not, therefore, one in whom we achieve our reconciliation with God, but one through whom we receive it as a free gift based on a finished work (cf. Rom. 5:10); and we love him, because he first loved us and gave himself for us.[18]

---

[17] James Denney, *The Death of Christ*, 2nd ed. (London: Hodder and Stoughton, 1911), 73.

[18] Packer, "What Did the Cross Achieve?," 77. This is what leads Packer to declare that "the taproot of our entire salvation, and the true NT frame for cataloging its ingredients, is our union with Christ himself by the Holy Spirit. That is, to be more precise, our implantation, symbolized by the under-and-up-from-under of water baptism, into the twin realities of Christ's own dying and rising (see Rom 6:1–11; Col 2:9–12). In this union we have a salvation that is not only positional through the cross in the terms just stated, and relational through our sustained faith-communion with our Lord, but is also transformational through the regenerating and indwelling Spirit, who stirs and motivates and empowers us to express our new hearts' desires in new habits of action and reaction constituting Christlike character ('the fruit of the Spirit' in Gal 5:22–23)" ("The Atonement in the Life of the Christian," 417).

Thus, he explains elsewhere:

> salvation in the Bible is by substitution and exchange: the imputing of men's sins to Christ, and the imputing of Christ's righteousness to sinners. By this means, the law, and the God whose law it is, are satisfied, and the guilty are justly declared immune from punishment. Justice is done, and mercy is made triumphant in the doing of it.[19]

Scripture is clear that the atonement displays God's righteousness (Romans 3). But how can a perfectly righteous God forgive and justify genuinely unrighteous people? The answer is in the provision of a substitutionary sacrifice. Anselm first spoke of this as a satisfaction of God's honor, and that is true. But the Reformers broadened the notion to insist that satisfaction restores God's glory through Christ's enduring all penal retribution for sin. So, yes, sin is punished as it is deserved. But it is punished in the person of a substitute, Jesus Christ.

We must also know that the atonement provided in Christ has the nature of a sacrifice in *blood* (Rom. 3:25; 5:9; Eph. 1:7; Col. 1:20; Heb. 9:11–14; 1 Pet. 1:19; 1 John 1:7; Rev. 1:5–6; 5:9). Some scholars have wondered whether the thought is that "the blood makes atonement for sin by in some way releasing a life-force which re-animates and re-energizes the sinner's relationship with God, which sin has somehow broken." But Packer responds, "That is pure fancy. There is no evidence to back such an idea." Indeed, every

> scriptural analogy and the whole attitude throughout the Old Testament to these animal sacrifices shows that the shedding of blood means the pouring out of life in a death of which the shed blood is witness. It is to exhibit death that the blood is presented at the altar. This alone is the basis on which God promised forgiveness of sin to his Old Testament people when they transgressed. So this alone is the meaning of blood-shedding in sacrifice. It is the laying down of life in death which atones.[20]

Therefore, the significance of sacrifice is not merely the laying down of life in death as such. It is that Christ has given up his life as a substitute in the place of guilty, death-deserving sinners.

Therefore, should someone query as to why Jesus had to die, the answer is not found in the placard placed above his head by Pontius Pilate,

---

[19] Packer, "Justification: Introductory Essay," 141.
[20] Packer, "Sacrifice and Satisfaction," 129.

on which he was mockingly declared to be the "King of the Jews." Rather "the stated cause of sentence and execution which the eye of faith sees is the bond that was our death warrant, which demanded our death for nonobedience."[21]

From all this we rightly conclude that the death of Christ by which men are saved and restored to fellowship with God took the form of a substitutionary sacrifice in blood. But is that all that can be said about the nature of his sufferings? No.

Penal Substitution

It is here that we find Packer at his exegetical and theological best. He is, without question, one of the most cogent and passionate defenders of what has become known as penal substitutionary atonement. By this, as we will shortly see in greater depth, we mean that Christ bore in our stead (there is substitution) the curse or divine retribution (there is the penal dimension) that hung over us as sinners. Packer is surely correct when he insists that this is Paul's final and fundamental category for understanding the cross. Packer goes so far as to suggest that "if the penal character of Christ's death be denied, the right conclusion to draw is that God has never justified any sinner, nor ever will."[22]

But would not this model pit the Father against the Son, severing all unity within the Godhead? Far from it. Packer reminds us that when the Son took to himself human nature and began his life on this earth, "his sense of being the Father's Son was unaffected, and he knew and did his Father's will, aided by the Spirit, at all times."[23] Therefore,

> since all this was planned by the holy Three in their eternal solidarity of mutual love, and since the Father's central purpose in it all was and is to glorify and exalt the Son as Savior and Head of a new humanity, smarty-pants notions like "divine child abuse" as a comment on the cross are supremely silly and as irreverent and wrong as they could possibly be.[24]

Both the Old Testament and the New together bear witness that God's retributive justice falls fully on those whose sins are not covered by a sub-

[21] Ibid., 132.
[22] Packer, "Justification: Introductory Essay," 142.
[23] Packer, "Penal Substitution Revisited," 22.
[24] Ibid.

stitutionary blood sacrifice: in the Old Testament it was the sacrifice of an animal; in the New it is the sacrifice of the true Lamb of God, Jesus Christ. "Penal substitution, therefore, will not be focused properly till it is recognized that God's redemptive love must not be conceived—misconceived, rather—as somehow trumping and displacing God's retributive justice, as if the Creator-Judge simply decided to let bygones be bygones."[25] Both love and justice are equally on display in the death of Christ. It was the love of God that made provision in the Son of God for the justice of God to be satisfied.

So what then is meant by saying that this work of substitution was of the order of a penal sacrifice? Packer explains:

> The notion which the phrase "penal substitution" expresses is that Jesus Christ our Lord, moved by a love that was determined to do everything necessary to save us, endured and exhausted the destructive divine judgment for which we were otherwise inescapably destined, and so won us forgiveness, adoption, and glory. To affirm penal substitution is to say that believers are in debt to Christ specifically for this, and that this is the mainspring of all their joy, peace, and praise both now and for eternity.[26]

To be sure, penal substitution does not attempt to explain the mechanics of how the suffering of one man in time could atone for the sins of many men for eternity. It is, instead, a model that seeks to account for a mystery according to which the remission of my sins and my reconciliation with God came to pass because Christ bore on the cross the penalty that was my due.

Thus Packer builds his biblical case for penal substitution on the assumption of several interlocking truths. First, God's holiness and justice require that rebellion against his perfect law be dealt with retributively, namely, in the suffering of both spiritual and physical death. Second, we humans can do nothing about this. We are helpless to atone for self and are thus wholly at a loss to escape the wrath of God that our sin has incurred. Third, Jesus Christ, the incarnate God-man, has taken our place under judgment and received in himself the penalty that was our sentence, thereby laying the foundation for our pardon and immunity from divine prosecution. Fourth, each human must look in faith outside and away from self to Christ and his cross as the sole ground of forgiveness and future hope.

---

[25] Ibid., 24.
[26] Packer, "What Did the Cross Achieve?," 77.

At the core of this scenario is the assurance that were it not for Christ enduring the penalty we deserved, we would be hopeless. "How it was possible for him to bear their penalty they do not claim to know, any more than they know how it was possible for him to be made man[;] but that he bore it is the certainty on which all their hopes rest."[27] What we do know is that in this saving scenario there exists a genuine solidarity between Christ and those for whom he died.

> We who believe have died—painlessly and invisibly, we might say—in solidarity with him because he died, painfully and publicly, in substitution for us. His death for us brought remission of sins committed "in" Adam, so that "in" him we might enjoy God's acceptance; our death "in" him brings release from the existence we knew "in" Adam, so that "in" him we are raised to new life and become new creatures (cf. Rom. 5–6; 2 Cor. 5:17, 21; Col. 2:6–3:4).[28]

Penal Substitution Is Propitiatory

To better grasp Packer's theology of atonement we should begin by noting that he places all theories or models into three broad categories.

The first includes theories that see *the cross as terminating primarily on human beings*,

> whether by revealing God's love to us, or by bringing home to us how much God hates our sins, or by setting us a supreme example of godliness, or by blazing a trail to God that we may now follow, or by so involving mankind in his redemptive obedience that the life of God now flows into us, or by all these modes together.[29]

In all these theories, our primary problem isn't guilt and the need for forgiveness. That is dealt with as we make ourselves forgivable through a subjective transformation wrought by the example of the cross.

Then, second, are those theories that see *the cross as terminating primarily on the spiritual forces of wickedness*, Satan and his demonic cohorts in particular. Man's plight is primarily the darkness and spiritual bondage

---

[27] Ibid., 84.
[28] Ibid., 86. Penal substitution, then, is a mystery, "a reality distinct from us that in our very apprehending of it remains unfathomable to us: a reality which we acknowledge as actual without knowing how it is possible, and which we therefore describe as incomprehensible" (ibid., 57).
[29] Ibid., 71.

imposed by these forces. As Jesus defeats them, we are caught up in his victory. The forgiveness of sins plays at best a secondary role in the nature of our salvation. First and foremost is the need to be delivered from the forces of darkness that blind, bind, and entangle us. These are the works of Satan from which Christ came to set us free (see 1 John 3:8).

Finally, there are those theories that see *the cross as terminating primarily on God*. The great benefit of this final approach is that it encompasses the other two. It is only because God in Christ has dealt with his wrath against us and has forgiven us our sins that we are genuinely motivated to embrace a new life of humility, love, and service. And whatever influence demonic forces exert over us is itself the result of our guilt and the state of condemnation under which we labor. Thus, "on this view" (Packer's view, I might add), "Christ's death has its effect first on God, who was hereby *propitiated* (or, better, who hereby propitiated himself), and only because it had this effect did it become an overthrowing of the powers of darkness and a revealing of God's seeking and saving love."[30]

Thus, for Paul, this penal substitutionary sacrifice by which Christ bore our penalty and endured the curse of divine retribution for sin is the essence of the atonement. Certainly, Paul "celebrates the cross as a victory over the forces of evil on our behalf (Col. 2:15) and as a motivating revelation of the love of God toward us (2 Cor. 5:14–15), but if it had not been an event of penal substitution, it would not for him have been either of these."[31]

We could put it this way: At the heart of atonement is blood sacrifice. At the heart of blood sacrifice is substitution. And the substitution in view must be penal in nature (that is, involving punishment) if we are to be forgiven of the guilt our sins incurred. And at the heart of this penalty which Christ endured in our stead is the notion of propitiation, which Packer insists is itself the very core of the gospel. "If a query is raised on the grounds that the *word* 'propitiation' appears in the New Testament only four times [see Rom. 3:21–26; Heb. 2:17; 1 John 2:1–2; 4:8–10], the reply must be that the *thought* of propitiation appears constantly."[32] Indeed, so central is this reality to any notion of atonement that a gospel without propitiation at its heart is "another gospel" than the one Paul preached, and thus deserving of his angry "anathema" (Gal. 1:8, 32).

---

[30] Ibid., 72.
[31] Packer, "Penal Substitution Revisited," 25.
[32] J. I. Packer, "The Heart of the Gospel," in Dever and Packer, *In My Place Condemned He Stood*, 42.

What precisely is meant by the term? Some would argue that it is synonymous with "expiation," but Packer demurs.

> Expiation is an action that has sin as its object; it denotes the covering, putting away, or rubbing out of sin so that it no longer constitutes a barrier to friendly fellowship between man and God. Propitiation, however, in the Bible, denotes all that expiation means, *and the pacifying of the wrath of God thereby.*[33]

Of course, many have protested this notion that God's wrath is pacified or his justice satisfied through the sufferings of Jesus. We've already mentioned C. H. Dodd in this regard, who argued, in effect, that there is in God's nature no such thing as anger provoked or elicited by human sin, and thus no need or possibility of propitiation. But anyone who takes the Bible seriously cannot so easily dismiss the reality of divine wrath. It is everywhere present in both Testaments as a personal attribute of God in which his righteousness reacts retributively against all unrighteousness. Propitiation simply, but gloriously, means that this wrath has been quenched by the sacrificial death of Jesus for our sins, whereby he pacified or satisfied God's holy opposition and anger against us. This is why Packer contends that "so far from the manifestation of God's wrath in punishing sin being morally doubtful, the thing that would be morally doubtful would be for him *not* to show his wrath in this way."[34] Which is to say, would a God who could so readily overlook the depravity and callous disregard of righteousness be worthy of our adoration and admiration? The answer is no.

Packer also keeps us mindful that propitiation is always, from first to last, a work of God himself. We do not propitiate God, and never could, not even should we suffer for eternity. Rather, God propitiates himself by his own loving action in Christ.

> The idea that the kind Son changed the mind of his unkind Father by offering himself in place of sinful man is no part of the gospel message—it is a sub-Christian, indeed an anti-Christian, idea, for it denies the unity of will in the Father and the Son and so in reality falls back into polytheism, asking us to believe in two different gods. But the Bible rules this out

[33] Ibid., 32.
[34] Ibid., 35.

absolutely by insisting that it was God himself who took the initiative in quenching his own wrath against those whom, despite their ill-desert, he loved and had chosen to save.[35]

From this Packer concludes that propitiation simply means that God loved the objects of his wrath so much that he gave his own Son (cf. John 3:16), to the end that he by his blood should make provision for the removal of his wrath against them (on this see especially 1 John 4:10).

The Extent of Christ's Atoning Sacrifice

Packer cannot escape the conclusion to which penal substitution invariably takes us, that in his death Christ died for some but not all sinners, namely, those who ultimately are saved by believing in his work for them at Calvary. He explains: "But if Christ specifically took and discharged my penal obligation as a sinner, does it not follow that the cross was decisive for my salvation not only as its sole meritorious ground, but also as guaranteeing that I should be brought to faith, and through faith to eternal life?"[36] This is simply another way of saying that the *nature* of Christ's atoning death controls its *extent*. Packer believes that penal substitution shuts us up to two and only two alternatives: either universal salvation or a definite substitutionary atonement in the place of the elect only. Those who deny this conclusion and contend that penal substitution for all mankind is possible must therefore deny that Christ's vicarious sacrifice ensures anyone's salvation. Why? Because "it is of the essence of their view that some whose sins Christ bore, with saving intent, will ultimately pay the penalty for those same sins in their own persons."[37]

Packer unravels this crucial truth for us in his introductory essay to John Owen's classic treatise *The Death of Death in the Death of Christ*.[38] The point of Owen's treatise and Packer's explanatory introduction is to reaffirm that "Calvary . . . not merely made possible the salvation of those for whom Christ died; it ensured that they would be brought to faith and their salvation made actual."[39] The notion that Christ died to save those who finally perish dishonors both God and his grace.

---

[35] Ibid., 36.
[36] Packer, "What Did the Cross Achieve?," 90.
[37] Ibid., 91.
[38] J. I. Packer, "Saved by His Precious Blood: An Introduction to John Owen's *The Death of Death in the Death of Christ*," in Dever and Packer, *In My Place Condemned He Stood*, 111–44.
[39] Ibid., 120.

It reduces God's love to an impotent wish and turns the whole economy of "saving" grace, so-called ("saving" is really a misnomer on this view), into a monumental divine failure. Also, so far from magnifying the merit and worth of Christ's death, it cheapens it, for it makes Christ die in vain. Lastly, so far from affording faith additional encouragement, it destroys the scriptural ground of assurance altogether, for it denies that the knowledge that Christ died for me (or did or does anything else for me) is a sufficient ground for inferring my eternal salvation; my salvation, on this view, depends not on what Christ did for me, but on what I subsequently do for myself.[40]

Conclusion

In summary, Packer explains how penal substitution theologically explains everything else that God accomplished on our behalf in Christ. Note the following sequence:

What did Christ's death accomplish? It *redeemed* us to God—purchased us at a price, that is, from captivity to sin for the freedom of life with God (Tit 2:14; Rev 5:9). How did it do that? By being a *blood-sacrifice* for our sins (Eph 1:7; Heb 9:11–15). How did that sacrifice have its redemptive effect? By making *peace*, achieving *reconciliation*, and so ending *enmity* between God and ourselves (Rom 5:10; 2 Cor 5:18–20; Eph 2:13–16; Col 1:19–20). How did Christ's death make peace? By being a *propitiation*, an offering appointed by God himself to dissolve his judicial wrath against us by removing our sins from his sight (Rom 3:25; Heb 2:17; 1 Jn 2:2; 4:10). How did the Savior's self-sacrifice have this propitiatory effect? By being a vicarious enduring of the retribution declared due to us by God's own law (Gal 3:13; Col 2:13–14)—in other words, by *penal substitution*.[41]

This, then, is truly the central reference point for all Christian living. Without it as a foundation for our relationship with God, and without the incentive and spiritual strength it gives us to pursue a life of Christ-exalting obedience, there simply is no Christian life. Or at least, none worth living.

---

[40] Ibid., 126.
[41] Packer, "The Atonement in the Life of the Christian," 416.

CHAPTER 3

AUTHORITY FOR CHRISTIAN LIVING

The Role of the Bible

The debate between Martin Luther (1483–1546) and Erasmus (1466–1536) on the nature of the human will is one of the more significant in the history of the Christian church. In the course of the dispute Erasmus declared a deep distaste for Luther's manner of expressing himself in positive and categorical terms. "So great is my dislike of assertions," wrote Erasmus, "that I prefer the views of the Sceptics wherever the inviolable authority of Scripture and the decision of the Church permit."[1] Luther was scandalized by this failure to appreciate the propositional nature of Christian faith and responded to Erasmus in typical fashion:

> To take no pleasure in assertions is not the mark of a Christian heart; indeed, one must delight in assertions to be a Christian at all! . . . Away, now, with Sceptics . . . let us have men who will assert. . . .
>
> Take away assertions, and you take away Christianity. . . .
>
> What Christian can endure the idea that we should deprecate assertions? That would be denying all religion and piety in one breath.[2]

Packer concurs with Luther and insists that

---

[1] Cited by J. I. Packer in "Luther against Erasmus," *Honouring the People of God*, vol. 4 of *The Collected Shorter Writings of J. I. Packer* (Carlisle, UK: Paternoster, 1999), 109.
[2] Ibid.

Christianity is . . . by its very nature an assertive, dogmatic faith. Luther knows, of course, that the world and the church are often bedevilled by a dogmatism which springs from nothing higher than pig-headedness, obscurantism, and sheer superstition, but he disclaims all intention of defending dogmatism of that sort. His point is not that it is never desirable to have an open mind, but simply that on the central issues of the Gospel—the person, place, and work of Jesus Christ, the sola gratia, and the way of salvation—an open mind, so far from being a true expression of Christian humility and self-distrust, is sub-Christian and indeed anti-Christian, for it argues ignorance, both theological and experimental, of the work of the Holy Spirit.[3]

The importance of this brief exchange between the two sixteenth-century giants is that it shows yet again how central to the theology of J. I. Packer is the notion of revealed, propositional truth as we find it in Scripture. Note again: Christianity is by its very nature, says Packer, "an assertive, dogmatic faith." But all such assertions and the dogmas to which they contribute derive first and fundamentally from the written Word of God. Human opinion, cultural trends, personal preferences, together with the discoveries of science, psychology, or whatever intellectual discipline one may cite, have their place, but they are and always will be a distant second to the Bible.

But isn't general revelation enough? Do we need a more direct and personal word from God in the Bible? While acknowledging the reality and importance of general revelation, whether in the visible order of creation (Rom. 1:18–23) or in the conscience of man (Rom. 2:12–16), Packer finds it redemptively inadequate. That is to say, general revelation

indicates that God punishes sin, but not that He pardons it. It shows forgiveness to be needed without showing it to be possible. It preaches the law without the Gospel. It can condemn, but not save. Any unbeliever who rightly understood it would be driven to despair. However clearly the content of general revelation was grasped, it would by itself provide no adequate basis for fellowship with God.[4]

We see clearly that biblical authority is no theoretical issue in the thought of Packer. That the Bible is inspired, inerrant, and authoritative

---

[3] Ibid.
[4] J. I. Packer, *God Has Spoken: Revelation and the Bible*, 3rd ed. (Grand Rapids: Baker, 1998), 55.

over the life of the Christian is of preeminent practical importance in Packer's perspective. It would not be going too far to say that one's view of Scripture quite literally governs and gives cognitive shape to everything genuinely Christian. There is no better illustration of this or more helpful way of introducing the focus of this chapter than an incident in Packer's own life that occurred in June 2002.

"Why I Walked"

The synod of the Anglican Diocese of New Westminster

> *authorized its bishop to produce a service for blessing same-sex unions, to be used in any parish of the diocese that requests it. A number of synod members walked out to protest the decision. They declared themselves out of communion with the bishop and the synod, and they appealed to the Archbishop of Canterbury and other Anglican primates and bishops for help.* [5]

Packer was one of those who walked out.

When asked why he walked out, he answered, "Because this decision, taken in its context, falsifies the gospel of Christ, abandons the authority of Scripture, jeopardizes the salvation of fellow human beings, and betrays the church in its God-appointed role as the bastion and bulwark of divine truth." In other words, it was Packer's confidence in the functional, life-directing authority of Scripture that led to this decision. "My primary authority," wrote Packer, "is a Bible writer named Paul. For many decades now, I have asked myself at every turn of my theological road: Would Paul be with me in this? What would he say if he were in my shoes? I have never dared to offer a view on anything that I did not have good reason to think he would endorse." Again we see that affirming biblical authority is meant not merely to provoke a debate but to give ethical direction to life. Regardless of what personal preferences one might have, irrespective of the cultural trends in play at the time, the Bible is the ethical standard by which Christians such as Packer judge their responsibility.

Packer then proceeds to exegete Paul's thought in 1 Corinthians 6:9–11 as justification for his decision to lodge this protest. There are only two ways in which we might miss Paul's point and his directives. One is to

---

[5] This and subsequent excerpts are taken from Packer's article in *Christianity Today*, "Why I Walked: Sometimes Loving a Denomination Requires You to Fight" (January 1, 2003): 46–50 (emphasis in the original).

embrace an artificial interpretation of the text in which Paul is conceived as speaking of something other than same-sex union. The second approach, notes Packer, "is to let experience judge the Bible." Experience suggests that homosexual behavior is fulfilling to some; therefore, the Bible's prohibition of it is wrong. But the appropriate response is that "the Bible is meant to judge our experience rather than the other way around," and "feelings of sexual arousal and attraction, generating a sense of huge significance and need for release in action as they do, cannot be trusted as either a path to wise living or a guide to biblical interpretation."

What is at stake in such a debate is the nature of the Bible itself. There are, notes Packer, fundamentally two positions that challenge each other:

> One is the historic Christian belief that through the prophets, the incar-nate Son, the apostles, and the writers of canonical Scripture as a body, God has used human language to tell us definitively and transculturally about his ways, his works, his will, and his worship. Furthermore, this revealed truth is grasped by letting the Bible interpret itself to us from within, in the knowledge that the way into God's mind is through that of the writers. Through them, the Holy Spirit who inspired them teaches the church. Finally, one mark of sound biblical insights is that they do not run counter to anything else in the canon. . . .
>
> The second view applies to Christianity the Enlightenment's trust in human reason, along with the fashionable evolutionary assumption that the present is wiser than the past. It concludes that the world has the wisdom, and the church must play intellectual catch-up in each gen-eration in order to survive. From this standpoint, everything in the Bible becomes relative to the church's evolving insights, which themselves are relative to society's continuing development (nothing stands still), and the Holy Spirit's teaching ministry is to help the faithful see where Bible doctrine shows the cultural limitations of the ancient world and needs adjustment in light of latter-day experience (encounters, interactions, perplexities, states of mind and emotion, and so on). Same-sex unions are one example. This view is scarcely 50 years old, though its antecedents go back much further.

The former view Packer calls "objectivist," and the latter "subjectivist."

> In the New Westminster debate, subjectivists say that what is at issue is not the authority of Scripture, but its interpretation. I do not question the

sincerity of those who say this, but I have my doubts about their clear-headedness. The subjectivist way of affirming the authority of Scripture, as the source of the teaching that now needs to be adjusted, is precisely a denying of Scripture's authority from the objectivist point of view, and clarity requires us to say so. The relative authority of ancient religious expertise, now to be revamped in our post-Christian, multifaith, evolving Western world, is one view. The absolute authority of God's unchanging utterances, set before us to be learned, believed, and obeyed as the mainstream church has always done, never mind what the world thinks, is the other.

What are represented as different "interpretations" are in fact reflections of what is definitive: in the one view, the doctrinal and moral teaching of Scripture is always final for Christian people; in the other view, it never is. What is definitive for the exponents of that view is not what the Bible says, as such, but what their own minds come up with as they seek to make Bible teaching match the wisdom of the world.

Each view of biblical authority sees the other as false and disastrous, and is sure that the long-term welfare of Christianity requires that the other view be given up and left behind as quickly as possible. The continuing conflict between them, which breaks surface in the disagreement about same-sex unions, is a fight to the death, in which both sides are sure that they have the church's best interests at heart.

That this is more than an intellectual battle is seen in the spiritual dangers to which the "subjectivist" view ultimately leads. Packer believes that to bless homosexual behavior is an explicit deviation from the biblical gospel and the historic Christian creed. The doctrines of creation, sin, regeneration, and sanctification are necessarily distorted in the effort to justify same-sex intimacy. Worse still, if, as Paul says, those who practice such sexual immorality will not "inherit the kingdom of God" (1 Cor. 6:10), it puts the eternal welfare of the individual at stake. Finally, says Packer, "it involves the *delusion* of looking to God—actually asking him—to sanctify sin by blessing what he condemns. This is irresponsible, irreverent, indeed blasphemous, and utterly unacceptable as church policy. How could I do it?"

Being unapologetically Anglican, Packer also finds in this dispute over the nature of biblical authority a threat to the tradition to which he and so many others over the centuries have been committed. To endorse, in writing, something that Scripture rejects as sin is disastrous. It is one thing to tolerate diversity on matters where Scripture is less than explicit. But "the New Westminster decision writes legitimation of sin into the diocese's constitutional standards." In effect, this is

> a decision that can only be justified in terms of biblical relativism, the novel notion of biblical authority that to my mind is a cuckoo in the Anglican nest and a heresy in its own right. It is a watershed decision for world Anglicanism, for it changes the nature of Anglicanism itself. It has to be reversed.

The manner in which Scripture functions as authoritative in Packer's belief and behavior is best seen in his appeal, once again, to Martin Luther at the Diet of Worms in 1521. Said the Reformer: "Unless you prove to me by Scripture and plain reason that I am wrong, I cannot and will not recant. My conscience is captive to the Word of God. To go against conscience is neither right nor safe [it endangers the soul]. Here I stand. There is nothing else I can do. God help me. Amen." "Conscience," Packer explains, "is that power of the mind over which we have no power, which binds us to believe what we see to be true and do what we see to be right. Captivity of conscience to the Word of God, that is, to the absolutes of God's authoritative teaching in the Bible, is integral to authentic Christianity." He quotes a statement often attributed to Luther (here slightly paraphrased):

> If I profess with the loudest voice and clearest exposition every portion of the truth of God except precisely that little point that the world and the devil are at the moment attacking, *I am not confessing Christ*, however boldly I may be professing Christ. Where the battle rages is where the loyalty of the soldier is proved, and to be steady on all the battlefield besides is merely flight and disgrace if he flinches at that point.[6]

I'm confident I have Packer's heart and mind on this when I say that the issue beneath the issue—namely, the nature and functional influence of biblical authority—is the watershed issue not merely for Anglicanism, but for Christianity as a whole. Everything that follows in this volume on the nature of Christian living is grounded upon and flows out of a belief

---

[6] The oft-quoted statement reflects Luther's ideas as expressed by a fictional character named Fritz in a historical novel by Elizabeth Rundle Charles, *Chronicles of the Schönberg-Cotta Family* (New York: Thomas Nelson, 1864), 276. It also captures the spirit of what Packer believes. See also http://creation.com/battle-quote-not-luther.

that what God has revealed in the written Word is binding on the consciences of all Christians and gives shape to their behavior on every issue, not merely same-sex marriage. Apart from an understanding of this principle, J. I. Packer on the Christian life will prove meaningless.

The Emergence and Development of Packer's View on Biblical Authority

The formative role that Scripture has played in Packer's view of the Christian life is captured most clearly in an interview he conducted with Joel Belz in 2008. Belz accidentally misplaced the recording of their conversation, only to have it resurface some five years later.[7] After being asked how his view of scriptural authority first emerged, Packer responded:

> The touch of God which helped me along that road took place six weeks after I converted. The Intervarsity [*sic*] people ran a Saturday night Bible study, and at this particular Saturday night Bible study an elderly gentleman with some eccentric views about the book of Revelation was speaking. . . .
>
> I think it was the reverence with which this curious old gentleman had handled Revelation 13. Not what he made of it, but it's the way that he squared up to the text—squeezing wisdom out of individual verses and phrases and studying the texts in the context and flow of the argument. I think it was that, though honestly I'm not quite sure. Anyway, something had triggered in me unawares. The Bible makes an impact on me which assures me that it is the Word of God pure. And being so it is bound to be all true and all trustworthy because God is. I think that is the way to say it—it's what Calvin called the witness of the Holy Spirit which I'd been enjoying for those six weeks but hadn't got around to verbalizing. When I got to verbalizing, I realized this isn't what I used to believe. It was a bit of a joke. I've stayed with that ever since and, as you know, stuck my neck out in all sorts of ways through pieces of writing to vindicate that position.

Belz followed up with a question about Packer's embracing of biblical inerrancy, a view not altogether popular or widespread in the United Kingdom at that time.

> If I remember rightly, it was more an assumption among the Intervarsity people than a matter for argument or debate, but it was their assumption. I

---

[7] J. I. Packer, "The Lost Interview," by Joel Belz, www.worldmag.org, December 7, 2013.

have a linear sort of mind, a lawyer's mind. When I believe something, I want to articulate it, so having become aware of it, I believed that the Bible is the Word of God. Yes, I have read some stuff that would help me to articulate it but I don't remember that anyone around me was particularly concerned to do that. Although, of course, in Intervarsity we knew that the other forms of Christianity in the university didn't involve trust in the Scriptures just like that, but in those days I didn't argue with them. That came later.

If Packer is known for anything these days, it is his unflinching stance on the inerrancy of the Bible. But how did he come to invest so much importance in it and so much energy in its defense? His initial contribution came in 1955 when he was asked to respond to criticisms aimed at Billy Graham. Many believed that Graham's affirmation of an inerrant biblical text was anchored in obscurantism and darkness of mind. Packer's written response came in the form of the book that did more than anything else to establish his reputation as a leading proponent of biblical inspiration and inerrancy: *"Fundamentalism" and the Word of God* (1958).[8]

Packer's Doctrine of the Functional Authority of the Biblical Text[9]

There are only three options when it comes to determining one's own belief and behavior. The first is to recognize *the Church as the authoritative guide to discerning God's will.* This is the view of Roman Catholicism. According to this view, "you should approach the Bible as a product of the church and identify mainstream church teaching with the biblical faith."[10] The practical effect is that "what the church says, God says." The second view is that *the individual himself is the final authority.* The Christian may regard his own ideas and imaginations as decisive when it comes to formulating both theology and ethics. "On this view," notes Packer, "Scripture and church teaching are essentially resource material to help us make up our own minds. Both should be known. But neither need be endorsed, for neither is infallible and both include chaff as well as wheat."[11] The principle in

---

[8] J. I. Packer, *"Fundamentalism" and the Word of God: Some Evangelical Principles* (Grand Rapids: Eerdmans, 1958).
[9] The adjective "functional" is intended to suggest that "God's authority in and through the revealed truth of the Bible must ever control and shape our belief and behavior" (J. I. Packer, *Taking God Seriously: Vital Things We Need to Know* [Wheaton, IL: Crossway, 2013], 40). Indeed, "true Christians are people who acknowledge and live under the word of God. They submit without reserve to the word of God written in 'the Book of Truth' (Dan 10:21)" (J. I. Packer, *Knowing God* [Downers Grove, IL: InterVarsity, 1973], 116).
[10] J. I. Packer, *Truth and Power: The Place of Scripture in the Christian Life* (Wheaton, IL: Harold Shaw, 1996), 30.
[11] Ibid., 31.

this case is that "what our own spirit says—that is, our reason, conscience and imagination—God says."[12] But as far as Packer is concerned, the only viable option, the only option that is consistent with the Bible's own testimony regarding itself, is that *Holy Scripture is decisive and authoritative.* Thus, what Scripture says, God says.

Thus Scripture, Packer insists, is the "transcript of divine speech."[13] In his article on "Inspiration," he unpacks the significance of this principle:

> Christ and his apostles quote Old Testament texts not merely as what, e.g., Moses, David or Isaiah said (see Mk. 7:10, 12:36, 7:6; Rom. 10:5, 11:9, 10:20, etc.), but also as what God said through these men (see Acts 4:25, 28:25, etc.), or sometimes simply what "he" (God) says (e.g., 2 Cor. 6:16; Heb. 8:5, 8), or what the Holy Ghost says (Heb. 3:7, 10:15). Furthermore, Old Testament statements, not made by God in their contexts, are quoted as utterances of God (Mt. 19:4f.; Heb. 3:7; Acts 13:34f.; citing Gen. 2:24; Ps. 95:7; Is. 55:2 respectively). Also, Paul refers to God's promise to Abraham and his threat to Pharaoh, both spoken long before the biblical record of them was written, as words which Scripture spoke to these two men (Gal. 3:8; Rom. 9:17); which shows how completely he equated the statements of Scripture with the utterance of God.[14]

This is the unshakeable foundation on which the very notion of authority is built. When Packer speaks of the authority of Scripture, his meaning is that it is the instrument by which God exerts his rule over our lives. Some reject this emphasis on the authority of the Bible out of fear that it would impose illicit restrictions on the individual's personal autonomy. Packer responds by reminding us that there are two ways of conceiving freedom. One "is to view freedom as secular, external and this-worldly. It is essentially a matter of breaking bonds and abolishing restrictions and hardships. It seeks freedom *from* or freedom *not to.*"[15] The second approach is distinctively Christian. Packer explains:

> It is evangelical, personal, and positive. It defines freedom persuasively, that is, in terms which (so it urges) all should recognize as expressing what they are really after. These terms relate not to externals, which vary from

[12] Ibid.
[13] J. I. Packer, *God Has Spoken: Revelation and the Bible*, 3rd ed. (Grand Rapids: Baker, 1998), 28.
[14] J. I. Packer, "Inspiration," in *The New Bible Dictionary*, ed. J. D. Douglas et al. (London: InterVarsity, 1962), 564.
[15] Packer, *Truth and Power*, 21.

age to age and person to person, but to the unchanging realities of the inner life. This definition starts with freedom *from* and freedom *not to*—in this case, freedom from the guilt and power of sin, and freedom not to be dominated by tyrannical self-will—but it centers on freedom *for*: freedom for God and godliness, freedom to love and serve one's Maker and fellow-creatures, freedom for the joy, hope and contentment which God gives to sinners who believe in Christ. . . . This approach sees freedom as the inner state of all who are fulfilling the potential of their own created nature by worshiping and serving their Savior-God from the heart. Their freedom is freedom not to do wrong, but to do right; not to break the moral law, but to keep it; not to forget God, but to cleave to him every moment, in every endeavor and relationship; not to abuse and exploit others, but to lay down one's life for them.[16]

At the heart of Packer's view of biblical authority is his insistence that we never think of Scripture statically but dynamically, that is to say, not merely as something that was spoken or recorded centuries ago but also as something God is saying today. The Bible speaks not merely to men in general but also to each particular person who reads or hears it in the present moment. Thus "Holy Scripture should be thought of as *God preaching*—God preaching to me every time I read or hear any part of it—God the Father preaching God the Son in the power of God the Holy Spirit."[17]

What Packer means by this is that divine revelation in Scripture is intensely personal. Indeed, he insists that the aim of Scripture is to create and sustain a relationship of interpersonal intimacy between God and his children. Whereas modern critics posit an antithesis between "personal" revelation and "propositional" revelation, Packer argues that *if* revelation is to be personal, it *must* be propositional. Revelation is certainly more than simply the communication of information about God, but it can never be less. "Personal friendship between God and man" (and we must never lose sight of the fact that this is the purpose of God's self-disclosure in the Bible) "grows just as human friendships do—namely, through talking; and talking means making informative statements, and informative statements are propositions."[18] This is no theological abstraction but the very foundation on which our reconciliation to God and our knowledge of him are based. How can God truly love us if he never declares it so? "To maintain that we

---

[16] Ibid., 22–23.
[17] Packer, *God Has Spoken*, 91.
[18] Ibid., 52.

may know God without God actually speaking to us in words is really to deny that God is personal, or at any rate that knowing Him is a truly personal relationship."[19]

This principle applies equally to God's activity in history. No event, of itself, can tell us anything definitively about God unless God himself reveals its meaning to us in words. We must rejoice in God's providential ways, confident that he is at work in our world and in our lives individually. But if these happenings are to be of saving value to us, God himself must inform us of them, and he must do so infallibly. All of history is, in some ultimate sense, God's work. But it remains mute and largely useless to us in any practical sense until such time as God talks to us about what it means. As Packer notes, "God's revelation is not through deeds without words (a dumb charade!) any more than it is through words without deeds; but it is through deeds which He speaks to interpret, or, putting it more biblically, through words which His deeds confirm and fulfil."[20]

Why Inerrancy?

Is inerrancy essential to biblical authority? Packer insists most emphatically that it is: "I said at the start that in the realm of belief, authority belongs to truth and truly only. . . . I can make no sense—no reverent sense, anyway—of the idea, sometimes met, that God speaks his truth to us in and through false statement by biblical writers."[21] Again, he explains in some detail why inerrancy is so crucial to any concept of the functional authority of Scripture:

> The importance of recognizing biblical inerrancy as a fact of faith is that, on the one hand, it reminds us that all Scripture is instruction in one way or another from the God of truth. On the other hand, it commits us to consistency in believing, receiving, and obeying everything that it proves to say. The more completely heart and mind are controlled

---

[19] Ibid., 53.

[20] Ibid., 72–73. Again, "no public historical happening, as such (an exodus, a conquest, a captivity, a crucifixion, an empty tomb), can reveal God apart from an accompanying word from God to explain it, or a prior promise which it is seen to confirm or fulfil. Revelation in its basic form is thus of necessity propositional; God reveals Himself by telling us about Himself, and what He is doing in His world" (ibid., 76–77).

[21] Packer, *Truth and Power*, 46. Packer clearly believes that "God's mind must be flawlessly communicated to the human mind in order for the will to be renewed and the imago Dei restored" (Don J. Payne, *The Theology of the Christian Life in J. I. Packer's Thought: Theological Anthropology, Theological Method, and the Doctrine of Sanctification* (Colorado Springs: Paternoster, 2006), 57–58.

by Scripture, the fuller our freedom and the greater our joy. God's free
servants know God and know about God. They observe God-taught
standards and restraints in living and in relationships. They trust
God's promises and in the power of Bible certainties live out their days
in peace and hope. Modern man needs to hear more of this message of
freedom from the church. The church needs to learn again how basic
that message is the truth of the inerrancy of Scripture, on which the
fullness of biblical authority depends.[22]

Thus, once again, biblical *veracity* and biblical *authority* are bound up together. "Only truth can have final authority to determine belief and behavior," says Packer.

And Scripture cannot have such authority further than it is true. A factu-
ally and theologically untrustworthy Bible could still impress us as a pre-
sentation of religious experience and expertise, but clearly, if we cannot
affirm its total truthfulness, we cannot claim that it is all God's testimony
and teaching, given to control our convictions and conduct.[23]

Let's return for a moment to the notion of genuine "freedom" and the
way in which Packer conceives its relationship to the authority of Christ
through his written Word:

True freedom—freedom from blind-mindedness and sin, freedom for
God and righteousness—is found where Jesus Christ is Lord in living personal fellowship. It is under the authority of a fully trusted Bible, however, that Christ is most fully known, and this God-given freedom most
fully enjoyed. Any degree of skepticism about the portrait of Christ, the
promises of God, the principles of godliness, and the power of the Holy
Spirit, as biblically presented, has the effect of enslaving us to our own
alternative ideas about these things, and thus we miss something of the
freedom, joy, and vitality that the real Christ bestows.[24]

This concept of how Scripture functions to exert its authority over the
lives of God's people requires that one put aside any notion of what the individual "prefers" or would "like" to be true. "Let it be said, loud and clear,
that this 'I like' mindset guarantees that all concepts of God that we form by

---

[22] Packer, *Truth and Power*, 53.
[23] Ibid., 134.
[24] Ibid., 55.

our speculation and wishful thinking will be seriously wrong."[25] Packer's appeal is that we turn our back on the world of theological guesswork and dreams, and concentrate wholly on the Bible where God bears witness to himself that we might know him as he truly is.

The effect this bears on the teaching ministry of the local church is massive. Indeed, it is a fundamental characteristic of evangelicalism

> to insist that both the church and the individual Christian must live by the Bible (that is, by appropriate contemporary application of bib-lical principles); that the proper task of the teaching and preaching office that God has set in the church is to explain and apply the Scrip-tures; and that all beliefs, disbeliefs, hopes, fears, prayers, praises, and actions of churches and Christians must be controlled, checked, and where necessary reshaped—*reformed*, to use the good old word—in the light of what God is heard saying as the Spirit brings biblical principles to bear.[26]

Inerrancy, then, is crucial because where it is not affirmed, "Scripture will not all be taken with all seriousness, elements of its teaching will inevi-tably be ignored, and the result . . . is bound to be a certain diminution of supernatural Christian faith."[27]

The Word of God as the Means of Fellowship

As noted earlier, the notion of the Bible's inspiration, together with its in-errancy and functional authority in and over the life of every Christian, is far from a purely theological abstraction. In fact, it serves to create and mediate intimate fellowship between God and the believer. Here is Packer's explanation of this vitally important truth:

> The word which God addresses directly to us is (like a royal speech, only more so) an instrument, not only of government, but also of fel-lowship. For, though God is a great king, it is not his wish to live at a distance from his subjects. Rather the reverse: He made us with the intention that he and we might walk together forever in a love relation-ship. But such a relationship can exist only when the parties involved

[25] J. I. Packer and Carolyn Nystrom, *Praying: Finding Our Way through Duty to Delight* (Downers Grove, IL: InterVarsity, 2006), 21.
[26] J. I. Packer, "Encountering Present-Day Views of Scripture," in *Honouring the Written Word of God*, vol. 3 of *The Collected Shorter Writings of J. I. Packer* (Carlisle, UK: Paternoster, 1999), 6.
[27] Ibid., 19.

know something of each other. God, our Maker, knows all about us before we say anything (Ps 139:1–4); but we can know nothing about him
unless he tells us. Here, therefore, is a further reason why God speaks
to us: not only to move us to do what he wants, but to enable us to know
him so that we may love him. Therefore God sends his word to us in the
character of both information and invitation. It comes to woo us as well
as to instruct us; it not merely puts us in the picture of what God has
done and is doing, but also calls us into personal communion with the
loving Lord himself.[28]

Thus, in Packer's way of thinking, the authority of Scripture must never
be restricted to the notion that God is teaching us what to believe and
thereby putting our minds straight. Most certainly it is that; but it is far
more. It is also a matter of capturing the hearts of his people in order
that they might live in fully committed discipleship to Jesus as Lord.
Says Donald Payne, Packer "believes that humans connect with the person of God through understanding the rational content of the mind of
God. Scripture is so closely allied with God's mind that to know God
personally is impossible apart from the rational content of Scripture."[29]
Payne rightly concludes from this that, in Packer's thought, "inerrancy
forms the basis not only for the possibility of absolutely accurate trans-
mission of information from God's mind to the human mind but also
for the possibility of meaningful obedience to God."[30] Theology, for
Packer, must therefore be motivated and governed by concrete practical
and pastoral intentions.[31]

But how might we have assurance that this written text, which we believe to be inerrant and authoritative, is in fact from God? Here Packer reveals his dependence on Calvin's notion of the *internal witness of the Holy
Spirit*. But of what sort is this "witness" that derives from the Spirit? Packer
explains with characteristic clarity:

The result of this witness is a state of mind in which both the Savior and
the Scriptures have evidenced themselves to us as divine—Jesus, a divine

---

[28] Packer, *Knowing God*, 110.
[29] Donald J. Payne, "J. I. Packer's Theological Method," in *J. I. Packer and the Evangelical Future: The Impact of His Life and Thought*, ed. Timothy George (Grand Rapids: Baker Academic, 2009), 58.
[30] Ibid.
[31] "As I have often told my students," writes Packer, "theology is for doxology and devotion—that is, the praise of God and the practice of godliness" (*Concise Theology: A Guide to Historic Christian Beliefs* [Carol Stream, IL: Tyndale House, 1993], xii).

person; Scripture, a divine product—in a way as direct, immediate, and arresting as that in which tastes and colors evidence themselves by forcing themselves on our senses. In consequence, we no longer find it possible to doubt the divinity of either Christ or the Bible.

Thus God authenticates Holy Scripture to us as his Word—not by some mystical experience or secret information privately whispered into some inner ear, not by human argument alone (strong as this may be), nor by the church's testimony alone (impressive as this is when one looks back over two thousand years). God does it, rather, by means of the searching light and transforming power whereby Scripture evidences itself to be divine. The impact of this light and power is itself the Spirit's witness "by and with the Word in our heart." Argument, testimony from others, and our own particular experiences may prepare us to receive this witness, but the imparting of it, like the imparting of faith in Christ's divine Saviorhood, is the prerogative of the sovereign Holy Spirit alone.[32]

Catechesis and Application

The focus of our study of Packer's concept of biblical authority has been the way it functions to shape both our belief and our behavior. There can be no authentically *Christian* living apart from the Word of God exerting its power over our minds and directing and shaping our wills. This "functional" authority of the Bible is seen, finally, in the way Packer conceives of catechesis and application. A brief word is in order regarding each.

Earlier we saw that Packer self-identifies as a "latter-day catechist."[33] Such language likely strikes the contemporary evangelical as odd, if not unintelligible. What does Packer mean by it, and how does it help us grasp more fully the functional authority of the inerrant Word?

Packer is convinced that the conservative evangelical world is, "if not starving, at least grievously undernourished for lack of a particular pastoral ministry that was a staple item in the church life of the first Christian centuries and also of the Reformation and Counter-Reformation era in Western Europe."[34] He is speaking of the ministry of *catechesis*, which "consists of intentional, orderly instruction in the truths that Christians are called to live by, linked with equally inten-

---

[32] Ibid., 14.
[33] J. I. Packer, "Reflection and Response," in George, *J. I. Packer and the Evangelical Future*, 174.
[34] Packer, *Taking God Seriously*, 10.

tional and orderly instruction on how they are to do this."[35] Contrary to the assumption of many, Christianity is not instinctive to any human being. No one casually and without effort attains to the truths about God and Christ. The Christian "faith" (and here the word "faith" is used objectively, of the normative body of teaching that sets apart Christianity from all rival religious claims) must be learned, and learning requires that someone teach. For this reason Packer insists that some form or strategy for systematic instruction is absolutely essential for healthy church life. He calls this *catechesis*.

Catechesis is simply Packer's word for "discipling." It is designed to show "how right belief requires right living through an active faith that responds to Christ crucified, risen, and enthroned, and that likewise responds to all that is and will be ours in and through him, and to the plans of God the Father that undergird this salvation and this hope."[36] Packer does not insist on any particular method of delivering this instruction, whether through questions and answers or a more direct didactic strategy, such as the traditional lecture. His concern is simply that real learning takes place. Should one inquire of him concerning what content to include, he has developed a ten-point syllabus from which he himself provides instruction:

1. the authority of the Bible
2. the reality of the Trinity
3. the sovereignty of God
4. the tragedy of humankind (sin)
5. the majesty of Jesus Christ, Savior and Lord (life, death, resurrection, return)
6. the necessity of faith
7. the necessity of holiness (life of repentance and good works and thankful praise to God)
8. the centrality of the church[37]
9. the circuitry of communion (the means of grace = Scripture, prayer, fellowship, sacraments)
10. the ultimacy of doxology

[35] Ibid. Packer develops this most extensively in the book he coauthored with Gary Parrett. See J. I. Packer and Gary A. Parrett, *Grounded in the Gospel: Building Believers the Old-Fashioned Way* (Grand Rapids: Baker, 2010).
[36] Ibid., 11.
[37] "No individual may cut loose from the church and act as if he or she is, so to speak, the only pebble on God's beach" (Packer, "Reflection and Response," 180).

Preaching can itself be one form of catechesis, assuming that it is grounded in and governed by the biblical text and not merely an opportunity for the preacher to espouse his own ideas, regardless of how explicitly he may baptize them in biblical language and imagery. Packer simply does not envision meaningful spiritual growth happening apart from the Word explained and applied, for it is in preaching that "the presence and power of God are being experienced. The preaching mediates an encounter not merely with truth, but with God himself."[38]

Consider, for example, what he says about the "application" of the Word in preaching. Would that every man who aspires to teach and preach God's Word might carefully and prayerfully consider Packer's recommendation on how it should be applied. The question we must ask of God's Word expounded and explained is this:

What difference should it make to our thinking, our resolves, our emotional attitudes, our motivation, and our view of our own spiritual state at this moment? More fully: if this principle is truth that God teaches and guarantees, then the following questions arise:

1. What particular judgements, and ways of thinking, does it require of us, and what habits of mind and particular opinions does it forbid us to entertain, and charge us to change if they are part of our life at present? (This is application to the mind.)

2. What particular actions, and what types of virtuous behaviour, does it require of us, and what vicious acts and habits does it forbid, and tell us to renounce herewith? (This is application to the will.)

3. What does it teach us to love, desire, hope for, insist on, and rejoice in, and what does it direct us to hate, abhor, fear, shrink from, and be sad at? (This is application to those emotionally freighted dispositional attitudes that Puritans called "affections.")

4. What encouragements are there here to embrace righteousness, or a particular aspect of righteousness, and persevere in it, and what discouragements are there here to dissuade us from lapsing into sinful habits and actions? (This is application at the level of motivation.)

5. How do we measure up to the requirements of this truth at this moment? And what are we going to do about our present shortcomings here, as self-scrutiny reveals them? And what conformity to the truth's requirements do we find in ourselves, for which we ought to thank God? And how do we propose to maintain and increase that conformity? (This

---

[38] J. I. Packer, "From the Scriptures to the Sermon," in *Honouring the Written Word of God*, 286.

is application for self-knowledge and self-assessment, as a step towards [s]alutary adjustments to our life.).[39]

This is the pastoral and preaching agenda to which J. I. Packer has devoted his entire academic and ministerial career. His aim has been not merely to instruct aspiring pastors, church leaders, and theologians in the principal truth of Scripture, but also to challenge and then lead them into the rigorous and life-changing application of it to all of life. Countless are the men and women, this author included, who have been blessed by his efforts.

---

[39] J. I. Packer, "The Preacher as Theologian," in *Honouring the Written Word of God*, 314–15.

CHAPTER 4

THE SHAPE OF CHRISTIAN LIVING

What Is Holiness?

One struggles to think of an author since J. C. Ryle (1816–1900) and his classic work *Holiness* who has articulated more clearly than J. I. Packer a biblical vision for personal godliness. Whereas Packer is widely known for his views on the inerrancy of Scripture and the sovereignty of God in both salvation and evangelistic outreach, as well as his emphasis on the practical benefits for today's church of seventeenth-century English Puritanism, his greatest contribution may well be his near-exhaustive and thoroughly biblical portrayal of the nature, necessity, and means for growth in Christlike holiness of life. Holiness, Packer insists, is not merely for the clergy or the missionary laboring among an unreached people group, or for those who feel "called" to a uniquely religious life. Holiness is the calling of every Christian and must never be regarded as an optional add-on. It is required of everyone who professes to know Christ. Far from tangential to Christian experience, holiness is itself the goal of our redemption. Thus "holiness, as a sign and expression of the reality of one's faith and repentance, and of one's acceptance of God's ultimate purpose, is genuinely necessary for one's final salvation."[1]

Packer often reminds us that the Christian life is more than merely a physical journey from the cradle to the grave. It is also, and more

---

[1] J. I. Packer, *Rediscovering Holiness* (Ann Arbor, MI: Servant, 1992), 36.

importantly, an inner spiritual journey into the knowledge of God and Christ. Moreover, it is a journey that requires we steer a careful course "between two opposite extremes of disaster. On the one hand, there is the legalistic hypocrisy of pharisaism (God-serving outward actions proceeding from self-serving inward motives), and on the other hand, there is the antinomian idiocy that rattles on about love and liberty, forgetting that the God-given law remains the standard of the God-honoring life."[2]

The proper and more biblically grounded course direction is into ever-increasing conformity to Jesus himself, to live and think and feel and act and react as he did. Jesus is himself the perfect man, the one in whom the image of God is most completely embodied, and our holiness is authentic only to the degree that we are progressively reshaped to resemble him in all ways. Thus, the aim for our lives must be his righteousness in us: his love for the unlovely, his humility in place of pride, his self-denial as over against self-seeking; wisdom and boldness and self-control, together with faithfulness to the Father and strength under pressure—these, says Packer, are among the "good works" (Eph. 2:10) for which we have been both created and, by new birth, re-created of the Spirit.

Defining Holiness

How do we define *holiness?* The term *holy* in both Hebrew and Greek means separated and set apart for God. The word *consecrated* might well function as a synonym. When the word is predicated of humans, it implies both devotion to God in loving and sacrificial service and assimilation to him in the sense that the believer imitates God, pursues Christlike behavior, and is, by the power of the Spirit, gradually conformed to the image of the Son. Packer insists, rightly so, that to be holy one must take God's moral law, as revealed in Scripture, as our rule and God's incarnate Son, Jesus Christ, as our model. Here is Packer's extended definition:

> Holiness is consecrated closeness to God. Holiness is in essence obeying God, living to God and for God, imitating God, keeping his law, taking his side against sin, doing righteousness, performing good works, following Christ's teaching and example, worshiping God in the Spirit, loving and serving God and men out of reverence for Christ. In relation to God,

---

[2] Ibid., 95.

holiness takes the form of a single-minded passion to please by love and loyalty, devotion and praise. In relation to sin, it takes the form of a resistance movement, a discipline of not gratifying the desires of the flesh, but of putting to death the deeds of the body (Galatians 5:16; Romans 8:13). Holiness is, in a word, God-taught, Spirit-wrought Christ-likeness, the sum and substance of committed discipleship, the demonstration of faith working by love, the responsive outflow in righteousness of supernatural life from the hearts of those who are born again.[3]

This notion of Christ-centeredness as one's way of life is at the heart of what Packer understands the Bible to teach us regarding holiness. It is a matter of obeying Christ's commands and listening to his Word, of loving him and seeking to please him. Those who are most committed to holiness think little, if at all, of holiness in the abstract, but rather have set their hearts and minds on Jesus Christ and have established their goals and dreams with their Lord as central and supreme.

How is this love to God and mankind to find expression? "The answer is by keeping God's commands and holding to his revealed ideals for human life—in other words, by keeping his law, as interpreted for Christians in the New Testament. Law keeping out of love is the true path of holiness."[4] We might then sum up this notion of holiness by describing it in terms of transformation through consecration. As one is set apart and unto God by sovereign, saving grace, one is progressively changed from within so that the life without might assume the shape of Christ himself. "So the substance of our holiness is the active expression of our knowledge of the grace that separated us sinners to God through Christ our Saviour and is now transforming us into Christ's image."[5]

Versions of Holiness

Perhaps the most helpful way to get to the heart of Packer's vision for the Christian life is by taking careful note of three principal versions of holiness that he identifies in the history of the Western church: Augustinianism, Wesleyan perfectionism, and Keswick (pronounced Kez-ick) theology.

[3] J. I. Packer, *Keep in Step with the Spirit* (Old Tappan, NJ: Fleming H. Revell, 1984), 96–97.
[4] Ibid., 165–66.
[5] Ibid., 103. We also see that "personal holiness is personal wholeness—the ongoing reintegration of our disintegrated and disordered personhood as we pursue our goal of single-minded Jesus-likeness; the increasing mastery of our life that comes as we learn to give it back to God and away to others" (Packer, *Rediscovering Holiness*, 93).

Augustinianism

Packer himself self-consciously identifies with what he calls the Augustinian model. Its most fundamental principle is that all of Christian living is
initiated, sustained, and consummated by the internal operation of God's
grace. Not only does God in grace elect and redeem the sinner, but his grace,
through the inner operation of the Holy Spirit, enables the individual to
believe in, hope in, and love God and others, worship God, and obey the
divine law as it is revealed in Scripture. Augustine is famous for praying,
"Command what you wish, but give what you command."[6] Packer endorses
this perspective.

The Augustinian approach also places great emphasis on humility. It
insists, Packer explains, "that there is need for *the most deliberate humility*,
self-distrustful and self-suspicious, in all our fellowship with God."[7] Why?
Because God is holy and we are not!

> We were born sinful in Adam, and sinful inclinations, dethroned but not
> yet destroyed, still remain in us now that we are in Christ. We are con-
> stantly beset by the seductions, deceptions, and drives of lawless pride
> and passion, of defiant self-assertion and self-indulgence. . . . So we need
> to get down very low before our Saviour God and to cultivate that sense
> of emptiness, impotence, and dependence that Jesus called poverty of
> spirit (Matthew 5:3).[8]

Clearly, Packer is adamantly opposed to any form of sinless triumphalism.

Augustinianism also insists that there is an ever-present need for conscious activity on the part of the individual in every area of life. Augustine,
and Packer in his wake, is adamantly opposed to any notion of passivity
that undermines the willful engagement of the Christian in resisting temptation and pursuing obedience. It is the very nature of indwelling sin to
make us apathetic, slothful, and reluctant when it comes to those good
works that God has ordained for our lives. There can never be an excuse for
spiritual slackness in the Christian life. Augustinianism, therefore, is the
polar opposite of all forms of quietism or stillness which holds "that you
cannot do anything that pleases God till, over and above the directives of
Scripture and common sense and the calls to action issued by knowledge

---

[6] Augustine, *Confessions*, trans. R. S. Pine-Coffin (New York: Penguin, 1961), 40 (10.29).
[7] Packer, *Keep in Step with the Spirit*, 124.
[8] Ibid., 124. On this theme in Packer, see *Weakness Is the Way* (Wheaton, IL: Crossway, 2013).

of your neighbor's needs, you have a specific inward urge from the Spirit to make a move."[9]

Packer insists on what he calls "the reality of spiritual change," in which there is substantive growth and moral advancement. By God's grace the believer is energized to obey, to put to death the deeds of the flesh (Packer and the Puritans before him prefer the term *mortification* of sin), and to move ever onward in progressive growth into Christlikeness. Thus Augustinians

> see God's work of grace as first renewing the heart and then progressively changing the whole person, from the inside out, so to speak, into the image of Jesus in humility and love. So they expect Christians to show forth increasingly the fruit of the Spirit, however contrary these character qualities might be to their natural temperament and inclination.[10]

Although they reject any form of sinless perfection in this life, Augustinians like Packer expect Christians to experience victory over the variety of temptations that come our way and by the Spirit's power to "mortify" the deeds of the body (see Rom. 8:13; Col. 3:5). The goal, though never achieved in perfect consummation in this life, is "to drain the life out of besetting sins, so that they beset no longer."[11] Essential to this view of holiness is the belief that in Romans 7:14–25, Paul is providing an account of his personal experience with God's law at the time of writing. I will devote all of chapter 6 to Packer's view of this text.

There are several other important features of this version of holiness. For example, the Augustinian perspective is uncompromising in its emphasis on God's moral law as setting the standard by which the family of God is to be governed. Also, as noted earlier, this view is very realistic about what we can attain in this life, resisting any form of this-life perfectionism. However, this does not diminish the expectation that God will provide help to face each day's challenges and strength for obedience to what he has required of us.

Wesleyan Perfectionism

Wesleyan perfectionism, a second version of holiness, provokes Packer's strong opposition, despite his appreciation of Wesley in many ways.[12]

---

[9] Packer, *Keep in Step with the Spirit*, 125.
[10] Ibid., 126.
[11] Ibid.
[12] For more on Packer's thoughts on Wesley, see his largely positive assessment in "The Glory of God and the Reviving of Religion: A Study in the Mind of Jonathan Edwards," in *A God Entranced*

Packer finds no biblical evidence for a second transforming work of grace, distinct from and ordinarily subsequent to the new birth.[13] According to Wesley's vision of the Christian life, God roots out of a Christian's heart all sinful motivation with the result that the whole of one's mental and emotional energy is redirected into love for others and for God. The Christian is henceforth free from any contrary or competing affections. Packer argues that Wesley himself came to believe that

> perfection, understood as a state of heart in which love to God and man is all (a state to which in any case the Holy Spirit will bring believers when they leave the body at death), may be wrought instantaneously in us in this life through our exercise of the same kind of insistent, expectant, empty-handed, full-blooded, promise-claiming faith as was previously the means of our justification.[14]

Contrary to popular misconceptions of what Wesley taught, this isn't absolute and irrevocable sinlessness. Rather, it is the experience of perfect love, "not, that is, as 'Adamic' or 'angelic' faultlessness, but as advance into and then within, the state of concentrated, integrated, passionate, resolute godliness for which mankind was both made and redeemed." Perfection, as Wesley would have it,

> is a state, but it is not static; it is a state of wholeheartedly going on with God in obedient worship and service that are fueled by love and love alone. It is, in essence, a quality of inward life rather than of outward performance. One who is perfect in Wesley's sense may still lack knowledge, err in judgment, and hence act foolishly.[15]

So why does Packer not find this persuasive? First, it lacks biblical proof. The scriptural texts to which Wesley appeals are either promises of what God will yet do in and for his people in the future, at the consumma-

---

Vision of All Things: The Legacy of Jonathan Edwards, ed. John Piper and Justin Taylor (Wheaton, IL: Crossway, 2004), 82–86.

[13] Nevertheless, Packer does say: "That, in God's mercy, momentous post-conversion experiences come to some Christians, bringing assurance, liberty of heart, new spiritual joy and energy, with new power for life and witness, is beyond doubt. These, however, seem to be the particular discretionary dealings of a gracious heavenly Father with his individual children. They are not universal requirements, not prescribed patterns of experience for all, not hoops through which every Christian must try to jump. Those who have had no momentous 'second experience,' therefore, should not see themselves as necessarily inferior to those who have been thus blessed. History confirms that some of God's finest servants have been enriched in this way, while others, equally fine, have not" (*Rediscovering Holiness*, 112).

[14] Packer, *Keep in Step with the Spirit*, 135.

[15] Ibid.

tion of the age and glorification of the body, or statements about one's very real deliverance from sin in the present, partial though it be. Packer also believes that Wesley's system proffers an unrealistic theological rationale. As he explains, if sin is a "thing" that must be rooted out of a person, "it ought to be impossible for a 'perfect' or . . . 'sanctified' person to be 'lured and enticed by his own desire' in temptation (James 1:13–15); for whence can come such desire—inordinate, unloving, self-serving, God flouting— when sin, according to the theory, has been rooted out of him."[16]

Packer also finds the practical implications of this view to be un- edifying. He rightly asks how Christians can be realistic about their continual struggles with sin when they believe sin has already and alto- gether been rooted out of them. Such a view would require an idealistic detachment from the real world and a constant battle with cognitive dis- sonance. When one's view of oneself (and of others) doesn't measure up to the heartaches, failures, and relational tensions that life invariably brings, the resultant distress and confusion can be devastating. Finally, there simply is no way to reconcile Wesley's vision of holiness with Paul's all-too-realistic assessment of his condition as a mature Christian man as found in Romans 7:14–25.

Keswick Theology

So, while he rejects Wesleyan perfectionism, might there be something of a theological halfway house that Packer finds more appealing? Early in his Christian life he encountered what initially promised the very remedy he so desperately desired. But Keswick theology ultimately failed in every way. And what precisely is Keswick theology?

According to the Keswick version of holiness, each believer may enter upon a "higher life" in which, "though one's sinful heart remained as it was before, the down drag of wrong desire and moral weakness is effec- tively nullified."[17] The faith by which this is attained entails a passivity in which one deliberately does nothing. A person simply "rests" in the power of Christ as he works his way in him or her through the Holy Spirit.

There is certainly a surface appeal in Keswick theology: it appears to promise that through an act of self-renunciation, surrender, and whole- souled faith, one can be elevated beyond the daily struggle with personal

[16] Ibid., 141.
[17] Ibid., 146.

sin and temptation. As we saw in an earlier chapter, Packer's encounter with John Owen awakened him to the fact that the Christian life is an ongoing, daily struggle with indwelling sin, not a passive yielding in which one renounces effort altogether. Owen's approach was realistic and relieved Packer of the pressure of attaining to this higher life of holiness. The Christian life, therefore, is pursued not by a passive reliance on the Holy Spirit but through obedience in an ongoing battle with indwelling sin.

According to Donald Payne,

> the Keswick movement propagated a piety in which conscious struggle aimed directly against sin or at Christian maturity is seen as a rejection of God's grace for the Christian life and, consequently, ill-fated. The focus of Keswick piety is a direct reliance on the Holy Spirit to carry one through struggles with temptation and sin, with the promise that when every area of life has been completely surrendered to God, one can experience a regular sense of victory over those struggles.[18]

But Packer, largely through the influence of Owen, came to see that sanctification "is experienced . . . not as a gift to be received by a passive act of faith, but by trusting engagement of the regenerated will in active obedience as the will is empowered by the Holy Spirit."[19]

Packer identifies one of the principal difficulties for Keswick adherents, namely, their *understanding of Christian faith.*

> What they meant by faith . . . was, first, believing consciously and persistently that one is indeed dead to sin and alive to God; second, relying consciously and persistently on Christ through the Holy Spirit to defeat sin and prompt righteousness in one's life on a moment-by-moment basis; and third, making specific use of the Spirit's power in every temptation to evil by specifically asking Christ to raise one and keep one raised above that temptation.[20]

Thus, any effort on the part of the individual will fail. Consequently, and wrongly so, they condemned all conscious exertion toward obedience on the part of the believer as indicative of self-reliance, and all effort to do right as the work of the flesh. Thus, says Packer,

---

[18] Don J. Payne, *The Theology of the Christian Life in J. I. Packer's Thought: Theological Anthropology, Theological Method, and the Doctrine of Sanctification* (Colorado Springs: Paternoster, 2006), 77n11.
[19] Ibid., 103.
[20] Packer, *Keep in Step with the Spirit*, 147.

if when sinful urges come, you set yourself to resist them directly (they said), you will be beaten by them, but if you hand them over to Christ to defeat, he will do so for you, and you will go on unscathed. From the inner passivity of looking to Christ to do everything will issue a perfection of performance.[21]

It would appear that Keswick teaching is at its core a modified version of Wesleyan perfectionism. The primary difference is that the former view excludes the unrealistic claim that all sin can be successfully uprooted from the sanctified Christian heart in this life.

Packer's critique of the Keswick model is swift and thorough. Several aspects of his indictment should be noted. First, the Keswick view has *a limited understanding of holiness*, one that

centers upon the essentially negative ideal of a life free from the tensions of moral reach (aspiration) exceeding moral grasp (achievement) and from the censures of conscience for not having done all one should. Unbroken joy and tranquillity are the goals set, and these prove to be linked not so much with achieving righteousness as with avoiding the sense of moral failure. . . . [But] to make present happiness one's present purpose is not the path of biblical godliness. A quiet, sunny, tidy life without agony, free from distress at the quality of one's walk with God and one's work for others, is not what Scripture tells us to aim at or expect, and Scripture will not justify us if we do.[22]

Second, the Keswick *assurance of total victory over all known sin* far exceeds anything that the New Testament teaches us to expect in this world (Packer would direct our attention to such texts as Rom. 7:14–25; Gal. 5:17; 1 John 1:8–10). Indeed,

the Christian's present righteousness is relative; nothing he does is sinlessly perfect yet. Behind his best performances lies a heart too little fervent and motives too mixed, and as Jesus' judgments on the Pharisees show, it is morally unreal to evaluate an agent's acts without regard for his motives and purposes (see Matthew 6:1–6, 16–18; 23:25–28).[23]

It is only "the very insensitive and the mentally unbalanced" mind that would ever imagine itself having achieved a condition in which everything

---

[21] Ibid.
[22] Ibid., 153.
[23] Ibid., 154.

he or she does is sinlessly perfect. It is one thing for the New Testament to assure us of an increasing degree of freedom from known sins. It is something else altogether to claim that the biblical authors promise total victory over them all prior to the consummation.

Third, the Keswick model is also undermined by its *insistence on passivity*. The Keswick view, or what Packer also calls quietism,

> holds that all initiatives on our part, of any sort, are the energy of the flesh; that God will move us, if at all, by inner promptings and constraints that are recognizably not thoughts and impulses of our own; and that we should always be seeking the annihilation of our selfhood so that divine life may flow freely through our physical frames.[24]

But this is not the vision of the Christian life portrayed by the apostle Paul in Philippians 2:12–13. There we see that

> the Holy Spirit's ordinary way of working in us is through the working of our own minds and wills. He moves us to act by causing us to see reasons for moving ourselves to act. Thus our conscious, rational selfhood, so far from being annihilated, is strengthened, and in reverent, resolute obedience we work out our salvation, knowing that God is at work in us to make us "... both ... will and ... work for his good pleasure" (Philippians 2:13).[25]

Far from releasing the Spirit to work freely within us, passivity serves only to quench and resist him.

> Souls that cultivate passivity do not thrive, but waste away. The Christian's motto should not be "Let go and let God" but "Trust God and get going!" So if, for instance, you are fighting a bad habit, work out before God a strategy for ensuring that you will not fall victim to it again, ask him to bless your plan, and go out in his strength, ready to say no next time the temptation comes. Or if you are seeking to form a good habit, work out a strategy in the same way, ask God's help, and then try your hardest.[26]

This is precisely the sort of biblical realism and practical wisdom that one finds consistently in Packer's approach to the Christian's ongoing war with sin.

---

[24] Ibid., 155.
[25] Ibid., 156.
[26] Ibid., 157.

The fourth and final shortcoming of the Keswick model is one that Packer himself learned all too well in his early days as a believer. From a pastoral perspective, this view of Christian holiness is *spiritually and emotionally destructive* as individuals agonize why they cannot overcome sin, being told repeatedly that it is simply because they have not fully yielded or wholly consecrated themselves. The cycle of this concept of "faith," followed by failure, and then again by a renewed act of passive dependence, is a virtual recipe for disaster.

Holiness Is an Affair of the Heart

One will look in vain in the vast corpus of Packer's writings on holiness for anything that remotely approximates what we know as legalism. Holiness for the biblical authors, and thus for Packer, has to do with our hearts. Mere outward conformity to a moral standard, even a biblical one, will ultimately produce pride and self-reliance. The biblical vision of holiness begins with the understanding that the heart is "the center and focus of one's inner personal life: the source of motivation, the seat of passion, the spring of all thought processes and particularly of conscience."[27] In other words, "holiness starts inside a person, with a right purpose that seeks to express itself in a right performance. It is a matter, not just of the motions that I go through, but of the motives that prompt me to go through them."[28] Packer's understanding of the progressive transformation and purity of the heart is central to his vision for the Christian life, something nowhere more clearly stated than in the following:

> Purity of heart is indeed a matter of willing one thing, namely to live every day of one's life loving God.
>
> How then should we spell out the dimensions of purity of heart? It is a matter of saying and meaning what originally the psalmist said: "Whom have I in heaven but you? / And there is nothing on earth that I desire besides you" (Ps 73:25)—nothing, that is, that I would not consent to lose if adhering to God required it. Thus, it is a matter of wanting and valuing "fellowship . . . with the Father and with his Son Jesus Christ" (1 Jn 1:3) more than I want or value anything else in this world. Again, it is a matter of developing, as Jonathan Edwards developed, "a God-entranced vision of all things," so that the thought of everything being God's property

---

[27] Packer, *Rediscovering Holiness*, 22.
[28] Ibid.

and in God's hands, and of God as in reality doing all things well, despite short-term appearances, brings unending joy. And it is a matter of making known and loving and pleasing and praising God my life task, and of seeking to lead others into the same God-glorifying life pattern. This is the motivational attitude that is reflected and expressed in all authentic prayer. Without it our calling on God, however regular and orderly, will truly and sadly be by-path praying.[29]

Packer goes so far as to define holiness as the "redirecting" of the desires of the heart in the sense that the believer experiences a detachment from created things in order that his or her longings might be attached through Christ to the Creator. Then, to the extent to which we increasingly long to love and know God and to please him and exalt his glory in every way, our behavior will express a corresponding change. This in turn serves to intensify and strengthen the desire itself, such that the daily habits of life for which the New Testament calls become increasingly ingrained in the depths of our being.

One of the more instructive paradoxes of the Christian life to which Packer alerts us is the fact that as we grow in holiness of both heart and hand, the distress and pain of sin only intensify. Many have embraced the unbiblical notion that with personal growth in godliness there comes a diminishing sense of the presence of sin and the pain that it typically evokes. But Packer reminds us that the more holy and mature one becomes, the more offensive and painful sin is to their hearts.

Those . . . who have been instructed in God's law and gospel, as found in the Bible, will ordinarily have a more vivid awareness of their sinfulness, and of their particular sins, because the divine light that shines on them from Scripture to show them to themselves is brighter. This is one reason (there are others) why converted Christians regularly experience deeper conviction of sin after their conversion than they knew before, and why one dimension of spiritual growth . . . is growth downward into a more thorough humility and more radical repentance. Though not much is said about this nowadays, a deepening sense of one's sinfulness remains a touchstone of the genuine Christian life.[30]

Packer is saying that an inescapable principle of the spiritual life is that

---

[29] J. I. Packer and Carolyn Nystrom, *Praying: Finding Our Way through Duty to Delight* (Downers Grove, IL: InterVarsity, 2006), 40.
[30] Packer, *Rediscovering Holiness*, 52–53.

the farther you go, or the deeper you progress, the greater is your sense of distance from where you know you should ultimately be. As your desires for God expand and increase, as your longing for greater intimacy deepens, you become ever more conscious of how far you have yet to go in knowing and loving God as you ought. Again,

> intense distress at one's continuing imperfection, in the context of an intense love of goodness as God defines it and an intense zeal to practice it, is the clearest possible sign of the holiness of heart that is central to spiritual health. The paradox—too hard a nut, it seems, for some to crack—is that increase of real holiness always brings increase of real discontent, because of what has not yet been achieved.[31]

Holiness Requires the Empowering Presence of the Holy Spirit

Spiritual growth, very much like its counterpart in the physical or biological realm, is typically what Packer envisions as a gentle and largely imperceptible process. Although one rarely sees it or feels it happening, it is not unusual for believers to realize at differing stages of life that they are different from what they once were. This difference, we must observe, is altogether the result of the Spirit's empowering work. In keeping with his overall commitment to Reformed theology and its focus on the sovereignty of God's work in and for the believer, Packer insists that

> holiness of life is not precisely a human achievement, however much it demands of human effort. It is a work of the Holy Spirit, who prompts and energizes the human effort as part of it. It is a supernaturalizing of our natural lives, a matter of becoming and so of being what we are as new creatures in Christ—a living out behaviorally of what God is working in us transformationally. We do not sanctify ourselves. . . . Self-reliance is not the way of holiness, but the negation of it. Self-confidence in face of temptation and conflicting pressures is a sure guarantee that some sort of moral failure will follow."[32]

That being said, we must never forget that the Holy Spirit works through *means*. That is to say, holiness is not something imparted immediately, as if by divine infusion, independent of what the biblical authors

---

[31] Ibid., 222.
[32] Ibid., 91–92.

call us to pursue, but rather precisely through or by means of those spiritual responsibilities and rituals set forth in Scripture. By this Packer has in view such things as the preaching and hearing of God's revealed truth in Scripture, worship (both corporate and private), prayer, fellowship with other Christians, and the celebration of the Eucharist. More will be said of the biblically ordained means of sanctification later on, but it is crucial that we keep in mind their necessity in the pursuit of holiness.

The Experience of Holiness Is One of Conflict

If there is a consistent theme or thread that runs through Packer's teaching on the Christian life it is the notion of *realism*. By this he has in mind, among other things, the inescapable conflict that we encounter throughout the duration of our earthly sojourn. At no time should the Christian expect to emerge from the struggle against indwelling sin or attain a level of holiness that insulates us from the onslaught of Satan and external persecution. Such an expectation is the sort of wildly unbiblical and escapist dream that Packer abhors. All such versions of holiness only serve to inflict the believer with disillusionment and will eventually demoralize his efforts as daily experience runs consistently counter to his misguided idealism.

The life of holiness, then, is something of a school in which we daily learn the hard lessons that only personal experience can teach us. That is to say, "holiness, like prayer (which is indeed part of it), is something which, though Christians have an instinct for it through their new birth, . . . they have to learn in and through experience."[33] Indeed, "prayer and holiness are learned in a similar way as commitments are made, habits are formed, and battles are fought against a real opponent."[34]

The experience of learning to be holy is like "an educational process that God has planned and programmed in order to refine, purge, enlarge, animate, toughen, and mature us. By means of it he brings us progressively into the moral and spiritual shape in which he wants to see us."[35] The school of holiness, therefore, is God's "spiritual gymnasium" for reshaping and rebuilding his children into the moral likeness of Jesus Christ. And like any other form of disciplined exercise, the process is often fraught with

---

[33] Ibid., 15.
[34] Ibid.
[35] Ibid., 16.

difficulty and danger. We find no better embodiment of this than in the experience known as "the dark night of the soul." Again, Packer always the realist, warns us that on occasion

> God brings on dryness, with resultant restlessness of heart, in order to induce a new depth of humble, hopeful openness to himself, which he then crowns with a liberating and animating reassurance of his love—one that goes beyond anything that was sensed before. As Christ's humiliation and grief on the cross preceded his exaltation to the joy of his throne, so over and over again humbling experiences of impotence and frustration precede inward renewing, with a sense of triumph and glory, in the believer's heart. Thus, with wisdom adapted to each Christian's temperament, circumstances, and needs, our heavenly Father draws and binds his children closer to himself.[36]

The Experience of Holiness Is One of Lifelong Repentance

There is no holiness or Christian life that does not have repentance at its core. Repentance is not merely one element in conversion, but a habitual attitude and action to which all Christians are called. It is, argues Packer, a spiritual discipline central to and inseparable from healthy holy living. But what is it? How should it be defined? What are its characteristic features? A close reading of Packer reveals that he understands repentance to entail a number of interrelated themes.

The most important dimension in godly repentance is the fundamental alteration in one's thinking with regard to what is sin and what God requires of us in terms both of our thoughts and actions. Repentance thus begins with a recognition of the multitude of ways in which our thinking and attitude and belief system are contrary to what is revealed in Scripture. We are by nature and choice misshapen and warped in the way we evaluate truth claims. What we cherish, on the one hand, and detest, on the other, are fundamentally at odds with God's value system, and repentance must begin with an honest confession that such is the case.

But merely acknowledging where our thinking has gone wrong is only the first step in genuine repentance. The most sincere of apologies is at best only a start down the pathway of repentance. There must follow a change in behavior. There must be a conscious and consistent abandonment of

---

[36] Ibid., 100–101.

those courses of action to which our sinful and rebellious thinking gave rise. Thus repentance

> signifies going back on what one was doing before, and renouncing the misbehavior by which one's life or one's relationship was being harmed. In the Bible, repentance is a theological term, pointing to an abandonment of those courses of action in which one defied God by embracing what he dislikes and forbids. . . . Repentance [thus] means altering one's habits of thought, one's attitudes, outlook, policy, direction, and behavior, just as fully as is needed to get one's life out of the wrong shape and into the right one. Repentance is in truth a spiritual revolution.[37]

There is also an emotional or subjective sorrow and remorse that true repentance requires. Merely feeling sorry for one's sins is not itself repentance, but it is impossible for repentance to occur in the absence of a deep conviction, and its attendant anguish, for having lived in defiance of God. Thus whereas one may well, and indeed should, feel regret for a life of sin, repentance is never complete until one actively turns away from those former dark paths in order to face, embrace, love, thank, and serve God. Whatever feeling is entailed in repentance, it must lead one to forsake all former ways of disobedience. To acknowledge one's guilt before God is one thing; to abandon those actions that incurred such guilt is another, absolutely essential, dimension in genuine repentance. Thus there is in repentance not only a backward look at the former life from which one has turned but also a commitment both in the present and for the future to pursue Christ and to follow him in a life of devoted discipleship. Throughout the process the believer is also examining his heart and habits to ensure that nothing of the old ungodly ways is making its way back into his life.

Packer also sees *humility* as a necessary constituent element in repentance. "What we have to realize is that we grow up into Christ by growing down into lowliness (humility, from the Latin word *humilis*, meaning low). Christians, we might say, grow greater by getting smaller."[38] There is hardly a more counterintuitive or countercultural notion than this, yet that is what sets apart the Christian from all forms of mere religion or secular models of personal improvement. When the biblical authors speak of humility and repentance, they have in view "a progress into personal small-

---

[37] Ibid., 123.
[38] Ibid., 120.

ness that allows the greatness of Christ's grace to appear. The sign of this sort of progress is that they increasingly feel and say that in themselves they are nothing and God in Christ has become everything for their ongoing life." Repentance, then, entails a "continual shrinkage of carnal self"[39] as one seeks the enlargement of the fame of Christ.

Cultivating a lifelong mind-set of repentance begins with one's understanding of God. On the one hand, Christians are fascinated and enthralled with the transcendent glory of God's grace and love. But they are equally captivated, with a slightly different effect, by his holiness and justice and purity. "This characteristically Christian sense of the mercy and the terror (fear) of the Lord," Packer explains for us,

> is the seed-bed in which awareness grows that lifelong repentance is a "must" of holy living. That awareness will not grow under any other conditions. Where it is lacking, any supposed sanctity will prove on inspection to be flawed by complacency about oneself and short-sightedness about sin. Show me, then, a professed Christian who does not see and insist on the need for ongoing repentance, and I will show you a stunted soul for whom God is not as yet the Holy One in the full biblical sense. For such a person, true Christian holiness is at present out of reach.[40]

True repentance, then, begins when a Christian is enabled by God's gracious power to transition out of self-delusion, or what modern psychologists might call denial, into what the Bible describes as heartfelt conviction of sin. This in turn leads to the abandonment of self-centered disobedience and is replaced by a God-centered life in which the Savior is honored, his people are served, and his revealed Word is obeyed.

Self-Examination versus Introspection, and Our Battle with Pride

We have not left the subject of repentance, but now turn to yet another facet of what it means and how we grow deeper in it. In this regard, Packer has great insight and excellent advice for us when it comes to the discipline of self-examination and our battle with pride.

> Whereas introspection, whether it ends in euphoria or in the gloom of self-pity and self-despair, can become an expression of self-absorbed

---

[39] Ibid., 121.
[40] Ibid., 132.

pride, self-examination is the fruit of God-centered humility, ever seeking to shake free of all that displeases the Father, dishonors the Son and grieves the Holy Spirit, so as to honor God more. Thus self-examination is a fundamentally healthy process, leading into repentance, where mere introspection can leave us just feeling sorry for ourselves.[41]

One particular area where we need regular self-examination concerns humility and its mortal enemy, pride. Simply put, proud people rarely repent; only the humble do. To detect whether humility is growing in us, notes Packer,

we can prayerfully invite God's help in self-examination as we ask ourselves such questions as: Am I able to joyfully perform tasks in my church that have little or no visibility? Do I regularly credit others for their labor? Can I value and enjoy people who are not normally considered respectable? Are my thoughts toward the difficult people in my life infused with grace? Do I give my spouse first choice of TV channel, room temperature or vacation? Are my prayers usually on behalf of other people? Is it relatively easy for me to give my time or my money—and tell no one about it? Do I see every opportunity not as an earned right but as a gift from God? Do I cut short thoughts of comparing myself favorably with others? Do I honor others with my thoughts, words and actions? To the extent that we can honestly say yes to questions like these, we are beginning to learn humility toward others—and so to conquer the sin of pride.[42]

On the other hand,

humility cannot be fully detected or measured by direct inspection, for trying to inspect our own humility is itself a yielding to pride (which is why it was so grotesque when a listener said after a talk: "I'm so glad you spoke on humility; that's my strong point, you know!"). The most we can ever do is concentrate on negating and mortifying the various expressions of pride we are already aware of, and on asking our Lord to show us what more negating and mortifying needs to be done. That is a request that the God who watches us even as he watches over us, and who maintains his perfect knowledge of us in all matters where we do not truly know ourselves (that means, in every matter without exception all our lives!) is fully equipped to answer.[43]

---

[41] Packer and Nystrom, *Praying*, 125.
[42] Ibid., 130.
[43] Ibid.

"Humble yourselves, therefore, under the mighty hand of God so that at the proper time he may exalt you" (1 Pet. 5:6).

The Experience of Holiness Is a Communal Affair

And what might the local church have to do with holiness? Packer's robust belief in the centrality of local church life is a much-needed corrective to the Lone Ranger mentality of many within the professing Christian world today. The perspective of the New Testament is decidedly corporate, communal, and church-centered, while at the same time preserving authentic individuality. The gospel embraces and upholds the latter, says Packer, insofar as our present decisions most assuredly affect our eternal destiny. When it comes to salvation, each person stands alone before God. No one, Packer insists,

> can make those decisions for someone else, and no one can enter the kingdom of God by hanging on to someone else's coat-tails. The individuality that consists of a sense of personal identity and responsibility Godward is a Christian virtue, making for wise and thoughtful behavior, and is a necessity for mature life and growth in Christ.[44]

At the same time, New Testament Christianity will have nothing to do with *individualism*,

> which is actually a proud unwillingness to accept a place in a team of peers and to be bound by group consensus. The gospel condemns individualism as disruptive of the life of the divine family, the new community of believers together that God is building in each place where individual Christians have emerged. Harmonious consensus, undergirded by brotherly love, is to be the goal for every church, and individualism is to be overcome by mutual deference.[45]

Salvation in Christ necessarily entails solidarity with others who in like manner have been incorporated into the spiritual organism we know as the body of Christ. Our true identity, then, is both as individuals and as members of a collective body known as the church.

Often, those who resist the call to identify with other Christians and claim that they find local church life to be stifling and oppressive are simply

---

[44] J. I. Packer, "Evangelical Foundations for Spirituality," *Serving the People of God*, vol. 2 of *The Collected Shorter Writings of J. I. Packer* (Carlisle, UK: Paternoster), 266.
[45] Ibid.

guilty of pride and self-sufficiency. God will not prosper the arrogance "of those who think they can get along without other Christians' help. Spiritual isolationism is in his eyes not a virtue but a vice; only through mutuality of dependence, ministry and pastoral care do Christians really grow and churches really go forward."[46] When God saved us, togetherness and mutual dependence were designed to be our manner of life and the means of our spiritual growth. Whereas there is always a place for occasional solitude, as Jesus himself modeled for us, the normal Christian life is decidedly a corporate participation with others in the pursuit of holiness and the glory of God.

What this means is that the local church functions as a means of grace, a divinely ordained instrument through which God communicates his presence and power for life. Sadly, though, "the popular pietist way is to value church services and parachurch gatherings as we value gas stations and parties and maybe college lectures too: we show up in order (in one sense or another) to fill up and then go on our way without any sense of continuing commitment to the source of the filling."[47] The ministry of grace, the means of growth into Christlike conformity, and the primary sphere for other-oriented service are within the local church. This is what Packer rightly describes as that "active habitual togetherness" into which God works to draw all Christians.[48] His design is that our community and togetherness become a means for our mutual blessing. This occurs only as we each share with one another what we have received through Christ. This is especially good news for those who feel weak and resourceless. Strength is gained for spiritual battle through the interaction and interdependence of Christian fellowship. Those who live in isolation from the body of Christ will inevitably suffer moral and spiritual atrophy.

Many struggle to grasp this reality for the simple fact that they still do not understand the meaning of *fellowship* as the word is used in Scripture. Fellowship is simply *"seeking to share with others* what God has made known to you, while letting them share with you what they know of him, as a means of finding strength, refreshment and instruction for one's own soul."[49] It is therefore "through fellowship and in fellowship one's own soul is refreshed and fed by the effort to communicate one's knowledge of divine things, to come and pray for others, and to receive from God through them."[50]

---

[46] Packer and Nystrom, *Praying*, 238.
[47] Ibid., 252.
[48] Ibid., 246.
[49] Ibid., 14.
[50] Ibid., 15.

In the context of this sort of honesty and vulnerability we see biblical accountability in operation. Only here can Christians truly exercise the mutual confession referenced in James 5:16. There we are exhorted to confess our sins to one another and to pray for one another so that we might be healed. Packer helpfully points out that James

> is talking not of the formalities of institutionalized absolution, but of the intimacies of Christian friendship in what are nowadays called "accountability relationships." In accountability relationships, one cares for another in a context of open sharing of lives: sad things like failures and falls, as well as glad things like deliverances and successes. Confession of sins within pastoral friendships of this kind is an important expression of repentance. Embarrassment should not be allowed to hold us back.[51]

Packer's concluding counsel is that we "choose togetherness," by which he means that radical experience of community embraced by those who know they are spiritually inseparable and eternally one in Christ. These are folks whose relationship with each other is rooted in praise and prayer and the study of God's Word together. On that basis, says Packer,

> *Choose* not to be held back by shyness, embarrassment, social convention or any form of personal inhibition (attitudes anchored not in concern for dignity and good taste, as some make themselves believe, but in a panicky fear of vulnerability). *Choose* to give and receive love on a basis of humble and mutual openness. *Choose* to commit yourself to a congregation long term, to identify as fully as you can with its goals and members, to open your life and your home to your fellow believers, and to give help wherever help is needed. In short, choose *togetherness*, and choose wholehearted, closely bound involvement in the congregation's worshiping life of prayer and praise as the central element of that togetherness. For this and nothing less than this is the will of God.[52]

The Sacraments and Sanctification

What possible connection is there between the celebration of water baptism and the observance of the Lord's Supper, on the one hand, and our growth as Christians in conformity to the image of Christ, on the other?

---

[51] Packer, *Rediscovering Holiness*, 142.
[52] Packer and Nystrom, *Praying*, 257–58.

Although many Christians would respond with a blank and uninformed stare, J. I. Packer finds in the answer a controlling key to both individual and corporate holiness. Coming from an evangelical view of Scripture and a traditional Anglican ecclesiology, Packer understandably embraces a high view of these sacraments and the role they play not only in local church worship but also, and perhaps especially, in the progressive spiritual growth of Christian men and women. Perhaps we should begin with what he understands regarding the nature of such sacraments and then move to how they serve to stimulate and strengthen Christian growth.

As over against the traditions of Roman Catholicism, Packer insists that Christ has commanded observance of only two, not seven, "rites" that serve as "bonds of unity" within the believing community of God's people. "In them," he notes,

> material items—water in one case, bread and wine in the other—become significant signs of his own saving ministry to us who as believers engage in the ritual actions. Both actions symbolize the restoring, through Christ's reconciling sacrifice, of our relationship with the Father and the restoring, in Christ by the Holy Spirit, of our love for God and godliness, through the untwisting of our moral nature by sovereign regeneration. The one is a rite of cleansing and initiation (baptism), and the other a rite of sustenance and continuance (the Lord's Supper).[53]

But we must not be misled by Packer's use of the word "signs" or the verb "symbolize," as if he were suggesting that baptism and communion exert no influence on the believer other than to direct our mental focus to the theological truths they express. Insofar as baptism and the Lord's Supper give expression to the fundamental truth of the gospel, they serve "to evoke, confirm, and strengthen faith in Christ."[54] Here Packer has in view the sacraments as "means of grace." As instruments of his sanctifying (not justifying) grace in the lives of the redeemed, God employs these two realities

> to strengthen faith's confidence in his promises and to call forth acts of faith for receiving the good gifts signified. The efficacy of the sacraments to this end resides not in the faith or virtue of the minister but

---

[53] J. I. Packer, *Taking God Seriously: Vital Things We Need to Know* (Wheaton, IL: Crossway, 2013), 150.
[54] J. I. Packer, *Concise Theology: A Guide to Historic Christian Beliefs* (Carol Stream, IL: Tyndale House, 1993), 205.

in the faithfulness of God, who, having given the signs, is now pleased to use them.[55]

Both baptism and communion are thus viewed as "mysteries" in the sense that they are "visible disclosures of God's saving work through Christ both past and present," and are used by God to "accentuate their recipients' *assurance* that God has his grip on their lives."[56] Both ordinances "point to, celebrate, and serve to solidify the unique Spirit-and-faith bond with [God] himself that is the believer's umbilical cord, so to speak, linking him or her with the life in Christ that begins here and is enjoyed in its fullness hereafter."[57]

But precisely how do they accomplish such ends? As for communion, Packer argues:

> In thus ministering assurance the Supper truly functions on the principle that seeing is believing—in other words, that contemplating and actually consuming the sign confirms confidence that one is sharing in the thing signified. And with baptism it is similar: remembering, or being reminded of, one's baptism as a fact of one's past confirms the believer's certainty of being dead and risen with Christ in the present, and hence of being called here and now to live out the new life that God has imparted.[58]

If one should ask why physical, tangible substances are employed, Packer would direct our attention to the fact that sense experience has a unique capacity to assure us of the spiritual realities to which each sacrament corresponds. Thus we recognize the importance of Jesus's commanding material actions with material objects. He does not simply say, "Remember me," or "You are united with me by faith in my life, death, and resurrection." He goes further and says, "Remember me by eating the bread and drinking from the cup." The physical action of ingesting a material substance is employed by the Spirit to deepen and intensify our faith and assurance regarding the spiritual reality to which those objects direct our attention. Likewise, with baptism, both the visible experience of coming under the water momentarily and the tangible

---

[55] Ibid., 210.
[56] Packer, *Taking God Seriously*, 130.
[57] Ibid., 128.
[58] Ibid., 130.

feeling of the water's cleansing effect on the body quicken the mind and strengthen our confidence in the inseparable unity we have with Christ and the purging of our guilt by his shed blood.

We turn now to the meaning of each ordinance. Packer speaks of baptism as "a speaking sign, a symbol carrying a message; what Augustine calls a visible word from God."[59] And what, precisely, is the message conveyed? Or we might ask, what sort of "change" does the "under-and-up ritual of baptism" symbolize?[60] It is that the risen and reigning Christ has made us and is making us something radically different from what we used to be. It reminds us that

> the power that made the world has made us into new creations (2 Cor. 5:17), terminating our old, self-centered, naturally sinful mode of existence and, to borrow again Paul's elegant horticultural image, grafting and implanting us into our risen Lord—plugging us into him, as we might less elegantly put it—with new desires, new powers, and new joys directly resulting. In terms of Paul's spiritual ontology, which tells us how God who brought about this change sees and knows his own handiwork, we have been co-crucified and co-resurrected with and in Christ (see Gal. 2:20; Eph. 2:5–6; Col. 2:11–13).[61]

But there is also in baptism a divine initiative that precedes any and all human response. In other words, "baptism should be seen as an embodied divine promise that is at the same time a call and a claim from all three persons of the Trinity." This is bound up in the fact that we are baptized "in the name of" the Father, the Son, and the Holy Spirit. The one baptizing is asserting that the person being baptized is consecrated to and given over to the triune God as his or her joint owners. The Christian, says Packer, is thus forevermore under new management! In sum,

> The blessings that this under-water-and-up-from-under ritual visibly signs and seals—that is, displays as really real and personally offered—are for those who thankfully embrace the fact that now they belong to the Father as his adopted children, to the Son as his pur-

---

[59] J. I. Packer, *Growing in Christ* (Wheaton, IL: Crossway, 1994), 99.
[60] Packer, *Taking God Seriously*, 138. "The symbolism of first going under water as a sign of saying goodbye to the style of life one is renouncing and then coming up from under as a sign of starting a new life pattern is clearly expressed, and that evidently is what is important. The washing symbolism shows that this commitment is conceived within the frame of an absolution from the past that sets one free for the new beginning. The rite is thus one of termination, initiation, and commencement" (ibid., 128).
[61] Ibid., 138.

chased possession, and to the Holy Spirit as subjects for his ministry of transformation.[62]

When it comes to the Eucharist, Packer is no fan of transubstantiation of the elements or even any notion of a special, somehow localized attachment of Christ's glorified body to the bread and wine. There simply is no physical presence of Christ's body as, in, with, or through the bread and wine. When Jesus spoke the words of institution ("this is my body . . . this cup that is poured out for you is the new covenant in my blood," Luke 22:19–20), the verb "is" clearly means "represents" or "symbolizes."

> The idea that Jesus's words worked like a wizard's spell, changing bread, and perhaps wine too, whether through addition or transmutation, into something other than what they were, has had a good run for its money, but seems impossible, if only because Jesus himself as he spoke was still with them, personally unchanged.[63]

Is there any sense, then, in which Christ may be said to be *present* in communion? Yes, says Packer, in much the same sense in which he promised to be with us in Matthew 18:20 and 28:20 ("And behold, I am with you always, to the end of the age"). Packer's own explanation is important to note:

> It is the presence of the triumphant, sovereign Savior, who is *there* in terms of his objective omnipresence and *here* in terms of being always alongside each believer with a sustaining and nurturing purpose. Clarity requires us to say, then, that Christ is present *at*, rather than *in*, the Supper. Though not physical, his presence is personal and real in the sense of being a relational fact. Christ is present, not in the elements in any sense, but with his worshippers; and his presence is effected, not by the quasi-magic of ritual correctly performed by a permitted person, but by the power of the Holy Spirit, who indwells believers' hearts to mediate Christ's reality to them. It is not a passive but an active presence, known not by what it feels like (often it is, in any ordinary sense of the word, unfelt), but rather by what it does.[64]

Thus when we together, in faith, partake of the bread and wine, they are understood as a pledge or divine assurance of the reality and provision of

---

[62] Ibid., 136.
[63] Ibid., 152.
[64] Ibid., 162.

the beneficial spiritual effects to which they point. We remember Christ in his atoning death, which is to say that we call him to mind in joyful praise, prayer, and gratitude for the gift of forgiveness and eternal life. Packer contends that when we take the elements, we should envision them coming from Christ's hand as his guarantee that in love he will continue to nourish us spiritually forever.[65]

This is no abstract intellectual reflection on past events. Packer directs our attention to 1 Corinthians 10:16–17, where Paul's use of the word "participation" indicates that "the ritual eating and drinking that Christ prescribed brings spiritual nourishment to us through unitive involvement with him in the shedding of his lifeblood and the giving of his body to be broken."[66] In this way Christ draws believers into identification with his own risen life. From this union, through the Holy Spirit, "spiritual vitality flows: health and strength for devotion and service; inner resources of love, ability, and power that we continue to discover within ourselves throughout our lives."[67] There is, therefore, something profoundly transformative that occurs in the Christian. The sacrament sanctifies!

One of the principal ways in which baptism serves to sanctify is by reminding us of our identity and hence our primary loyalty. Baptism vividly signifies that we are inseparably one with Christ in his death and resurrection. Just as the wearing of a uniform encourages members of the armed forces to recall that their first loyalty is to country and their first task is to obey their commanding officers, so remembering that we have been baptized enables us to keep our Christian commitment in sharp focus. That is to say, the recognition and remembrance that we have been baptized should constantly impress on our hearts the irrevocable commitment to Christ and his purposes that we have publicly expressed. Continuing with his military metaphor, Packer says that baptism is "an enlistment ceremony, publicly transacting a pledge of loyalty whereby one undertakes to be, as the Prayer Book puts it, 'Christ's faithful soldier and servant' for life."[68]

Our responsibility to embrace the daily demands of Christian obedience is likewise reinforced by the reality of our baptism. Thus, "thinking

---

[65] "What we need more than anything else at the Lord's Table is a fresh grasp of the glorious truth that we sinners are offered mercy through faith in the Christ who forgives and restores, out of which faith comes all the praise that we offer and all the service that we render" (J. I. Packer, "The Gospel and the Lord's Supper," in *Serving the People of God*, 49). Indeed, "this everlasting gospel of salvation for sinners is what in Scripture the Lord's Supper is all about" (ibid.).

[66] Packer, *Taking God Seriously*, 153.

[67] Ibid., 153–54.

[68] Packer, *Growing in Christ*, 112.

of our baptism will keep our nose to this particular grindstone."[69] This is the intended practical effect of Paul's words in Romans 6:1–14. There the apostle contends that because we have been buried and raised with Christ in baptism, we may not continue in sin, as if by doing so we might in some convoluted way cause the glories of God's grace to abound. This is essentially the same message we find in Colossians 2:8–3:17, where Paul argues that because we have been buried and raised with Christ in baptism, "we must not lapse into Christless, worldly, 'natural' religion, with its legalism and superstition, but must let Christ's supernatural risen life find expression in us in the breaking of bad habits and the hammering out of a new, Christlike character."[70]

Faithful and frequent participation in the Lord's Supper likewise empowers the will to resist sin and strive, in God's grace, after holiness. Thus, "as a good meal energizes the body, so our Savior [via the elements of the table] energizes us for renewed ventures in faith and love, faithfulness and obedience, worship and service."[71] Regular table fellowship with Christ also serves to awaken and solidify the assurance of our salvation. Each time we partake,

> we should be saying in our hearts, "as sure as I see and touch and taste this bread and this wine, so sure is it that Jesus Christ is not a fancy but a fact, that he is for real, and that he offers me himself to be my Saviour, my Bread of Life, and my Guide to glory. He has left me this rite, this gesture, this token, this ritual action as a guarantee of this grace; He instituted it, and it is a sign of life-giving union with him, and I'm taking part in it, and thus I know that I am his and he is mine forever." That is the assurance that we should be drawing from our sharing in the Lord's Supper every time we come to the table.[72]

If this chapter has defined holiness, then we now must ask how it might be attained. By what process? Through what means? To that subject we now turn as we examine Packer's concept of sanctification.

---

[69] Packer, *Taking God Seriously*, 144.
[70] Packer, *Growing in Christ*, 99–100.
[71] Packer, *Taking God Seriously*, 162.
[72] Packer, "The Gospel and the Lord's Supper," 50.

CHAPTER 5

THE PROCESS OF CHRISTIAN LIVING

The Meaning and Means of Sanctification

J. I. Packer is not the sort of man who worries about his legacy. Rather, his focus in life and ministry these many years has been one of sustained faithfulness. He is largely devoid of concern for his reputation and image (I say "largely" rather than "altogether" because Packer himself repeatedly insists that no one in this life attains the perfection of heart and motive that will come only at the return of Christ). That said, I suggest that Packer will be remembered primarily for his contribution to our understanding of the meaning and means of sanctification. His written work on such topics as the atonement, the inerrancy of Scripture, the nature and character of God, how to evangelize in light of divine sovereignty, and the role of Puritan theology in the contemporary church is well known. But he has written more extensively and with unparalleled insight on the dynamics of Christian living than on any other subject.

So when Packer talks and writes about sanctification, what is he talking *about*? I'll let him answer that question for himself: "We are talking about God's work of character change in Christians; about the life of God in the soul of man; about the fruit of the Spirit; about the outworking in our behavior—our new, supernatural life—that is hid in Christ with God."[1]

---

[1] J. I. Packer, *Hot Tub Religion* (Wheaton, IL: Tyndale House, 1987), 165.

As we have noted before, Packer believes that sanctification is primarily about the inner transformation of our dispositions, our desires, our inclinations, or what he here calls our "character." It is about the very life of God himself manifesting its transformative influence in the soul of man (taking his cue from Henry Scougal's book *The Life of God in the Soul of Man* [1677]).[2] But this internal change in how we think, feel, and yearn, and especially in what we assign ultimate value, must express itself in a change in behavior. The evidence of the life of the Spirit within is the fruit of the Spirit without. The "outworking in our behavior" is not an optional, sidebar matter in sanctification. Sanctification, as we shall come to see, is holistic and encompasses the entirety of life, from internal motivation to external conduct.

But Packer is far from finished in explaining what sanctification is about. When we talk about sanctification, we are also talking "about God working in us to make us will and act for his good pleasure."[3] Apart from the antecedence of God's grace, enabling and equipping the human will to choose and act in a way that pleases God, there is no hope for authentic transformation. There may well be a shift in habits of life or in external conformity to a moral standard, but the sort of conduct that pleases God is conduct that is powered by God. This is more than abstract theologizing, for from it Packer derives a concrete strategy for daily obedience. Knowing that God is always *prior*, that his enabling grace always precedes even our most strenuous pursuit of godliness, supplies us with a strategy. He explains it this way:

> This suggests the proper procedure every time a new act of obedience is called for. First, take it to God in prayer, acknowledging your own lack of strength for it and asking to be enabled from on high. Then go into action, expecting to be helped, and you will find that you are. Then thank God for the help you received. It is by this pattern of humble, dependent activity that our salvation is worked out. It is thus that we shall grow in grace.[4]

And to what end is this growth designed? The answer brings us back again to the question, when we talk about sanctification, what are we talking *about*? "We are talking about the family likeness that God the Father

[2] See Packer's introduction to Scougal's book in *Puritan Portraits, J. I. Packer on Selected Classic Pastors and Pastoral Classics* (Fearn, Ross-Shire, UK: Christian Focus, 2012), 37–45.
[3] Ibid.
[4] J. I. Packer, *Rediscovering Holiness* (Ann Arbor, MI: Servant, 1992), 193.

wants to see in all his adopted children: the family likeness that is Christ-likeness, displaying the love, humility, and righteousness that constitute the moral image of the Son who is himself the image of the holy Father."[5] This is a recurring theme in Packer's understanding of spiritual and moral change: it is always change from what we currently are into what Jesus Christ is.

Finally, in talking about sanctification, at least in terms of how Packer conceives it,

> we are talking about God supernaturalizing our lives, and causing us to behave in ways in which left to our own resources we never could have behaved. We are talking about an ongoing spiritual mystery. If regeneration is a work of new creation, sanctification is a work of new formation. If regeneration is a new birth, sanctification is a new growth.[6]

Packer is quick to remind us, and he does so repeatedly, that sanctification is not natural morality, as if it were little more than the exchange of one set of rules for another. Rather, sanctification is

> supernatural conformity to the moral and spiritual likeness of Jesus Christ. Sanctification is not mystical passivity, as our use of the slogan "let go and let God" has too often implied, but is active moral effort energized by prayerful and expectant faith. We look for help in practicing righteousness, and we receive it. Nor is sanctification a solitary achievement. Rather, it is to be worked out and expressed in the close and demanding relationships of the Christian church, primarily the local congregation.[7]

The Influence of John Owen

The most enlightening approach to Packer's grasp of sanctification comes from his own conversion and the subsequent teaching to which he was exposed. In his introduction to John Owen's *The Mortification of Sin*, he describes how he was taught from the beginning of his Christian life that there are two kinds of Christians, "spiritual" and "carnal" (based on the terminology of 1 Cor. 3:1–3 in the KJV). Spiritual Christians are those who experience sustained peace and joy, together with a consistent inner

---

[5] Packer, *Hot Tub Religion*, 165.
[6] Ibid.
[7] Ibid., 173.

confidence, as well as regular victory over temptation and sin, all this in a way unattainable by those who are carnal. So, believing himself to be most assuredly carnal, what was Packer to do? He explains:

> There is a secret, I was told, of rising from carnality to spirituality, a secret mirrored in the maxim: Let go, and let God. . . . The secret had to do with being Spirit-filled. The Spirit-filled person . . . is taken out of the second half of Romans 7, understood . . . as an analysis of constant moral defeat through self-reliance, into Romans 8, where he walks confidently in the Spirit and is not so defeated.[8]

So how is one to be filled with the Spirit and thus escape from the bondage of "carnality" into the freedom and joy of "spirituality"? It begins, so Packer was taught, with self-denial, but not the sort of which Jesus spoke in Luke 9:23. In the latter case the call is for the negating of self-will and self-assertion, the sort of self-centeredness that characterizes all who are descended from Adam. The self-denial to which Jesus calls his followers is the abandonment of egocentricity and those patterns of behavior that begin and end with the praise of one's own identity and efforts. Such orientation to self is rooted both in the fallen nature of humanity and in conscious rebellion against God. But that is not what Packer was hearing from his mentors. What he understood them to teach was the need to deny "personal" self so that, says Packer, "I could be taken over by Jesus Christ in such a way that my present experience of thinking and willing would become something different, an experience of Christ Himself living in me, animating me and doing the thinking and willing for me."[9]

But that was only the first step in the path to a Spirit-filled life, a life that he was assured would be free from the seemingly perpetual struggle with indwelling sin. He continues:

> The rest of the secret was bound up in the double-barrelled phrase *consecration and faith*. Consecration meant total self-surrender, laying one's all on the altar, handing over every part of one's life to the lordship of Jesus. Through consecration one would be emptied of self, and the empty vessel would then automatically be filled with the Spirit so that Christ's power within one would be ready for use. With consecration was to go faith, which was explained as looking to the indwelling Christ moment

---

[8] Packer, *Puritan Portraits*, 78.
[9] Ibid., 78–79.

by moment, not only to do one's thinking and choosing in and for one, but also to do one's fighting and resisting of temptation. Rather than meet temptation directly (which would be fighting in one's own strength), one should hand it over to Christ to deal with, and look to Him to banish it.[10]

And the result? For Packer, it was most assuredly not the victorious life about which he had heard so much, but an inescapable defeat that threatened his emotional and spiritual health.

But what happened? I scraped my inside, figuratively speaking, to ensure that my consecration was complete, and laboured to "let go and let God" when temptation made its presence felt. . . . [But] the technique was not working. Why not? Well, since the teaching declared that everything depends on consecration being total, the fault had to lie in me. So I must scrape my inside again to find whatever maggots of unconsecrated self-hood still lurked there. I became fairly frantic.[11]

In another place, Packer says of this path and its possible outcome, "I might well have gone off my head or got bogged down in mystical fanaticism."[12]

As mentioned in chapter 1, it was then that by God's providence Packer came across an old clergyman's library in which he found an uncut set of John Owen's works.[13] He cut the pages of volume 6 and began to read *The Mortification of Sin*, and God used what the great Puritan had written three centuries earlier to sort out the mess in which the young Packer found himself. "Here," said Packer, "was God's chemo for my cancered soul."[14] What Owen showed Packer was that sin "is a blind, anti-God, egocentric energy in the fallen human spiritual system, ever fomenting self-centred and self-deceiving desires, ambitions, purposes, plans, attitudes, and behaviours."[15] But now that Packer was a regenerate believer, born again, a new creation in Christ, the sin that formerly dominated his life had been dethroned, even though it was not yet destroyed altogether. "It was marauding within me all the time," writes Packer, "bringing back sinful desires that I hoped I had

---

[10] Ibid., 79.
[11] Ibid., 79–80.
[12] J. I. Packer, *A Quest for Godliness: The Puritan Vision of the Christian Life* (Wheaton, IL: Crossway, 1990), 12.
[13] How significant was the influence of Owen on Packer, both then and now? "I do in fact think," said Packer, "that Owen has contributed more than anyone else to make me as much of a moral, spiritual and theological realist as I have so far become" (ibid., 84).
[14] Ibid., 80.
[15] Ibid.

seen the last of, and twisting my new desires for God and godliness out of shape so that they became pride-perverted too. Lifelong conflict with the besetting sins that besetting sin generates was what I must expect."[16]

The remedy, as we have already had occasion to see, was first to have a vivid and lively sense of God's holiness firmly embedded in one's mind. Second, Owen reminded Packer that sin desensitizes the believer to its presence and wickedness. Sin functions like spiritual novocaine, numbing one's heart to the horror of self-centeredness and rebellion against God. Thus, one must "watch—that is, prepare to recognise it, and search it out within you by disciplined, Bible-based, Spirit-led self-examination."[17] The Christian must then rivet his attention on the living Christ and the love displayed for us on the cross. At all times throughout, Packer counsels, we are to pray, asking God for the strength to say no to sin's otherwise persuasive appeal and to fortify oneself against bad habits by forming good ones in their place. Finally, one must energetically and persistently plead with Christ to kill the sinful impulse against which he or she is fighting.

The Synergy of Sanctification

All spiritual growth begins with the reality of regeneration, an entirely monergistic act of God's grace in bringing to life the formerly dead soul. Subsequent growth in grace means going on from there in the sense that the newly born-again believer now lives out in ever-increasing moral maturity the life that God has implanted within. That faith in Christ, which is itself the fruit of the new birth, brings to the believing soul justification by grace alone. The result, says Packer, is that we are now "God's children. His law is now our family code and no longer an oppressive burden as it was before we were converted. It is now an expression of our Father's will which we delight to keep because we want to please the One who loved us and saved us."[18]

Sanctification is also, in one sense, the work of God. God is the one who is at work, gradually demolishing our bad habits and the wicked ways of the old man in Adam. God is the one who is actively constructing with us good and godly new habits of Christlike action and reaction. We must never lose sight of the fact that it is God who is making us new. "God

---

[16] Ibid.
[17] Ibid., 81.
[18] J. I. Packer, "The Means of Growth," in *Serving the People of God*, vol. 2 of *The Collected Shorter Writings of J. I. Packer* (Carlisle, UK: Paternoster, 1998), 285.

is doing something entirely supernatural in our lives. God is changing us into the image of the Lord Jesus. This cannot be explained in natural terms. It is the work of grace and of his indwelling Holy Spirit."[19] However, sanctification is also

> in one sense synergistic—it is an ongoing cooperative process in which re-generate persons, alive to God and freed from sin's dominion (Rom. 6:11, 14–18), are required to exert themselves in sustained obedience. God's method of sanctification is neither activism (self-reliant activity) nor apathy (God-reliant passivity), but God-dependent effort (2 Cor. 7:1; Phil. 3:10–14; Heb. 12:14).[20]

In other words, there is the human side of willing obedience in addition to the divine work of enabling grace. Thus sanctification

> is both a gift (that is one side: God working in us to renew and transform us) and a task (the task of obedience, righteousness and pleasing God). And we must never so stress either of the two sides that we lose sight of the other. Think only of the task, and you will become a self-reliant legal-ist seeking to achieve righteousness in your own strength. You will not make any headway at all. Think only of the work of God in your life, and the chances are that Satan will trick you into not making the necessary effort and not maintaining the discipline of righteousness so that, in fact, even as you rejoice in the work of God in your life, you will be dishonour-ing it by your slackness. Hold both sides of the matter together in your mind, if you want your living to be right.[21]

Sanctification as the Transformation of Inner Motives and Dispositions

How precisely does the Spirit "change" us? What exactly has happened and is happening in the human soul that serves to set us apart for God and the new life to which we have been saved? It is here that Packer appeals to the notion of spiritual "union" with Christ, a much-neglected doctrine of the faith. By virtue of this mysterious union the very quality and energy of Christ's human life becomes our own. There is hardly a statement in Packer's writings that can rival the following in terms of the explicit way in

---

[19] Ibid.
[20] J. I. Packer, *Concise Theology: A Guide to Historic Christian Beliefs* (Carol Stream, IL: Tyndale House, 1993), 170–71.
[21] Packer, "Predestination and Sanctification," in *Serving the People of God*, 320.

which he articulates the dynamics of this event. We would do well to read it carefully. God in sovereign grace, says Packer,

> unites the individual to the risen Lord in such a way that the dispositional drives of Christ's perfect human character—the inner urgings, that is, to honour, adore, love, obey, serve and please God, and to benefit others for both their sake and his sake—are now reproduced at the motivational centre of that individual's being. And they are reproduced, in face of the contrary egocentric cravings of fallen nature, in a dominant way, so that the Christian, though still troubled and tormented by the urgings of indwelling sin, is no longer ruled by those urgings in the way that was true before. Being under grace, the Christian is freed from sin . . . ; the motivational theocentricity of the heart set free will prompt the actions that form the habits of Christ-likeness that constitute the Spirit's fruit (Gal. 5.22f.), and thus the holiness of radical repentance (daily abandonment of self-centred self-will), childlike humility (daily listening to what God says in his Word, and daily submission to what he sends in his providence), and love to God and humans that honours and serves both, will increasingly appear. This thorough-going intellectual and moral theocentricity, whereby Christians come to live no longer for themselves but for him who died and rose to save them (cf. 2 Cor. 5.15), is first God's gift and then the Christian's task, and as such it is the foundation not only of sound ethics but also of true spirituality.[22]

This is nothing short of breathtaking! Note again: sanctification is that process in which the "dispositional drives of Christ's perfect human character"—that is to say, the "inner urgings" of our Lord that led him to honor, adore, love, and obey the Father—are now "reproduced at the motivational centre" of the believing heart, enabling us to do the same (not perfectly, of course, but principally). Thus, when the question is asked, what is actually happening in the process of sanctification? Packer's answer is:

> Motivationally, within the heart, the change is an implanting in us of the inclinations of Christ's perfect humanity through our ingrafting into him: this produces in us a mind-set and lifestyle that is not explicable in terms of what we were before. The Spirit-born person, as Jesus indicated, cannot but be a mystery to those who are not born again themselves; they can form no idea of what makes him tick (cf. John 3:8).[23]

---

[22] J. I. Packer, "Evangelical Foundations for Spirituality," in *Serving the People of God*, 259.
[23] Ibid., 265.

By this means, then, the "new creation" in Christ (2 Cor. 5:17) undergoes a progressively substantive, what one might even call essential or metaphysical, transformation. The believer does not cease to be human (nor does he become divine), but rather becomes authentically human in the sense that his nature, inclination, longings, and loves gradually conform to those of the incarnate Christ.

Before leaving this topic, we must note another matter. Packer is firmly opposed to any notion of sanctification that restricts itself to external behavior. It is indeed extremely important that the Christian behave as Christ did, that one respond to his or her enemies with restraint and gentleness, that one refrain from sexual immorality, that one speak only to edify and encourage others, that one not retaliate when persecuted, and that one not succumb to the allure of ill-gotten gain, just to cite a few examples. In other words, living in visible obedience to the moral law of God is essential. But it is not enough. It is tragically possible for a person to conform in every outward way just noted, all the while the heart is impatient and angry, and lust rages uncontrolled. One can conceivably give every appearance to the eye of man that he or she cares for the welfare of those in distress, while simultaneously despising them in the heart. One might live a comparatively simple life, largely devoid of the physical opulence that characterizes much of our society today, while yet in the grip of materialism.

Packer's point is that genuine and godly sanctification must include the attitude of the heart and not simply those concrete actions visible to the naked eye. Holiness is more than outward conformity to a law, more than adherence to a set of ethical rules, even when those rules are divinely imposed. As noted above, holiness of life begins at the level of motivation and the transformation of our inmost urgings, inclinations, desires, loves, and longings. As these take on the character of Christ's, one's behavior undergoes a corresponding alteration.

Misconceptions Identified and Corrected

One should not be surprised that such a momentous transformation would be subject to misunderstanding and distortion. Packer provides several helpful reminders of what this supernatural change is and is not. We would do well to heed his warnings.

He begins with the reminder that the change or transformation that we experience in the course of Christian living "is neither instantaneous nor total in this lifetime. Rather, the change takes place through progressive mastery of the motivation by redeemed impulses."[24] As much as we might wish it otherwise, and as fervent as some are in insisting that sinless perfection is attainable prior to the consummation,

> the biblical teaching is rather that the Christian's total self is progressively renewed and restored throughout the sanctifying process—refocused on God, reintegrated with God at the center, reconstructed in character, habits, and reaction patterns, sensitized to God's values, redirected into God-glorifying purposes, and made more alert to others' needs and miseries.[25]

Yet another correction that Packer brings to our attention is in response to the misguided notion that the born-again believer has two natures, an old one and a new one. Christians are often exhorted to obey the latter while denying the former. Sometimes, notes Packer,

> this is illustrated in terms of feeding one of your two dogs while starving the other. The misleading thing here is not the reminder that we are called to holiness and not to sin, but that the idea of "nature" is not being used as it is used both in life and in Scripture (see, for example, Rom 2:14; Eph 2:3). The point is that "nature" means the whole of what we are, and the whole of what we are is expressed in the various actions and reactions that make up our life. To envisage two "natures," distinct sets of desires, neither of which masters me till I choose to let it, is unreal and bewildering, because it leaves out so much of what actually goes on inside me. The clearer and more correct thing to say . . . is this: we are born sinners by nature, dominated and driven from the start—and most of the time unconsciously—by self-seeking, self-serving, self-deifying motives and cravings. Being united to Christ in new birth through the regenerating work of the Spirit has so changed our nature that our heart's deepest desire (the dominant passion that rules and drives us now) is a copy, faint but real, of the desire that drove our Lord Jesus.[26]

Packer also identifies for us two extremes in relation to Christian living to which people often gravitate. He refers to one as *rhapsody without realism*. This is seen in folk who concentrate "totally on devotional exercises,

[24] Don J. Payne, *The Theology of the Christian Life in J. I. Packer's Thought: Theological Anthropology, Theological Method, and the Doctrine of Sanctification* (Colorado Springs: Paternoster, 2006), 169.
[25] Packer, *Rediscovering Holiness*, 111–12.
[26] Ibid., 83–84.

experiences of divine love, ecstasies of assurance, expressions of their own love to God, and the maintaining of emotional warmth and excitement in all their approaches to him and communion with him. Of this ardor, they feel, true holiness essentially consists."[27] As wonderful as this sounds,

> they fall short when it comes to love of neighbor, sometimes even love for their own families. The problem with these people is not that they are insincere, but that their tunnel vision, born of their all-absorbing passion to know, love, and praise God, keeps them from seeing that holiness involves being a responsible realist in the life-situation in which God has placed you. . . . Rhapsody without realism is not Christlike, and it is a failure in holiness rather than a form of it.[28]

This notion of being a "responsible realist" may well be the distinguishing characteristic of Packer's concept of genuine holiness.

A second group tends toward the opposite end of the spectrum, *rule keeping without relating*. Holiness is effectively reduced to a life of law keeping. Such folk are meticulously honest and careful, and insist on correctness in all areas of life, whether at home or at business. They are

> meticulously conscientious in shunning evil and avoiding activities classed as worldly (smoking, drinking, dancing, gambling, use of make-up, etc.); meticulously insistent on maintaining God's truth and fingering error and sin in any company; and their passion to be correct by the code merits unfeigned admiration and applause. But relationally they are cool and distant people, who see rule-book righteousness as the essence of holiness and who concentrate on formal correctness of conduct rather than personal closeness either to God or their fellow human beings.[29]

True holiness, however, "is the healthy growth of morally misshapen humans toward the moral image of Jesus Christ, the perfect man."[30] Note the three elements in Packer's construct. It begins with the recognition of humanity's inherent depravity. We are, he says, "morally misshapen." But, second, we are carried and sustained by God's grace in a process of "growth." For the true believer, there is always progress. Moral stagnation is the sign of unbelief. A true Christian will always struggle against the

---

[27] Ibid., 163–64.
[28] Ibid., 164.
[29] Ibid., 164–65.
[30] Ibid., 165.

downdrag of sin, but the presence of struggle is itself the sign of spiritual life. Finally, there is a goal, namely, conformity to the "moral image of Jesus Christ, the perfect man." This growth, says Packer,

> is an all-around personal wholeness, God-centered, God-honoring, hum-ble, loving, service-oriented, and self-denying, of a kind that we never knew before. One-sidednesses are corrected, undeveloped and under-developed aspects of our personhood are brought into action, and the likeness in us of the moral beauty of Christ's character begins to appear. Moral beauty, like every other kind of beauty, is largely a matter of parts being balanced within the whole, in this case virtues and strengths of character. . . . [Thus] the Christian ideal is of a renewed person in whom love of God and his neighbor; love of God's law and of his fellowship; love of the Father, the Son, and the Spirit; love of worshiping God and of work-ing for God; love of righteousness and love of sinners, blend together in balance. Disproportion and imbalance in the formation of our spiritual identity are not a mode of holiness, but a negating of it.[31]

Yet a similar polarity is seen in those who envision the Christian life as being all about doctrine, for whom "discipleship revolves around the study of theology."[32] Do not misunderstand Packer here. He is himself a theolo-gian of the highest order who regularly insists that apart from the study of God's Word and the doctrines of the church throughout its history there can be no spiritual change. So when he speaks this way, he has in mind those who would reduce Christian living to nothing more than theologi-cal precision and intellectual accuracy. "He or she is not much concerned about experience, not very active in obedience and service of others, and not distinguished for a radically changed life. But the head is always busy with theological questions, and is full to overflowing with doctrine."[33]

Then there is the equally "unnatural development of the Christian who knows very little doctrine and cares very little about doctrine . . . , but who thinks of Christianity as a matter of constantly churned-up feelings and exciting experiences."[34] For such people, Christianity is all experience, all feeling, all thrill, with little or no concern for objective truth. To these Packer would also add the "Christian activist: the restless do-gooder whose

---

[31] Ibid., 165–66.
[32] Ibid., 168.
[33] Ibid.
[34] Ibid.

interest is not in doctrinal truth nor in the devotional disciplines of the spiritual life, but in programs, organizations, and world-changing tasks of one sort or another."[35]

But the life of Christlike consecration to God, in which there is genuine health in the human soul,

> requires of each of us a balanced threefold concern, for truth, for experience, and for action. Where this proportioning of zeal has not yet become habitual, personal spiritual development is lopsided, just as when one's Christian life is a matter of rhapsody without realism, or rule-keeping without relating.[36]

Thus what we need, says Packer, is a wide-angled picture of holiness in which we avoid reducing godliness to a single dimension but seek instead for a more holistic transformation of head, heart, and hand.

If there is a single biblical text that encompasses most of what Packer is trying to teach us, it is 2 Corinthians 3:18, where Paul declares that "we all, with unveiled face, beholding the glory of the Lord, are being transformed into the same image [that is, Christ's image] from one degree of glory to another." What this means, simply put, is that "through the Holy Spirit's agency, we become like the One we look at as we absorb the gospel word. Each step in this character-change . . . is a new degree of glory, that is, of God's self-display in our human lives."[37] As someone has rightly said, beholding is a way of becoming.[38] To this end Packer also cites Paul's exhortation in Romans 12:1–2 that we "present" our bodies to God "as a living sacrifice, holy and acceptable to God," which is our "spiritual worship." Rather than being conformed to this world, we are to "be transformed by the renewal" of our minds.

> Paul's thought is that by our self-offering, we open ourself to God, and thereby bring to an end any resistance to the indwelling Holy Spirit that may have been in us before. As a result the planned and promised supernaturalizing of our inner life through our sharing in Christ's risen life will proceed unhindered.[39]

---

[35] Ibid., 169.
[36] Ibid., 169–70.
[37] Ibid., 171.
[38] See, for example, John Piper, "Letter to an Incomplete, Insecure Teenager," http://www.desiringgod.org/blog/posts/letter-to-an-incomplete-insecure-teenager.
[39] Packer, *Rediscovering Holiness*, 171–72.

Thus Christlike holiness means, among other things, the development of good habits simultaneous with the breaking of bad ones, resisting the temptation to sin, and controlling ourselves when provoked by those who attack us. This can only be done as we put to death the deeds of the flesh (Rom. 8:13). "This too is hard. It is a matter of negating, wishing dead, and laboring to thwart, inclinations, cravings, and habits that have been in you . . . for a long time. Pain and grief, moans and groans, will certainly be involved, for your sin does not want to die, nor will it enjoy the killing process."[40] How radically different this is from the Keswick model of passive yielding that initially promised great hope to Packer but ultimately proved vacuous.

Earlier I mentioned that Packer is consistently opposed to any notion of Christian growth that is restricted to external conformity, devoid of internal change. Similarly, the secret to resisting the sins of the flesh is the mortification of those inner impulses that give rise to them. Packer explains:

> Outward acts of sin come from inner sinful urges, so we must learn to starve these urges of what stimulates them (porn magazines, for instance, if the urge is lust; visits to smorgasbords, if the urge is gluttony; gamblings and lotteries, if the urge is greed; and so on). And when the urge is upon us, we must learn, as it were, to run to our Lord and cry for help, asking him to deepen our sense of his own holy presence and redeeming love, to give us the strength to say "no" to that which can only displease him. It is the Spirit who moves us to act this way, who makes our sense of the holy love of Christ vivid, who imparts the strength for which we pray, and who actually drains the life out of the sins we starve.[41]

We must also avoid the mistake of thinking that spiritual growth will always be easy to recognize. Since the primary locus of growth is the heart, what Packer calls "the dispositional and dynamic core of our selfhood,"[42] it isn't something visible to others. This doesn't mean that we can never discern the presence of spiritual growth. There are countless occurrences in life, such as unanticipated crisis or devastating loss, that can reveal to us all sorts of things about the state of our souls. And one of the things we may see in such instances, with resultant praise and gratitude to God, is the growth of our spiritual stature in Christ.

---

[40] Ibid., 175.
[41] Ibid.
[42] Ibid., 179.

People also mistakenly think that spiritual transformation is uniform, that all Christians will progress at the same rate, to the same degree, and typically respond to life's challenges and sin's temptations in the same way. But "the changes and developments in individuals that sanctifying growth involves vary from one to another in speed, in degree, and in what we may call internal proportioning."[43]

It is also a serious mistake to think that growth in godliness is automatic, as if merely being born again guarantees that transformation for which we have all been saved. Those who are saved *will* be transformed, but not independent of their cooperative response to the grace of God operative within them. And let us never be deceived into thinking that with growth in Christ there comes protection from harm or insulation against the spiritual and even physical attack of the Enemy. Sanctification does not shield us from the pressures, pains, or routine daily distresses in one's Christian life. The fact is that Christians should no more anticipate exemption from suffering, hindrances, and the hatred of the world than did Jesus or Paul.

The Signs of Spiritual Life

We've spent considerable time and space identifying the misconceptions of spiritual growth. So, if we now have some idea of what sanctification isn't, what *is* it? What does growth in grace look like? Packer directs our attention to several important signs.

The first sign "is a growing delight in praising God, with an increasing distaste for being praised oneself. . . . And the higher one goes in praising God, the lower one will go in one's own eyes."[44] Sign two "is a growing instinct for caring and giving, with a more pronounced dislike of the self-absorption that constantly takes without either caring or giving."[45] In addition to these two indicators, there is a third, namely, a growing passion for personal righteousness, with ever-increasing distress over the godlessness and immorality of the world in which we live. Add to this a keener sense of Satan's strategies and the multitude of ways he seeks to blind the minds of the unbelieving, lest they believe the gospel of the glory of God in Christ Jesus (cf. 2 Cor. 4:4).

Packer directs our attention to three additional signs of spiritual life. The child of God who is making significant progress in spiritual transformation

---

[43] Ibid., 183.
[44] Ibid., 188.
[45] Ibid.

will experience a growing zeal for God's name and fame and will be ever more willing to endure whatever resistance or ridicule may come with taking an unpopular stand on behalf of kingdom values. There is also in the true child of God "a greater patience and willingness to wait for God and bow to his will, with a deeper abhorrence of what masquerades as the bold faith, but is really the childish immaturity, that tries to force God's hand."[46]

Finally, there is in the born-again life the presence of heartfelt *joy*. If there is one predominant caricature of Reformed thinkers (such as Packer) that yet lingers in the imagination of both Christians and nonbelievers, it is that they are devoid of genuine joy, or at least highly suspicious of it. Yet nothing could be further from the truth. Packer unmistakably and repeatedly locates joy at the heart of daily Christian living and one's relationship with Christ.

Perhaps this misconception is due to a misunderstanding of what precisely is meant by joy. All too often we've let the culture define it rather than the Bible. When the Scriptures speak of joy, there is nothing of fun and games or the lighthearted mood of the person who is the life of the party. Joy is not the telling of jokes or carefree levity. Rather, "joy is a condition that is experienced, but it is more than a feeling; it is, primarily, a state of mind. Joy, we might say, is a state of the whole man in which thought and feeling combine to produce total euphoria."[47] It first flows out of the assured conviction that one is loved by God. Likewise, it is inextricably tied to one's relationship with Jesus Christ. Thus, when we are exhorted to "rejoice in the Lord," the meaning is that we are to rejoice because we belong to Christ and are through faith in him at peace with God as Father. Joy is the invariable fruit of having been made an heir of glory and being brought into a relationship of forgiveness and freedom.

When the apostle Peter spoke of joy that is "inexpressible and filled with glory" (1 Pet. 1:8) he did not envision an experience unrelated to the mind or theological truth. Indeed, it is only insofar as we "believe in him" that we are capable of rejoicing in this manner and to this degree. Or, as Packer says:

> The secret of joy for believers lies in the fine art of Christian thinking. It is by this means that the Holy Spirit, over and above his special occasional visitations in moments of joy, regularly sustains in us the joy that marks

[46] Ibid., 189.
[47] Packer, *Hot Tub Religion*, 147.

us out as Christ's. Our Lord Jesus wants our joy to be full. Certainly, he has made abundant provision for our joy. And if we focus our minds on the facts from which joy flows, springs of joy will well up in our hearts every day of our lives; and this will turn our ongoing pilgrimage through this world into an experience of contentment and exaltation of which the world knows nothing.[48]

Packer, in line with the seventeenth-century Puritans who influenced him so greatly (more on this later), reminds us often that there is inestimable joy in denying ourselves and taking up our cross to follow Christ in daily sacrifice and discipleship. We are to "rejoice" when our enemies persecute and slander us, for great is our reward in heaven. The radical call of Jesus to cut off the offending hand and to gouge out the sinful eye (a spiritual hyperbole, of course, to emphasize the lengths to which we must be willing to go in mortifying the deeds of the flesh) does not undermine our joy but serves and strengthens it. Notwithstanding the disdain of a secular world or the ridicule of the power elite, Packer would have us always remember that "holiness is essentially a happy business."[49]

---

[48] Ibid., 159.
[49] Packer, *Rediscovering Holiness*, 87.

CHAPTER 6

THE STRUGGLE OF CHRISTIAN LIVING

The Battle with Indwelling Sin (Romans 7)

There is simply no way to exaggerate the significance of Paul's experience in Romans 7 for the way in which J. I. Packer understands the struggle of Christian living. In particular, verses 14–25 have had a formative influence in Packer's theology of the Christian life:

[14] For we know that the law is spiritual, but I am of the flesh, sold under sin. [15] For I do not understand my own actions. For I do not do what I want, but I do the very thing I hate. [16] Now if I do what I do not want, I agree with the law, that it is good. [17] So now it is no longer I who do it, but sin that dwells within me. [18] For I know that nothing good dwells in me, that is, in my flesh. For I have the desire to do what is right, but not the ability to carry it out. [19] For I do not do the good I want, but the evil I do not want is what I keep on doing. [20] Now if I do what I do not want, it is no longer I who do it, but sin that dwells within me.

[21] So I find it to be a law that when I want to do right, evil lies close at hand. [22] For I delight in the law of God, in my inner being, [23] but I see in my members another law waging war against the law of my mind and making me captive to the law of sin that dwells in my members. [24] Wretched man that I am! Who will deliver me from this body of death? [25] Thanks be to

God through Jesus Christ our Lord! So then, I myself serve the law of God
with my mind, but with my flesh I serve the law of sin.[1]

Romans 7 is one of the most disputed passages in all of Scripture.
The debate rages over such questions as: Who is this "man" whom Paul
describes? Is he a Christian or a non-Christian? Does Paul portray for us
here what some might call the "normal" Christian life, or is this a portrayal
of what we were before being born again, a condition from which, by the
grace of God, we have been delivered? Is the Christian life one of severe
struggle and frequent defeat, or is it one of triumph over sin and victory
over the flesh? Or are these questions themselves misleading? Is there a
third or middle way between these two extremes?

Before we look at Packer's interpretation, a brief overview of the options is in order. One view of Romans 7 insists that the man described by
Paul in verses 14–25 is regenerate or born again. But there are a number
of variations within this perspective, only two of which I'll note. People
such as Augustine, Martin Luther, John Calvin, John Owen, John Murray,
and John Stott, just to mention a few, believe that the experience of verses
14–25 is one which even the most sanctified and mature of believers may
expect to encounter until the resurrection of the body. The battle Paul describes is thus one we all should expect to fight until Jesus returns. As we'll
shortly see, this is Packer's view.

Others insist that Paul is describing an experience that may be overcome
through growth and maturity in the faith. The goal is to exchange the conflict of Romans 7 for the victory of Romans 8. In other words, 7:14–25 describes the Christian who has failed to avail himself of the power of the Holy
Spirit. This believer's experience may be "normal" in the sense that many
languish in this condition, but it is by no means "normative"; God has provided us with everything necessary to live victoriously over such sin. Thus,
according to the first of these two perspectives, verses 14–25 describe the life
of the believer at all times, whereas the second view envisions moving out of
immaturity and into a more triumphant, victorious, higher Christian life. It
is this latter view that Packer was taught soon after his conversion.

---

[1] There are two primary places where Packer has addressed Paul's meaning in this text. See J. I. Packer,
"The 'Wretched Man' Revisited: Another Look at Romans 7:14–25," in *Romans and the People of God: Es-
says in Honor of Gordon D. Fee on the Occasion of His 65th Birthday*, ed. Sven K. Soderlund and N. T. Wright
(Grand Rapids: Eerdmans, 1999), 70–81; and "The 'Wretched Man' in Romans 7," in *Keep in Step with the
Spirit* (Old Tappan, NJ: Fleming H. Revell, 1984), 263–70, an earlier version of which chapter is found in
J. I. Packer, "The 'Wretched Man' of Romans 7," *Studia Evangelica* 2 (1964): 621–27.

Another interpretive option is that Paul is describing someone who is unregenerate. Under this major heading, some see this as Paul's *autobiographical* account of his own preconversion experience, either as understood by him at the time of his non-Christian life and later recorded, or as understood in retrospect when he was writing Romans. According to the latter, Paul looks with Christian eyes on his former, non-Christian state. He now discerns a discord or struggle that was present then but unrecognized at that time.

Others believe this is Paul's portrayal not of himself, but of *man* under the law. The "I" is not Paul himself but a stylistic form making for a more vivid picture than our colorless "one." Thus it is Paul's analysis of *human* existence apart from faith, either as seen by the non-Christian himself or as seen by the Christian, in this case Paul. A somewhat similar perspective, but with a slight difference in emphasis, is the position taken by Douglas Moo. He believes that verses 14–25 describe the situation of an unregenerate person.

> Specifically, I think that Paul is looking back, from his Christian understanding, to the situation of himself, and other Jews like him, living under the law of Moses. . . . Now, in vv. 14–25, he portrays his own condition as a Jew under the law, but, more importantly, the condition of all Jews under the law. Paul speaks as a "representative" Jew, detailing his past in order to reveal the weakness of the law and the source of that weakness: the human being, the *ego*.[2]

This view, in one of its many forms, was the position of the early church fathers and has found exponents in more recent times in James Denney, Herman Ridderbos, Robert Gundry, and as noted above, Douglas Moo.

A few argue that Paul is describing *both* the regenerate and the nonregenerate person. This would then be the experience of any morally earnest man, whether Christian or non-Christian, who seeks to obey God's law on his own without the resources and strength that grace and the Holy Spirit alone can provide. Leslie Mitton explains:

> Romans 7 may therefore be said to deal with the condition of a man who is trying to do right, as he understands what right is, but who is not "in Christ." Such a man may be one who has not yet been converted to Christ,

---

[2] Douglas J. Moo, *The Epistle to the Romans* (Grand Rapids: Eerdmans, 1996), 447–48.

or one who has relapsed from Christ. It is concerned, therefore, neither exclusively with what is past, nor with what is present, but with that which was true of Paul's past, and may become true of the present.[3]

Others arguing for some form of this view include Richard Longenecker, W. H. Griffith Thomas, and Anthony Hoekema.

John Stott argues for an unusual view that should also be classified here. He identifies three facts about the person in Romans 7 that he thinks cannot be avoided. (1) He is regenerate (born again). (2) Although regenerate, "he is not a normal, healthy, mature believer."[4] And (3) "this man appears to know nothing, either in understanding or in experience, of the Holy Spirit."[5] Thus Stott concludes that the "I" of Romans 7 is

> an Old Testament believer, an Israelite who is living under the law, including even the disciples of Jesus before Pentecost and probably many Jewish Christian contemporaries of Paul. Such people were regenerate. Old Testament believers were almost ecstatic about the law. . . . But these Old Testament believers who loved the law lacked the Spirit. . . . They were born of the Spirit, but not indwelt by the Spirit.[6]

Stott then suggests that

> some church-goers today might be termed "Old Testament Christians." . . . They show signs of new birth in their love for the church and the Bible, yet their religion is law, not gospel; flesh, not the Spirit; the "oldness" of slavery to rules and regulations, not the "newness" of freedom through Jesus Christ.[7]

Finally, a few argue that the "I" of Romans 7 is neither regenerate nor unregenerate. I'll mention two quite different variations on this approach. First, Martyn Lloyd-Jones argues that the "I" of Romans 7 is a man who is experiencing deep conviction of sin by the Holy Spirit and who therefore yearns to be holy but cannot. In other words, he is a man who is experiencing the *preparatory* work of the Holy Spirit, which eventually will lead to regeneration. Somewhat similarly, some take Romans 7 as an authentic record of Paul's

---

[3] C. Leslie Mitton, "Romans—vii. Reconsidered," in *The Expository Times* 65 (February 1954): 134.
[4] John R. W. Stott, *Romans: God's Good News for the World* (Downers Grove, IL: InterVarsity, 1994), 208.
[5] Ibid.
[6] Ibid., 209.
[7] Ibid., 210.

own experience during the period that culminated in his vision of Christ and conversion on the road to Damascus. The second variation of this view comes from Thomas Schreiner, who contends that "Paul does not intend to distinguish believers from unbelievers in this text."[8] The issue, he says, is the law's inherent inability to transform human beings, whether Christian or not.

Our concern, of course, is with how Packer reads this passage and the way in which it gives shape to his understanding of Christian living.

Packer on Paul

Packer believes that what we read here is a description of "the healthy Christian in honest and realistic self-assessment."[9] We should especially take note of his use of the word "healthy." If one were to ask Packer how Paul could possibly have given expression to such agonizing feelings of frustration and failure, especially amid his emphatic declarations in Romans 6 and 8 of the victory available to those in whom the Spirit lives and works, Packer would respond that Paul's language is not the result of his being a defeated sinner but precisely because he is a saint. In other words, sin has a numbing effect on the soul; it anesthetizes us to the conviction of the Spirit. Paul's apparent hypersensitivity to a sense of failure is due precisely to his having made such gracious and glorious progress in the Christian life, and even the slightest tinge of sin wreaks havoc on his heart.

Packer argues that Paul is providing us with an explanation of the relation between God's law and human sin. He summarizes this in three points. First,

> the effect of the law is to give knowledge of sin—not merely of the abstract notion of sin, but of the quasi-personal reality of sin as a driving force within us all, a spirit of rebellion and self-assertion against God, of pride and unwillingness to be dominated by anything or anybody from outside, and specifically of dislike and disobedience in relation to God's commands (7:7, 13; cf. 3:20).[10]

Second, the law gives this knowledge "by setting God's commands and prohibitions before us; for these first goad sin into active rebellion and

---

[8] Thomas R. Schreiner, *Romans*, Baker Exegetical Commentary on the New Testament (Grand Rapids: Baker, 1998), 390.
[9] Packer, "The 'Wretched Man' Revisited," 72.
[10] Ibid.

then enable us to see the specific shortcomings of motive and behavior into which sin has led us (7:8, 19, 23)."[11] Third, as good as it may be, being divine in origin, the law neither promises nor provides sufficient ability to fulfill the good it commands, nor is it capable of diminishing the presence of sin or freeing us of sin's power (7:9–11, 22–24).

Paul makes this point by using the first person singular in verses 7–13. He then moves from the aorist to the present tense in verses 14–25, where he

> describes the experience of a person who sees himself constantly failing to do the good that the law commands, and that he himself actually wants to do, and who through reflecting on this fact has come to see the bitter truth stated at the outset as the thesis of this section—"I am unspiritual [carnal, KJV; of the flesh, NRSV], sold as a slave to sin" (7:14).[12]

Packer points out something of vital importance for silencing objections to the view that this describes a regenerate man. He insists that "sold as a slave to sin" (Packer's rendering of the phrase) is *pictorial* rather than *theological* language. In other words, Paul is articulating quite vividly how the condition being described "feels" rather than expressing it in explicit and intentional theological terms. Packer insists that it is precisely because Paul is a Spirit-filled and Spirit-led man who loves God and his law that such moral failures feel as though he were a bond slave to sin. His heightened sensitivity to sin in his life accounts for this elevated and emotionally intense language. It is not, therefore, a technical affirmation that he is in fact still under the power of sin and under divine wrath.

Contrary to one of the views noted earlier, Packer believes that the notion that Paul is speaking in representative terms against the background of his own remembered experience—as if he were in some sense portraying himself as a typical Jew, or Adam, or a human being in Adam as such—is fundamentally misguided. Neither does he believe that Paul is "remembering himself as a Pharisee or personating a pagan moralist and so speaking for unregenerates who, whatever their idealism and moralism, fall short behaviorally and have not yet learned to thank God for Jesus Christ and to receive through him the free gift of pardon and acceptance."[13] Instead, Packer is convinced that Paul's "wretched man" cry

---

[11] Ibid., 72–73.
[12] Ibid.
[13] Ibid., 75.

is the mark of a healthy believer who loves God's law and aims to keep it perfectly, but finds that something within him whose presence is known only by its effects, namely indwelling sin, obstructs and thwarts his purpose; for it betrays him time and again into doing things which at the moment of action seem good but in hindsight appear bad—meaning unwise, unprincipled, unjust, unloving, thoughtless, faithless, cowardly, self-serving, disobedient, irreverent, and so on (see vv. 21–23). The wretchedness of the "wretched man" then springs from thus discovering his continued sinfulness, and from knowing that he cannot hope to be rid of indwelling sin, his unwelcome and troubling inmate, as long as he is in the body—that is, while his present life lasts.[14]

On this view the verb to be supplied in verse 24 is future tense: "Who *will* deliver . . ." Thanks be to God "who *will deliver* me" in the coming age when I get my resurrection body. Thus the thanksgiving has for its focus neither one's current state of having been justified nor the enabling power of the Spirit presently enjoyed. Rather, it is a declaration of personal Christian hope.

So, in Romans 7:14–25 Paul is describing not so much a *struggle*, says Packer, but a *discernment*. Paul becomes aware of his shortcoming—that he failed to do what he wanted and intended—and thus his text describes the reality of his frustration at this repeated discovery, rather than his despair over a struggle that brings repeated and persistent failure. Therefore, Paul is not describing complete moral failure, "as if behaviorally the 'wretched man' never gets anything right in any sense at all. The bewildered and distressed consciousness that Paul analyzes is simply of a very much desired perfection not being attained."[15] In other words, Paul is not telling us that the daily experience of this "wretched man" is as bad as it could be, but rather that it is not as good as it should be. On this view, then, "the 'wretched man' is Paul himself, spontaneously voicing his distress at not being a better Christian than he is, and all we know of Paul personally fits in with this supposition."[16]

The result of this reading is Packer's remarkably insightful and practical help in enabling us to grasp Paul's perspective, and what should also be our own when it comes to every believer's struggle with sin. It is a simple

---

[14] Ibid., 76.
[15] Ibid., 77.
[16] Ibid.

but pointed reminder that Paul is speaking to us within the framework of *inaugurated eschatology*. Packer's explanation here is a model of theological clarity and pastoral wisdom. What Paul has done is to bring us to the recognition

> that through the Spirit Christians enjoy the firstfruits, foretaste, initial installment, and dawning enjoyment of the life of the new aeon, the kingdom era of redeemed existence, while the old aeon, the era of existence spoiled by sin, continues, and the fullness of new aeon life remains future. The two ages overlap, and Christians are anchored in both, so that language proper to both is appropriate, indeed necessary, for describing their condition theologically. Justified by faith and "alive to God in Christ Jesus" (6:11), believers serve God "in the new life of the Spirit" (7:6, NRSV), as those who belong to the new aeon; but sin, the anti-God driving force whose dominion has marked and marred the old aeon from the start, still indwells them, holding them back and leading them away from the full-scale righteousness at which they now aim. Living simultaneously in both aeons and finding in themselves both dynamics, that of their own law-loving, new-aeon "inner being" (7:22; "inmost self," NRSV) and that of the law-opposing, old-aeon "sin living in me . . . within my members" (7:20, 23 [NIV]), Christians have a two-sided experience: the uplifting of the Spirit and the downdrag of sin both operate, and bewilderment results.[17]

Therefore, we must conclude, says Packer, "that in 7:14–25 Paul is describing, not a man in Adam, writhing under the condemnation of a law that he resents even as he acknowledges its authority, but a man in Christ, whose heart is now turned to love the law and to bewail only his inability to keep it perfectly."[18] This is what Packer means by "healthy" or "normal" Christian living. It bears repeating yet again that Paul's obvious emotional anguish as he contemplates his personal experience is not because he is a hopelessly enslaved sinner with little or no prospects for extricating himself from this wretched condition. Rather, he faces inner turmoil precisely because he is a mature and ever-growing saint. The greater and more influential the presence of transforming grace in his heart, the greater and more intensely painful the lingering reality of sin will prove to be. Whereas a life immersed in sin anesthetizes the soul, rendering it increasingly inca-

---

[17] Ibid., 77–78.
[18] Ibid., 80.

pable of feeling genuine conviction, a life in tune with the Holy Spirit and devoted to the supremacy of God's glory is ever more sensitive to even the least degree of sin committed.

One should by no means conclude from this that Packer has reverted to his earlier belief that the Christian might conceivably grow beyond the conflict that indwelling sin persistently provokes. When Packer speaks of ever-increasing maturity and godliness, he is not endorsing the view that the hope of the Christian in this life is to escape from the anguish of Romans 7 into the perfect peace of Romans 8. He is not describing a transition from "carnality" to "spirituality." He explains:

> But the desires that constitute the flesh in Paul's sense, though now dethroned, are not yet destroyed, and in many cases remain psychologically potent within us. Perfect accomplishment of what we want most heartily to do is still beyond us: at this point our reach exceeds our grasp. To be sure, we fight moral and spiritual battles with what we find inside us and we win victories; we make progress, cleansing ourselves "from every defilement of body and spirit, bringing holiness to completion in the fear of God" (2 Cor. 7:1). But here on earth the task is never finished. Everything we do appears in retrospect as something we could and should have done better, and whenever we measure our actual performance by Scripture, shortcomings stand out.[19]

Once again, to make the point with unmistakable clarity, the second half of Paul's statements in Romans 7, says Packer, refers

> to the involuntary down drag of indwelling sin in its myriad forms, obstructing, distracting, dissembling, deceiving and keeping us from doing, properly and purely, the things that we most want to do. Things our hearts know we should not do—little things, maybe, but grievous— repeatedly fool us into thinking we want to do them just this once or into doing them without thinking at all, and then we wake up to the fact that we have done, not the good we should have done, but things that were poor quality, much less than the best, and often downright bad. *This is an ongoing aspect of every Christian's experience as long as we are in this world.* So Christian living involves a permanent element of conflict and struggle, not only with temptations that come from outside but

---

[19] J. I. Packer and Carolyn Nystrom, *Praying: Finding Our Way through Duty to Delight* (Downers Grove, IL: InterVarsity, 2006), 274.

with impulses, urges, attitudes, moods and mental states that bubble up around the heart and to some extent block and derail our purpose of obeying and honoring God with perfect purity of heart and perfect precision of action.[20]

Is Assurance of Salvation Possible?

People often emerge from an exploration of Romans 7 and its bare-knuckled approach to the ongoing struggle with indwelling sin and wonder aloud: If this is true, is assurance of salvation even possible? If I must continually wage war with indwelling sin, may I ever enter into the joy of knowing I'm saved?

Packer would respond by arguing that it is impossible to envision a joyful and peaceful Christian life apart from the assurance of salvation. Every born-again child of God ought to find the inexpressible delight that comes from knowing that he or she is the recipient of God's unmerited mercy and saving favor. To confidently know that nothing can ever separate us from the love of God in Christ is the pinnacle of Christian assurance. To live in the fullness of the knowledge of Christ's immeasurable love for us, a knowledge that Paul says surpasses all human calculation (Eph. 3:18–19), is at the heart of living as a Christian in this world. But how does this come to pass? On what grounds may we rest assured that we stand in union with Christ and at peace with the Father?

Packer is quick to remind us that no one has a right to claim confidence in salvation who does not walk in the path of conscious and purposeful obedience to God. That is not to say that sinless perfection is the condition of assurance, but that when failures occur there is repentance, as previously defined. There is always the danger of self-deception that may even be of demonic origin. Therefore, inward assurance, says Packer, must always be checked and monitored by external moral and spiritual tests such as we find in 1 John. Do we consistently and happily embrace the truth that Jesus is God in human flesh? Do we demonstrate over time, in concrete acts of self-sacrifice and generosity, a love for the brethren? Are our lives marked by joyful obedience to the fullness of biblical revelation? These objective tests must combine with that more subjective, inner confidence to bring authentic assurance.

It is in this regard that Packer directs our attention to 2 Peter 1:3–11, where we learn that daily, progressive growth in sanctification is the only

---

[20] Ibid., 274–75 (emphasis mine).

way to make one's calling and election sure. Packer reminds us forcefully that texts such as 1 Corinthians 6:9–11; Galatians 6:7–8; and Ephesians 5:5–6 are wake-up calls to those unrepentantly unholy persons who claim to be born again but are clearly self-deceived. If they continue unabated on the path they are pursuing, only wrath and exclusion from God's kingdom await them. Therefore,

> if we value assurance (and Romans 8, which is an ecstatic exposition of the content of Christian assurance, must surely convince us that a valid assurance is of infinite worth), we must seek it by obeying the teaching to which we have been entrusted, and so reaping the fruit that consists of holiness, as Paul puts it in Romans 6:17 and 22. Feelings of confidence about our salvation need to be tested before they are trusted.[21]

I have been especially stirred and encouraged in this regard by Packer's portrait of the love of God in his classic work *Knowing God*. He points to Romans 5 in particular. Paul's declaration is that the hope we have put in Christ "does not put us to shame, because God's love has been poured into our hearts through the Holy Spirit who has been given to us" (Rom. 5:5). Packer draws our attention to three things. First, the word translated "poured" "suggests a free flow and a large quantity—in fact, an inundation. . . . Paul is not talking of faint and fitful impressions, but of deep and overwhelming ones." God is not stingy with his love but overflows in abundant kindness toward his children. Packer also highlights the tense of the verb in verse 5.

> It is in the perfect, which implies a settled state consequent upon a completed action. The thought is that knowledge of the love of God, having flooded our hearts, *fills them now*, just as a valley once flooded remains full of water. Paul assumes that all his readers, like himself, will be living in the enjoyment of a strong and abiding sense of God's love for them.

Finally, Paul wants us to know that the instilling of this knowledge "is described as part of the *regular ministry of the Spirit* to those who receive him—to all, that is, who are born again, all who are true believers."[22]

---

[21] J. I. Packer, *Hot Tub Religion* (Wheaton, IL: Tyndale House, 1987), 176–77.
[22] J. I. Packer, *Knowing God* (Downers Grove, IL: InterVarsity, 1973), 118.

Here we see how important and practical it is that we know God's love for us. For if we know it, we may rightly ask of ourselves:

> Why do I ever grumble and show discontent and resentment at the circumstances in which God has placed me? Why am I ever distrustful, fearful or depressed? Why do I ever allow myself to grow cool, formal and halfhearted in the service of the God who loves me so? Why do I ever allow my loyalties to be divided, so that God has not all my heart?[23]

---

[23] Ibid., 127.

CHAPTER 7

THE CATALYST FOR CHRISTIAN LIVING

The Person of the Holy Spirit

Among those regarded as contemporary champions of the Reformed faith, few have written more extensively or thought more deeply about the ministry of the Holy Spirit than has J. I. Packer. Our concern, of course, is with Packer's understanding of the role of the Spirit in Christian living, but the extent of his reflections on the broader work of the third person of the Trinity is remarkable. As a theological cessationist,[1] Packer has not been hesitant to voice numerous penetrating critical insights into errors he has detected in the broader Pentecostal/charismatic/Third Wave movement. At the same time, he has displayed a commendable openness in recognizing both the presence of God and the practical value of certain of its emphases. As is typical of Packer, his interaction with those with whom he differs is a model of Christian charity and a reflection of his desire to maintain unity within the broader body of Christ. Although not our primary focus in this chapter, a brief comment is in order regarding Packer's overall assessment of this now-global phenomenon[2] before turning to his wider understanding of the Holy Spirit in general.

---

[1] A cessationist is someone who believes certain revelatory and miraculous spiritual gifts ceased to be operative in the church soon after the death of the last apostle.

[2] Among Packer's many writings on the Holy Spirit and the contemporary charismatic renewal, the more helpful include "On Being Serious about the Holy Spirit," and "The Holy Spirit and His Work," in *Celebrat-*

The Holy Spirit and Charismatic Phenomena

Packer responds to those who are offended by charismatic phenomena with the observation that we are very apt to react "by abusing the whole movement and denying that there is anything of God in it at all. But how silly! And how nasty! This is a reaction of wounded pride and wilful prejudice, and as such is bad thinking in every way."[3] Not one to overlook what he considers serious extremes in certain segments of the charismatic world, Packer does at least acknowledge that "if charismatics err [and he believes they do], they err only by expecting to receive from God, whose face they seek, more than he has actually promised."[4] When one examines the fruit of the movement by biblical standards, says Packer,

> it becomes plain that God is in it. For, whatever threats and perhaps instances of occult and counterfeit spirituality we may think we detect round its periphery (and what movement of revival has ever lacked these things round its periphery?), its main effect everywhere is to promote robust Trinitarian faith, personal fellowship with the divine Saviour and Lord whom we meet in the New Testament, repentance, obedience, and love to fellow-Christians, expressed in ministry of all sorts towards them; plus a zeal for evangelistic outreach which puts the staider sort of churchmen to shame.[5]

In summary, and laying aside matters of detail, Packer believes that

> God has generated it [the charismatic movement] in order to counter and correct the death-dealing fashions of thought which, starting with theologians and spreading everywhere, for the past century have done damage by demurring at the truth of the trinity, diminishing the deity of Jesus Christ, and for practical purposes discounting the Holy Spirit altogether.[6]

---

ing the Saving Work of God, vol. 1 of The Collected Shorter Writings of J. I. Packer (Carlisle, UK: Paternoster, 1998), 205–9 and 211–35; "Mapping the Spirit's Path: The Charismatic Life," and "Mapping the Spirit's Path: Interpreting the Charismatic Life," in Keep in Step with the Spirit (Old Tappan, NJ: Fleming H. Revell, 1984), 170–99 and 200–34; "Piety on Fire," and "Theological Reflections on the Charismatic Movement," in Serving the People of God, vol. 2 of The Collected Shorter Writings of J. I. Packer (Carlisle, UK: Paternoster), 99–109 and 111–55.

[3] Packer, "Piety on Fire," 104.

[4] Ibid., 105.

[5] Packer, "Theological Reflections on the Charismatic Movement," 125.

[6] J. I. Packer, Rediscovering Holiness (Ann Arbor, MI: Servant, 1992), 52–53. Unlike many who, because of their disagreements with charismatic theology, tend to dismiss the movement altogether, Packer argues that "though charismatic theology in its usual forms is not viable, charismatic experience could and should be accounted for theologically in other terms and on that basis accepted as from God, and therefore valuable" (Celebrating the Saving Work of God, 233).

But our focus here is primarily on how Packer conceives the work of the Spirit in the process of individual sanctification. To that we now turn our attention.

Identifying the Primary Role of the Spirit

To what end or for what principal purpose was the Spirit of God poured out on the church of Jesus Christ? Packer answers this question by identifying several different, but complementary, ways in which evangelicals have understood the role of the Spirit. It's important to take note of the word "complementary" insofar as Packer envisions these various perspectives not as mutually exclusive, but rather as each one supplying a facet of the Spirit's work and thus filling out what may be lacking in any one point of emphasis. This isn't to say he is reluctant to identify what he believes is the "primary" role of the Spirit, but only to keep us mindful of the importance of a full-orbed theology (or what he calls "wide-angled" view) of the Spirit's ministry.

We begin with those who argue that the Spirit is primarily concerned with our experience of power, in the sense of God-given ability to fulfill all that God has commanded us to do, and indeed we genuinely want to do, but feel that we lack the strength to carry through to the end. Packer never suggests that there is something wrong with this. The New Testament says much about divine "power" for life and ministry. "What we are being told is that supernatural living through supernatural empowering is at the very heart of New Testament Christianity, so that those who, while professing faith, do not experience and show forth this empowering are suspect by New Testament standards."[7] Indeed, Packer would insist that the experience of spiritual power is a theme that should always be given prominence anytime the Christian faith is discussed.

Notwithstanding Packer's well-known cessationist theological stance and his understandable reservations about certain dimensions of the charismatic movement, he maintains without apology that the Christian life is and always must be what he calls "empowered." In an important chapter he contributed to the book *The Kingdom and the Power: Are Healing and the Spiritual Gifts Used by Jesus and the Early Church Meant for the Church Today?*,

---

[7] Packer, *Keep in Step with the Spirit*, 23.

Packer acknowledges the clear New Testament witness to the importance of power.[8] There are three specific realms in which the power of the Spirit is most readily needed and manifest. The first is the *physical* realm, which would include both miracles of nature and divine healings of all sorts. God's power is also to be sought and expected in *gospel communication.* Here Packer has in mind such texts as Luke 4:14; 24:47–49; Acts 1:8; 4:33; Romans 1:16; 15:18–19; 1 Cor. 1:17–18; and 2:4–5. Apart from the energizing presence of the Spirit, our words cannot be expected to accomplish anything of lasting spiritual value. Finally, Packer directs our attention to the Spirit's power at work in and through the believer to enable the child of God to *understand* divine revelation and to do what otherwise could not be done. With regard to this dimension of divine power in Ephesians 1:17–19, Packer points out that "it is not just power in the *message.* It is not just power through the *messenger.* It is power *in and upon those who believe,* making their life utterly different from what it was before. It is resurrection power—a matter of God raising with Christ those who have become willing to die with Christ."[9]

How, then, should the Christian approach God in prayer, and for what ought we all to be expectant when it comes to such displays of divine power through the Spirit? Packer is not without an answer.

First, Packer does not allow the excesses of some to undermine the importance of a robust belief in the supernatural and biblically circumscribed expectations of what God both can and may well do in our midst. Indeed, he contends that our expectations of seeing God's power in the transformation of peoples' lives are generally not as high as they should be. While acknowledging the somewhat justified reaction of the Protestant Reformers to the excessive claims of the Roman Catholic Church, he believes "the reformers' reaction against the supernatural in the lives of God's people in this age of the Holy Spirit was, frankly, more wrong than right."[10] As for what we've seen in the more recent charismatic renewal, "we should thank

---

[8] See J. I. Packer, "The Empowered Christian Life," in *The Kingdom and the Power: Are Healing and the Spiritual Gifts Used by Jesus and the Early Church Meant for the Church Today?,* ed. Gary S. Greig and Kevin N. Springer (Ventura, CA: Regal, 1993), 207–15.

[9] Ibid., 210. This is evidently what Packer has in mind when he describes the Spirit as he "who authenticates them [the Scriptures] to us as the Word of God; interprets them to us so that we see what they mean and know that the divine realities spoken of truly exist; applies to us the principles of believing and living that the Scriptures teach and illustrate; and animates us to respond to what we know in faith, worship, and obedience. They [biblical inerrantists] will underline again and again the incapacity of the fallen human mind to think rightly of God apart from the guidance of Scripture, and they will constantly emphasize that it is only as each one is the beneficiary of the Spirit's illuminating and interpreting ministry that they have any knowledge of divine things to share with others" ("The Holy Spirit and His Work," 219).

[10] Packer, "The Empowered Christian Life," 211.

God that expectations of supernatural healing and answer to prayer have risen during this past 30 or 40 years."[11]

Packer says this while simultaneously warning us not to undervalue the natural and the ordinary in Christian living. In other words, he rightly identifies one area in which too many in the charismatic movement have taken a truth and run with it recklessly. He has in mind the all-too-common failure to properly appreciate God's work in what we might call the mundane dimensions of daily life. His word for this mistake is *super-supernaturalism*. His comments on this point are well worth a close reading:

> [*Super-supernaturalism*] is my word for that way of affirming the supernatural which exaggerates its discontinuity with the natural. Reacting against flat-tire versions of Christianity, which play down the supernatural and so do not expect to see God at work, the super-supernaturalist constantly expects miracles of all sorts—striking demonstrations of God's presence and power—and he is happiest when he thinks he sees God acting contrary to the nature of things, so confounding common sense. For God to proceed slowly and by natural means is to him a disappointment, almost a betrayal. But his undervaluing of the natural, regular, and ordinary shows him to be romantically immature and weak in his grasp of the realities of creation and providence as basic to God's work of grace.[12]

Second, notwithstanding the widespread differences of opinion currently on the nature and duration of spiritual gifts, Packer believes it is right for Christians to aspire to use those gifts in powerful and useful ministry. At the same time, he is wise to remind us that gifts are secondary and that sanctity is primary. Or again, character must always take precedence over charisma. We need to realize that "there can be *gifts* without *graces*; that is, one may be capable of performances that benefit others spiritually and yet be a stranger oneself to the Spirit-wrought inner transformation that true knowledge of God brings."[13] Throughout the New Testament, when God's redemptive and sanctifying work in human lives is center stage, the ethical or moral always has priority over the charismatic. That is to say, the New Testament authors are far more concerned with the degree to which our lives reflect the image of Jesus Christ (as seen in love for one's enemies, humility, kindness, submission to the will of God, etc.) than they are with what spiritual gifts we possess.

---

[11] Ibid.
[12] Packer, *Keep in Step with the Spirit*, 193–94.
[13] Ibid., 31.

Packer's point is that "any mind-set which treats the Spirit's gifts (ability and willingness to run around and do things) as more important than his fruit (Christlike character in personal life) is spiritually wrongheaded and needs correcting."[14] He rightly warns us about those who see the doctrine of the Spirit as essentially about *performance*, in the sense of our public use of the charismata. Sadly, for such people the Spirit's ministry seems both to start and to end with the possession and employment of gifts. Packer is far from dismissing altogether this work of the Spirit in edifying both the individual and the corporate body of Christ. But there are problems with taking a *secondary* or subsidiary work of the Spirit and making it *central* to the purpose for which the Father commissioned him. Packer explains:

> First, magnifying lay ministry has led some laymen to undervalue and indeed discount the special responsibilities to which clergy are ordained and to forget the respect that is due to the minister's office and leadership. Second, emphasis on God's habit of giving saints gifts that correspond to nothing of which they seemed capable before conversion (and make no mistake, that really is God's habit) has blinded some to the fact that the most significant gifts in the church's life (preaching, teaching, leadership, counsel, support) are ordinarily natural abilities sanctified. Third, some have balanced their encouragement of extreme freedom in personal Christian performance by introducing extremely authoritarian forms of pastoral oversight, in some cases going beyond the worst forms of medieval priestcraft in taking control of Christians' consciences.[15]

There is something misguided in our reading of Scripture when we focus on the charismata as if they were the Spirit's primary ministry to us individually and thus the aspect of the Spirit's work on which we should set our highest concentration.

Third, every Christian should have a goal to be a channel of divine power into the lives of others who are hurting and in need. That being said, we need to guard ourselves from "the neurosis of needing to be needed—the state of not feeling you are worthwhile unless you are able to feel that others need you. That is not spiritual health. That is *lack* of spiritual health."[16]

Fourth, and following on a point made earlier, Packer cannot conceive of evangelistic success apart from the manifestation of divine power in and

---

[14] Ibid., 33.
[15] Ibid., 30.
[16] Packer, "The Empowered Christian Life," 213.

through the messenger. This does not mean he believes that for evangelism to be real it must always have a miracle attached to it, but neither should we shy away from the demonstration of God's power in awakening human hearts to the truth of the gospel.

Fifth, and finally,

> it is right to want to be divinely empowered for righteousness, for moral victories, for deliverance from bad habits, and for pleasing God. . . . The good news is that through the means of grace, all Christians *may* be so empowered. Through the Spirit, you and I may and must mortify the deeds of the Body. Through the Spirit, you and I may and must manifest the new habits, the new Christlike behaviors that constitute the fruit of the Spirit.[17]

All that being said (and Packer says it without hesitation), experience would suggests that when the power theme is made central to our thinking about the Spirit—to such an extent that it loses its anchoring in a deeper view of the Spirit's ministry with a different center—"unhappy disfigurements soon creep in."[18] It can tend

> to produce an egoistic, introverted cast of mind that becomes indifferent to community concerns and social needs. The Spirit's work tends to be spoken of man centeredly, as if God's power is something made available for us to switch on and *use* . . . by a technique of thought and will for which *consecration* and *faith* is the approved name.[19]

Then there are those for whom the doctrine of the Spirit centers, above all else, on what Packer calls *purifying* and *purgation*. By this he has in mind

> God's work of cleansing his children from sin's defilement and pollution by enabling them to resist temptation and do what is right. For these folk, the key thought is of the holiness that the Spirit imparts as he progressively sanctifies us, enabling us to mortify indwelling sin . . . and changing us ". . . from one degree of glory to another . . ." (2 Corinthians 3:18).[20]

Again, this crucial dimension of the Spirit's work is entirely biblical.

---

[17] Ibid., 214.
[18] Packer, *Keep in Step with the Spirit*, 26.
[19] Ibid.
[20] Ibid., 33–34.

We must not forget "the reality of conflict in the Christian life. You must realize," says Paul in Galatians 5:17 and Romans 7,

> that there are two opposed sorts of desire in every Christian's makeup. The opposition between them appears at the level of motive. There are desires that express the natural anti-God egoism of fallen human nature, and there are desires that express the supernatural, God-honoring, God-loving motivation that is implanted by new birth. Now because he has in him these opposite motivational urgings, one holding him back whenever the other draws him forward, the Christian finds that his heart is never absolutely pure, nor does he ever do anything that is absolutely right, even though his constant goal is perfect service of God springing from what the hymn calls "loyal singleness of heart." In this sense he is being prevented every moment from doing what he wants to do. He lives with the knowledge that everything he has done might and should have been better: not only the lapses into which pride, weakness, and folly have betrayed him, but also his attempts to do what was right and good.[21]

As Romans 7:17 reminds us:

> The Christian who thus walks in the Spirit will keep discovering that nothing in his life is as good as it should be; that he has never fought as hard as he might have done against the clogging restraints and contrary pulls of his own inbred perversity; that there is an element of motivational sin, at least, in his best works; that his daily living is streaked with defilements, so that he has to depend every moment on God's pardoning mercy in Christ, or he would be lost; and that he needs to keep asking, in the light of his own felt weakness and inconstancy of heart, that the Spirit will energize him to the end to maintain the inward struggle.[22]

But even in this emphasis there are dangers. The tendency of some is to become legalistic, pharisaic, overly scrupulous, and thus joyless and morbid and pessimistic about the possibility of moral progress.

What, then, is the essence, heart, and core of the Spirit's work? Is there one fundamental, baseline activity to which the Spirit's work of empowering, enabling, purifying, and presenting may be related? Or again, Packer wonders if there is a single divine strategy that unites all these facets of his

---

[21] Ibid., 35–36.
[22] Ibid. 37.

life-giving action as means to one end? He believes the answer is yes, and he finds it in the idea of *presence*. By this he means the work of the Spirit in making known to the believer and to the corporate experience of the church the very real and dynamic personal presence of the risen Christ. The aim of the Spirit in this ministry is to make Christ known, to facilitate and sustain our love for him, to awaken and energize faith in who he is and all he has promised to be and do for us. In sum, the Spirit is primarily devoted to stirring heartfelt praise and adoration of the Son.

When Packer uses the term "presence," he does not have in mind the divine attribute by which we know God to be everywhere simultaneously. In other words, this is not the presence of omnipresence, but rather of "God acting in particular situations to bless faithful folk and thus make them know his love and help and draw forth their worship."[23] In the new covenant the Spirit works constantly to provide believers with the experiential consciousness of Christ's presence in such a way that three things regularly happen:

> *First, personal* fellowship *with Jesus*, that is, the to-and-fro of discipleship with devotion, which started in Palestine, for Jesus' first followers, before his passion, becomes a reality of experience, even though Jesus is now not here on earth in bodily form, but is enthroned in heaven's glory. . . .
>
> *Second, personal* transformation *of character into Jesus' likeness* starts to take place as, looking to Jesus, their model, for strength, believers worship and adore him and learn to lay out and, indeed, lay down their lives for him and for others. . . .
>
> *Third, the Spirit-given* certainty *of being loved, redeemed, and adopted* through Christ into the Father's family.[24]

Packer thus defines the Spirit's primary work in terms of John 16:14 where Jesus, speaking of the Spirit, announces, "He will glorify me, for he will take what is mine and declare it to you." On this Packer largely bases his conclusion that no pneumatology

> is fully Christian till it exhibits all his many-sided work from the standpoint of, on the one hand, the Father's purpose that the Son be known,

---

[23] Ibid., 48. See Gen. 39:2; Ex. 3:12; 33:14–16; Josh. 1:5, 9 (see also Deut. 31:6, 8); Isa. 43:2, 5; Matt. 1:23; 28:20.

[24] Ibid., 49. By this final statement Packer means that assurance of salvation begins to "blossom in believers' hearts" (ibid.)

loved, honored, praised, and have preeminence in everything, and on the other hand, the Son's promise to make himself present with his people, here and hereafter, by giving his Spirit to them.[25]

Thus, the Spirit serves as something of a *christological floodlight*. The purpose of that light is not to draw attention to itself but to focus attention on that which it illumines. The Spirit is, so to speak, the hidden floodlight shining on the Lord Jesus Christ and drawing the attention of all preeminently to him. Thus,

> the Spirit's message to us is never, "Look at me; listen to me; come to me; get to know me," but always, "Look at *him*, and see his glory; listen to *him*, and hear his word; go to *him*, and have life; get to know *him*, and taste his gift of joy and peace." The Spirit, we might say, is the matchmaker, the celestial marriage broker, whose role it is to bring us and Christ together and ensure that we stay together.[26]

Not everyone in mainstream evangelicalism is comfortable with Packer's emphasis on the experiential dimension of life in the Spirit. All too many, he argues, are not well versed in this spiritual reality. In defending such phenomena, Packer is careful never to suggest that all Christians must experience the Spirit in precisely the same way and to the same extent or with the same frequency. The Spirit's actions are, and always will be, subject to the divine will. And such perceptions and experiences of the Spirit always presuppose and arise from biblical understanding. They must be identified by biblical criteria and interpreted by biblical theology. Furthermore,

> they are in themselves immediate and sovereign. They are not under our control; they can neither be demanded nor predicted; they simply happen as God wills. Ordinarily . . . these perceptions are given through the Spirit to the loving and obedient disciple in fulfillment of Christ's promise that the Father and the Son would come to him, stay with him, and show themselves to him (John 14:18, 20–23). The perceptions themselves (better so called than "experiences," although each truly is what we mean

---

[25] Ibid., 54.
[26] Ibid., 66. Elsewhere Packer contends that even to ask the question do you know the Holy Spirit? "is not biblically angled, for it is the Spirit's way to keep out of direct view, like a shy child hiding behind the door. So Christians never know the Spirit in the way they know the Son, and we can be led astray by questioning that suggests we do" ("Shy Sovereign," in *Celebrating the Saving Work of God*, 203).

by "an experience") bring great joy because they communicate God's great love. They belong to the inner life, as distinct from that of the outward senses by which we know men and things. They are to be distinguished from our knowledge of people and things, though it seems always to be via that knowledge, in memory if not in the moment of its being given, that perceptions of God occur.[27]

Some are inclined to identify such experiences with what the apostle Paul refers to as the "witness" of the Spirit (see Rom. 8:16). John also alludes to this ministry in 1 John 5:7–8. The way the Spirit bears witness to the truth

is first to make us realize that as Christ on earth loved us and died for us, so in glory now he loves us and lives for us as the Mediator whose endless life guarantees us endless glory with him. The Spirit makes us see the love of Christ toward us, as measured by the cross, and to see along with Christ's love the love of the Father who gave his Son up for us (Romans 8:32).[28]

In addition, this ministry of the Spirit enables us to grasp, in an often intensely intimate way, that it is through Christ that we are now God's children and thus are to think of God as Father and to address him in such fashion (Gal. 4:6).

Lest there be any confusion on this point, Packer is careful to define what he does and does not mean by the word *experience*. The witness of the Spirit, he writes,

is not ordinarily "an experience" in the sense in which orgasm, or shock, or bewilderment, or being "sent" by beauty in music or nature, or eating curry are experiences—dateable, memorable items in our flow of consciousness, standing out from what went before and what came after, and relatively short-lived. There are, to be sure, "experiences" in which the Spirit's witness becomes suddenly strong.[29]

In this regard he cites the experience of such men as Blaise Pascal and John Wesley. But the "witness" of the Spirit most often will come more gently, more subtly, and with deeper and long-lasting effects in the heart.

---

[27] Packer, *Keep in Step with the Spirit*, 72–73.
[28] Ibid., 77.
[29] Ibid., 77–78.

The Spirit of Sanctification

Our first concern, of course, is the role the Spirit of God plays in our progressive transformation into the image of Jesus. Although, as noted above, Packer does not envision this as the central or primary role of the Spirit, it is still essential to any and all spiritual growth in Christlike character and conduct. Packer comes straight to the point in this regard by reminding us that "all actual achievement must be ascribed to him [the Holy Spirit], however much self-denial and sweat it may have cost us. Without his controlling and empowering activity we would never be able to achieve any conquests of sin, or any reshaping of our lives in righteousness."[30] The Spirit is anything but optional in Christian growth. Without the Spirit, there may well be moral alteration in one's external habits, or changes in one's daily routine, together with the disciplined cultivation of new beliefs and patterns of behavior and relationship with others. But none of this will be of lasting spiritual value that unites us and conforms us to the moral image of Jesus unless the Holy Spirit is present throughout the process.

So, for example, Packer insists that the Spirit's work is multifaceted. The Spirit will work to bring to conscious awareness the nature and threat of the many forms that evil might take. He will alert us to the nature and potency of each temptation before we fall victim to it. He will keep in the forefront of our thinking the nature of Christ's love for us and the way it serves to motivate us to obedience and to cultivate deeper humility and gratitude for all he has done. The Spirit also deepens our desire to please the Lord in all of life and, at the same time, makes the thought of sinful irresponsibility and outright disobedience increasingly abhorrent.

Packer is, as always, pointedly realistic about our struggles. Though born anew by the Spirit, Christians' "fallen, Adamic instincts (the 'flesh') which, though dethroned, are not yet destroyed, constantly distract them from doing God's will and allure them along paths that lead to death (Gal. 5:16–17; James 1:14–15)."[31] In such instances, when we find within our hearts contrary urgings, sinful impulses, and thoughts that are inconsistent with the truth of God's Word, the Holy Spirit can be trusted to sustain our regenerate desires and purposes, not sinlessly, of course, but

---

[30] Packer, *Rediscovering Holiness*, 173. "All that we ever contribute to our own Christian lives, according to Paul [and Packer], is folly, inability, and need. Everything that is good, right, positive, and valuable, comes from Christ through the Spirit" (J. I. Packer, "The Holy Spirit and His Word," in *Celebrating the Saving Work of God*, 231).

[31] J. I. Packer, *Concise Theology: A Guide to Historic Christian Beliefs* (Carol Stream, IL: Tyndale House, 1993), 171.

consistently and to such a degree that genuine progress, even moral victory, becomes more the norm than the exception.

Sanctification by the Spirit, however, is not to be confused with any notion of psychological seizure or suspension of the believer's mental and volitional faculties. The Spirit does not override the routine operations of mind and body, as if by some ecstatic takeover we lose all conscious control of what we believe and how we behave. Thus, any perceived similarities between biblical sanctification and what typically occurs in various expressions of shamanism or in the trances of spiritistic mediums or New Age channeling must be thoroughly rejected. Packer insists that the role of the Spirit is to bring about a directed use of our natural powers in obedient, creative service of God, motivated by gratitude and a purpose of glorifying him for the grace he has given. In other words, whatever relational, behavioral, and directional changes are wrought in us by the Spirit, and however much they may exceed what would be possible for us were he not actively present in our lives, his consistent manner of operation is through, and never independent of, the believer's active, cooperative, responsible, and prayerful moral endeavor. As the image of God in Christ is being restored in us, no violence is imposed on the rational faculties or the volitional powers of the believer.[32]

The inescapable reality of our fallenness and the enslaving power of indwelling sin is a constant reminder that we can never hope to do anything right or pleasing to God unless he, through the Spirit, works in us to will and to do for his good pleasure. This realization will thrust us into utter dependence on the indwelling Christ, what Packer equates with the biblical notion of "abiding" in Christ. This gives direction to a clear and consistent strategy for our encounter with sin and temptation. As Packer explains it:

> Our living should accordingly be made up of sequences having the following shape. We begin by considering what we have to do, or need to do. Recognizing that without divine help we can do nothing as we should (see John 15:5), we confess to the Lord our inability, and ask that help be given. Then, confident that prayer has been heard and help will be given, we go to work. And, having done what we could, we thank God for the ability to do as much as we did and take the discredit for whatever was still

---

[32] Again, says Packer, "the Spirit within us works through our minds and wills and not apart from them (that is, he does not move us by physical force without persuasion, as one would move a stick or rock or robot)" (ibid., 232).

imperfect and inadequate, asking forgiveness for our shortcomings and begging for power to do better next time. In this sequence there is room neither for passivity nor for self-reliance. On the contrary, we first trust God, and then on that basis work as hard as we can, and repeatedly find ourselves enabled to do what we know we could not have done by ourselves. That happens through the enabling power of the Holy Spirit, which is the wellspring and taproot of all holy and Christ-like action. Such is the inside story of all the Christian's authentically good works.[33]

One can see from this how far Packer is removed from his initial embrace of Keswick theology. The realism that permeates his understanding of the Christian life is both refreshing and hopeful. Would that the church of Jesus Christ might lay hold of it and rejoice in the supply of the Spirit to equip us in the battle with sin.

---

[33] J. I. Packer, *Hot Tub Religion* (Wheaton, IL: Tyndale House, 1987), 180.

CHAPTER 8

POWER FOR CHRISTIAN LIVING

The Necessity of Prayer

Prayer is "a key to the whole business of living. What it means to be a Christian is nowhere clearer than here."[1] With that, we are introduced to what J. I. Packer thinks about the urgency, indeed, the absolute necessity, of prayer for living the Christian life. Most people with at least some exposure to his writings may be surprised to discover that he has placed such a high value on this facet of daily discipleship. Packer's name is not generally associated with the theology and practice of prayer, although he wrote an entire book devoted to it and would often address it at some length in his other writings.[2]

To gain a sense for how crucial a role prayer plays in our Christian experience, consider these statements by Packer:

> Our praying is the index of our spiritual life quality; the dictum credited to Murray McCheyne is right: "What a man is alone on his knees before God, that he is, and no more." Our lack of love for praying may be an indication of all-round spiritual debility.[3]

---

[1] J. I. Packer, *Growing in Christ* (Wheaton, IL: Crossway, 1994), 153.
[2] J. I. Packer and Carolyn Nystrom, *Praying: Finding Our Way through Duty to Delight* (Downers Grove, IL: InterVarsity, 2006). He also addresses prayer at length in *Growing in Christ*, 153–217, where he carefully analyzes the Lord's Prayer and its application to believers today.
[3] Packer and Nystrom, *Praying*, 145.

> Praying and sinning will never live together in the same heart. Prayer will consume sin, or sin will choke prayer.[4]

> I ask whether you pray, because *diligence in prayer is the secret of eminent holiness.*[5]

One need not read deeply into Packer on prayer before discovering that his understanding of its place in the Christian life is closely tethered to the theme of his best-known book, *Knowing God.* Simply put, if you don't know God, you can't pray to him, or at least not with any measurable degree of effectiveness. Knowing God—his character, personality, and patterns of behavior, together with how he thinks and feels and reacts—is the one thing that will make prayer a joy and a delight rather than religious drudgery. Packer would certainly agree that every problem in prayer is traceable to a misconception about God. If we pray less than we should, or not at all, it is probably because we are deficient in our knowledge of the true and living God. How we perceive God controls how we speak to him. Who we understand God to be will always control what we ask him to do.

In a somewhat obscure and, sadly, little-read study guide, Packer accounts for what is unquestionably the primary cause for so much prayerlessness in the body of Christ:

> Moving in evangelical circles as I do, I am often troubled with what I find. While my fellow believers are constantly seeking to advance in godliness, they show little direct interest in God himself. When they study Scripture, only the principles of daily personal godliness get their attention; their heavenly Father does not. It is as if they should concentrate on the ethics and dynamics of marriage and fail to spend time with their spouse! There is something narcissistic and, to tell the truth, nutty in being more concerned about godliness than about God. As it would not be nice to care more for our marriage than for the partner we have promised to love, honor, and cherish, so it is not nice to care more for our religion than for the God whom we are called to praise and please every day of our lives.[6]

In other words,

> people feel a problem about prayer because of the muddle they are in about God. If you are uncertain whether God exists, or whether he is per-

---

[4] This is Packer quoting approvingly the words of J. C. Ryle (*Praying,* 17).
[5] This is yet another quote from Ryle to which Packer appends his enthusiastic endorsement (ibid.).
[6] J. I. Packer, *Meeting God* (Downers Grove, IL: InterVarsity, 1986), 9.

sonal, or good, or in control of things, or concerned about ordinary folk like you and me, you are bound to conclude that prayer is pretty pointless, not to say trivial, and then you won't do it.[7]

Thus, Packer is surely correct in concluding that "the vitality of prayer lies largely in the vision of God that prompts it. Drab thoughts of God make prayer dull."[8]

Packer's theology of prayer is grounded not only in his concept of God, but also in his commitment to the authority of Scripture from which this knowledge of God is derived. It is, after all, only from Scripture that we learn who we are: our strengths and weaknesses, as well as our greatest and most pressing needs. These give shape to the content of our prayers. "The word," says John Owen, "is the instrument whereby the Holy Spirit reveals unto us our wants, when we know not what to ask, and so enables us to make intercessions according to the mind of God."[9] This fundamental principle is echoed in the words of R. C. Sproul:

> How does one pen love letters to an unknown God? How do the lips form words of praise to a nebulous, unnamed Supreme Being? God is a person, with an unending personal history. He has revealed himself to us not only in the glorious theater of nature, but also in the pages of sacred Scripture. If we fill our minds with his Word, our inarticulate stammers will change to accomplished patterns of meaningful praise. By immersing ourselves in the Psalms, we will not only gain insight into the how of praise, but also enlarge our understanding of the One whom we are praising.[10]

Prayer: A Duty or Delight?

Packer believes that immense spiritual benefit comes from setting aside a designated time and place for prayer. We need a regularly scheduled appointment for time alone with God. We can hardly expect to grow in our friendship with God apart from consistency in this spiritual discipline. There is also considerable wisdom in planning ahead precisely what we hope to articulate to God in terms of petition and request. At the same

---

[7] Packer, *Growing in Christ*, 155.
[8] Ibid., 167.
[9] John Owen, "A Discourse of the Work of the Holy Spirit in Prayer: With a Brief Inquiry into the Nature and Use of Mental Prayer and Forms," in *The Works of John Owen*, ed. William H. Goold, vol. 4 (London: Banner of Truth, 1967), 321–22.
[10] R. C. Sproul, *Effective Prayer* (Wheaton, IL: Tyndale House, 1984), 47.

time, we need to be vigilant lest the routine that we establish in our prayer lives becomes an end in itself. Such can only serve to promote a false sense of well-being, leading us to think that merely being punctual and faithful to the appointed times of prayer will lead to deeper intimacy with God. There is, then, always a struggle in the Christian experience of praying. It is a struggle to be consistent without being ritualistic, a struggle to be faithful without it degenerating into pride, and worse still, legalism. Packer describes it best:

> Routine prayer can actually come from a tired soul. It reduces prayer to an item to be ticked off in the checklist of things to do—preferably with as little mental and emotional engagement as possible. No one sets out to pray like that. But tired souls drop into the same semi-automatic mode of actions as tired bodies, and in that way prayer as a mechanical routine can become a mindless task that creates a sense of spiritual security that is false.[11]

This raises the important question of whether we pray from a sense of duty or from the delight that comes from intimacy with God. Packer is helpful in pointing out that duty and morality are the language of "ought" and "must" that often run counter to desire. They shouldn't, but they do. We are sinfully selfish creatures who must be told by God what is right and how we should live. But in heaven, where all sinful and selfish impulses will have been eradicated, desire and duty will converge. What we "ought" to feel and think and do will come spontaneously, as a matter of our deepest inner desires. No one spoke to this more clearly than C. S. Lewis. Here and now, said Lewis, prayer is a "duty," but will not be so in heaven. He explains:

> If we were perfected, prayer would not be a duty, it would be delight. Some day, please God, it will be. The same is true of many other behaviors which now appear as duties. . . . To practice them spontaneously and delightfully is not yet possible. This situation creates the category of duty, the whole specifically *moral* realm. . . . But . . . there is no morality in heaven. The angels never knew (from within) the meaning of the word *ought*, and the blessed dead have long since gladly forgotten it. . . . This also explains . . . why we have to picture that world in terms which almost seem frivolous. . . . We can picture unimpeded, and therefore delighted, action only by the analogy of our present play and leisure.[12]

---

[11] Packer and Nystrom, *Praying*, 14.
[12] C. S. Lewis, *Letters to Malcolm: Chiefly on Prayer* (London: Geoffrey Bles, 1964), 147–48.

Packer concurs:

> When we are resurrected in our finally perfect state, *duty* will be a word
> that we will not need. Thoroughgoing love (admiration, appreciation, val-
> uation, gratitude, goodwill), both to our triune God and to all our glorified
> fellow sinners, will be the spontaneous, wholehearted, unqualified and
> indefatigable expression of what we now are. All the thoughts that pass
> through and come from our minds will have at their center praise to God,
> all the time and all the way. And it will be *fun!*—pure, celestial, transcen-
> dent, glorious fun. We will never have enjoyed anything so much.[13]

Prayer: A Multifaceted Experience

Packer has much to say about the many-sided nature of prayer, and we will
benefit greatly by taking note of his observations.

Prayer as Petition

As far as Packer is concerned, so-called "wordless" prayer is a contradiction in terms. Of course, prayer need not be spoken aloud. Silent prayer is
perfectly biblical, so long as one's thoughts and meditations and requests
are cognitively intelligible. Related to the misguided notion that prayer can
be cast in a form devoid of words is the unbiblical notion that God is to be
conceived "as an impersonal presence rather than a personal friend."[14] But,
counters Packer, "there is no place for an unmediated flight of 'the alone to
the alone,' bypassing Jesus Christ and the Bible in order to go straight to a
noncognitive closeness to God in which the mind is emptied of all personal
thoughts about him, and indeed of all thoughts whatsoever."[15]

If prayer always engages the mind and is necessarily cast in words, for
what then should we ask? In answering this question, Packer turns to the
instruction of Jesus in the Gospel of John. There our Lord said to his disciples: "Whatever you ask in my name, this I will do, that the Father may be
glorified in the Son. If you ask me anything in my name, I will do it" (John
14:13–14). Again, Jesus appears to promise his followers who bear fruit and
abide in him that "whatever you ask the Father in my name, he may give it
to you" (John 15:16). And again, "Truly, truly, I say to you, whatever you ask
of the Father in my name, he will give it to you" (John 16:23). Is Jesus giving

---

[13] Packer and Nystrom, *Praying*, 117.
[14] Ibid., 65.
[15] Ibid.

his disciples and us a blank check, an invitation to pray for anything we wish with the guarantee that we'll get it? Packer answers:

> The thought from the text is that we should ask God for things that the Lord Jesus will also ask for on our behalf. We are to make requests to the Father that the Lord Jesus will back. Jesus will associate himself with us in our requests when our requests match what he wants for us. That is the meaning of asking in his name. Jesus looks forward to his disciples asking for things that can only become reality with his help and by his power, and that will make for his glory when they do. That is what it means to ask according to God's will, the will of the Father which the Son knows and does. We, God's adopted children, come to know his will through studying Scripture and brooding on its implications, and through directly seeking the Savior's face in prayer.[16]

But on what basis do we ask, or on what basis do we pray with confidence that he hears us and will answer us? Packer points to three truths. First, there is our knowledge that God is now our Father by adoption and grace. Earthly parents, who are anything but perfect—indeed they are often selfish and indifferent to others—nevertheless are generous and kind when their children express their needs and desires. How much more will our heavenly Father, perfect and free of the slightest taint of sin, give abundantly to his children when they seek his face. Second, Packer reminds us of the promises of God as set forth in Scripture. We can rest confidently that he who has spoken will always fulfill his word in such a way that we are blessed and he is glorified.

> It needs to be said with the greatest possible emphasis that God's promises, including those that relate to prayer, are utterly trustworthy, and uncertainty as to whether he will keep them in our own case, uncertainty that will of course keep our prayer half-hearted if it does not stop us praying entirely, is unbelief, and unbelief is sin.[17]

Finally, our purity of heart, itself the fruit of God's grace at work within us, entitles us to expect God to answer our petitions.

---

[16] Ibid., 154. "When Jesus says to his disciples, 'Ask whatever you wish, and it will be done for you' (Jn 15:7), he qualifies his invitation by adding controls: they must be abiding in him and his words in them, the request must be 'in his name,' that is, one that he endorses, and 'according to his will,' that is, fitting in with the cosmic plan for the good of his people and others of which we spoke earlier (Jn 14:13; 15:16; 1 Jn 5:14)" (ibid., 66).

[17] Ibid., 61.

But does God ever actually fail to answer our requests? Whereas most would say, "Yes, he often does," Packer demurs. He is persuaded that when it comes to the children of God, there is no such thing as unanswered prayer. We must have confidence from the start that our heavenly Father, whose wisdom is infinite and pure, always reserves the right to respond to our petitions for help in what he knows to be the best way and at the best time. Thus Packer insists that "when we speak of unanswered prayer, we often mean not answered according to the terms of our asking. But to call that 'unanswered' is misleading and irreverent."[18]

As Packer understands prayer, God always reserves the right to answer the requests he knows we *should* have made in regard to a particular need rather than the one we actually *did* make. Therefore, "to conclude that God is not answering our prayers unless he matches his answer precisely to the terms of our original request is another by-path; it does us no good to travel there."[19] What Packer is doing here is teaching us to think of prayer less in terms of a manipulative means of getting from God what we want and more as the means by which God gives us the good things that he purposes to give but that we are not always in a fit condition to receive. When understood in such terms, any notion that our prayers coerce God into doing something on our behalf that he otherwise knows to be not in our best interests twists and turns the biblical teaching in a direction never intended by its Author.[20] Here Packer breaks down this truth with his customary clarity:

> God's yes is regularly a case of "your thinking about how I could best meet this need was right"; his no is a case of "not that, for this is better"—and so is really a yes in disguise!—and his wait (which we infer from the fact that though we have asked for action, nothing yet has changed) is a case of "*wait and see*; I will deal with this need at the best time in the best way. Whether or not you will be able to discern my wisdom when I do act, that is what in fact I am going to do. Keep watching, and see what you can see."[21]

This is important enough to warrant further explanation. Packer is arguing that when we pray in confidence that God has our best interests at

---

[18] Ibid., 58.
[19] Ibid., 63.
[20] "If our reasoning was right, what he does is what we asked; if our wisdom failed, what he does is what we should have asked. He knows and does what is better in every situation—situations, remember, of which the prayers we have made are now a part" (ibid., 173).
[21] Ibid., 173–74.

heart, when we pray with a robust faith in his goodness and greatness, and when we humbly pray with expectations that are biblically authorized, all, mind you, with his ultimate glory in view, his answer to us is never going to be altogether negative. From God's perspective he is always responding positively. It may be that his answer is of a sort that we actually receive something better than what we had requested. Or it may be that the timing of its fulfillment is different from what we had hoped but clearly more suitable to our need. Packer also envisions a positive answer, though it appears negative to us, in which God's strategy for fulfilling our petition takes such a mysterious turn that it doesn't look like an answer at all. Be assured that it is an answer. Be assured that though we may not comprehend what God is doing, there may yet be a day when he enables us to see the greater good that his plan has accomplished.

Prayer as Conversation

Prayer is most assuredly a two-way conversation between God and his children. But the way in which Packer conceives this is somewhat at odds with what may be the predominant view among evangelicals. It assuredly is different from what most charismatic Christians would expect. Packer's contention is that God communicates to us in writing, through the inscripturated record of his will and ways in the Bible. We in turn communicate with God through direct speech, in prayer. Characteristic of Packer's generosity toward those with whom he disagrees, he concedes that there are undoubtedly "some Christians to whom God speaks in ways that he doesn't speak to us, but we think hearing an audible voice from God is rather rare."[22] Here is his extended explanation:

> Does God, then, really tell us things when we pray? Yes. We shall probably not hear voices, nor feel sudden strong impressions of a message coming through (and we shall be wise to suspect such experiences should they come our way); but as we analyze and verbalize our problems before God's throne, and tell him what we want and why we want it, and think our way through passages and principles of God's written Word bearing on the matter in hand, we shall find many certainties crystallizing in our hearts as to God's view of us and our prayer, and his will for us and others.[23]

---

[22] Ibid., 76.
[23] Packer, *Growing in Christ*, 156.

Prayer as Meditation

Packer also speaks of "brooding" in prayer, by which he means meditating. Meditative prayer is far from the mystical practice of emptying one's mind and yielding to the experience of mental passivity. What Packer calls for is that we fill our minds with truth from God's Word about God himself. Meditation is what Packer refers to as *directed thinking*, active mental exertion in faithful and sustained focus on Scripture, God, the beauty of creation, the truths of redemption, and all that has been revealed of Christ and his saving work. Packer also differentiates between our ordinary "brooding," which tends to be random, lack focus, and leave us confused, and that experience of meditation which enables us to gather together

> random ideas about God in his presence and under his eye in order to form clearly, orderly, vivid and nourishing thoughts about him. Again, the self-indulgent broodings into which we regularly fall are forms of moodiness that we could do without, whereas if we want to be healthy Christians the discipline of celebratory thinking that we call meditation is something that we *cannot* well do without. It is an art that all praying people need to master.[24]

Meditating on God's works, in both creation and redemption, is powerfully sanctifying. The psalmist declares:

> I will remember the deeds of the LORD;
>   yes, I will remember your wonders of old.
> I will ponder all your work,
>   and meditate on your mighty deeds. (Ps. 77:11–12)

Packer's interpretation of what the psalmist resolves to do is enlightening:

> By controlling his thoughts, sending them into a channel toward God, focusing on the great things God has done—in creation, in providence and in grace—and thus thinking in a directed, disciplined way, so that God fills his whole horizon, this psalmist, though embattled by life's circumstances, is able to stabilize himself. He started in trouble and admits that trouble in prayer, but he then meditates with stubborn persistence on the mighty works of God and so gets steady and strong again. The wonders of the exodus and the passage through the Red Sea (corresponding for

---

[24] Packer and Nystrom, Packer, *Praying*, 69.

Christians to the wonders of their redemption through Christ, their regeneration in Christ and their subsequent experiences of God's goodness)
are the mighty works that, as he reviews them, raise his mind above his
present pain and renew his hope for the future. That kind of God-centered
meditative prayer is an art that we need to learn from him.[25]

Whereas there is nothing magical about the way meditation can change
someone's mood,

reviewing what God has done in the past, both in the public history of
world redemption and church renewal and in our own personal experience, naturally brings encouragement, refreshment, patience, stability,
and hope; for nothing in God's character or commitment has changed,
and he can be trusted to keep his promises.[26]

Meditating on the Bible is absolutely essential for genuine and long-
lasting Christian growth. We must soak our souls in Scripture until, as
Spurgeon put it, "our blood is bibline." We must also "traverse the Bible in
terms of overall images of its nature as God's communication to us, and of
our due response as recipients of his messages. Images affect our imagination, and imagination is the midwife, if not the mother, of insight."[27]

Packer also encourages a form of *lectio divina* or "divine reading" of
the Word. A typical *lectio* meditation might involve four steps. It begins
with the reading aloud of a sentence or a paragraph of the biblical text.
The reading should be slow, as one has opportunity to taste and enjoy
the goodness of God revealed. It often helps to read the passage several
times, perhaps with a slightly different emphasis each time through.
The second step brings us back to the notion of meditation (*meditatio*)
or brooding over the text. Here one ponders each word, each phrase,
each image, all the while asking: What is God saying or doing? What is
he asking of me? How should my life be different in light of this truth?
How might I respond with humility and vulnerability to what God is
showing me?

The third step, says Packer, is *oratio*, or responding verbally to God by
praying the passage itself or rephrasing it in the form of petition or praise
or intercession. Lastly comes *contemplatio*, or contemplation,

---

[25] Ibid., 83.
[26] Ibid., 83–84.
[27] Ibid., 86.

a time of peacefully resting in God, waiting in silence in the divine presence with alert, hopeful expectancy. A new sharpness of focus on something may not be given, but then again it may. Practicing lectio divina takes time, perhaps thirty minutes to an hour for a single verse. But this slow prayerful reading of God's Word engages the mind and the heart with a refreshing force that the brisk march would easily miss.[28]

Prayer as Praise

Praise as a dimension of one's prayer life was initially quite puzzling to C. S. Lewis, and Packer once shared his bewilderment. Packer's question was this: "Is the prayer of praise—praise prayer, we will call it—anything more than a bargaining counter directed toward God? Why does God ask for it? What is the true point of it? Should humans bargain with God by attempting to trade gain for praise?"[29] Packer cites Psalm 54 as an example. There David appears to offer praise to God in exchange for being given victory in battle. In Psalm 88:10, Heman appears to offer praise as a bargain for life. This prompts Packer to ask again, "What kind of God trades protection for compliments?"[30]

Packer's effort to overcome this problem comes in the form of six alliterative words, linked in three pairs.

He first describes praise as "declaring and distancing." The idea here is that when we worship God in prayer, we declare outwardly and are persuaded inwardly that he is God and we are not! The very notion of supplication keeps us mindful of our "distance" from God, that he is in heaven and we are not, that he is transcendent and altogether other, while at the same time drawing us close to him and the blessings of his presence. So who stands to gain from the praise that emerges from prayer? Is it a weak and needy "god" whose ego is stroked when his servants speak openly of how great he is? Or is it those who pray, to whom God, as they pray, communicates his presence and power and new insights into his own greatness? Packer agrees with Lewis in affirming the latter.

> So we praise God in prayer. We declare his greatness to his face while on our knees, and in this act God bridges the distance between us and reveals himself to us. As we declare him to be very far above us, so we find him

---

[28] Ibid., 90–91.
[29] Ibid., 99.
[30] Ibid.

to be very close to us. He receives our praise; we receive his love. That is
how praise prayer works.[31]

Then, second, there is praise as "discipline and diet." Packer explains:

In this as in other matters, companionship quells inhibitions and cre-
ates incentives. As the discipline of bodily exercise becomes easier to give
your heart to in a gym, where you are surrounded by a whole crowd of
people exercising already, and as sticking to a prescribed diet becomes
easier when everyone at the table is on the diet with you, so you are swept
up into personal praise much more quickly and powerfully when you realize that praise—from angels, from glorified saints, and from all creation—is going on all around you.[32]

Packer also portrays praise as "duty and delight." Thus, in answer to the
question, why does God so constantly and insistently require us to praise
him? the answer is: "So that we may get into the habit of doing what in
heaven we will do spontaneously and wholeheartedly in and from and for
enjoyment of God. God's joy and our joy in praising will then coincide."[33]

The Prayer of Self-Examination

Packer draws an analogy between our physical health and our spiritual
well-being. Just as the body needs a regular checkup to make certain that
we are free from any fatal affliction, we likewise stand in need of a spiritual
examination to determine the state of our souls. There is a principle of
inertia in human nature, notes Packer, that leads us to think we are com-
fortably okay with whatever degree of growth we have until now experienced. It closes us off to the possibility of new things and blinds us to the
potential of spiritual illness. For this reason we are all in need of close
self-examination. He explains:

Whereas introspection, whether it ends in euphoria or in the gloom of
self-pity and self-despair, can become an expression of self-absorbed
pride, self-examination is the fruit of God-centered humility, ever seek-

[31] Ibid., 102–3.
[32] Ibid., 103.
[33] Ibid., 109. Although not a charismatic, Packer acknowledges that "we can hardly attend a contemporary Christian worship service without witnessing a high degree of delight in praising God, and feeling
drawn joyfully to join in. It would be a happy thing if all those congregations that maintain older styles
of corporate praise would make their own patterns of song equally potent and attractive" (ibid., 113).

ing to shake free of all that displeases the Father, dishonors the Son and grieves the Holy Spirit, so as to honor God more. Thus self-examination is a fundamentally healthy process, leading into repentance, where mere introspection can leave us just feeling sorry for ourselves.[34]

But there is a distinct danger in attempting to monitor our own humility. As we noted earlier in our discussion of the nature of repentance, the moment we light upon it and acknowledge some measure of its presence, we have yielded to the very pride from which we long to be free. The wiser approach is to focus on identifying the various ways in which pride expresses itself and labor in the power of God's grace to mortify such fleshly impulses.

The Prayer of Complaint

Must prayer always be a joyful and exhilarating experience? What of those seasons in life when God seems remote and our enemies appear to have the upper hand? Packer, ever the realist, acknowledges the legitimacy of giving vent in prayer to what can only be called our "complaints." He defines the latter as "a kind of speech that blends lamentation (raging, glooming and despairing over what is bad, frustrating and hurtful) with supplication (begging and pleading that someone will do something about it)."[35]

Many Christians fear the prayer of complaint. It strikes them as irreverent and ungrateful. Ought not the believer to gird up his loins, clench his fists, grit his teeth, knuckle under to the realities of divine providence, and simply keep his mouth shut? But the prayer of complaint is not only permissible; it is often essential. If you doubt the legitimacy of godly complaint, take a moment and consider these expressions found in the Psalms:

O LORD, rebuke me not in your anger,
nor discipline me in your wrath.
Be gracious to me, O LORD, for I am languishing;
heal me, O LORD, for my bones are troubled.
My soul also is greatly troubled.
But you, O LORD—how long?

---
[34] Ibid., 125.
[35] Ibid., 190.

Turn, O LORD, deliver my life;
    save me for the sake of your steadfast love.
For in death there is no remembrance of you;
    in Sheol who will give you praise?

I am weary with my moaning;
    every night I flood my bed with tears;
    I drench my couch with my weeping.
My eye wastes away because of grief;
    it grows weak because of all my foes. (Ps. 6:1–7)

How long, O LORD? Will you forget me forever?
    How long will you hide your face from me?
How long must I take counsel in my soul
    and have sorrow in my heart all the day?
How long shall my enemy be exalted over me? (Ps. 13:1–2)

But I call to God,
    and the LORD will save me.
Evening and morning and at noon
    I utter my complaint and moan,
    and he hears my voice. (Ps. 55:16–17; see also Psalms 38, 79, 88)

And thus what Packer describes as our "complaint prayers" are

not mere self-centered whining that life has not treated us right. Instead, our complaints are those of dependent children, running in fear and in hurt to our almighty Father, who rules all things. God, if he chooses, will relieve our pain. And if, for nurture's sake, he chooses not to do so, even then we are to snuggle and nestle into his arms, knowing that Father God loves us, hears our complaints and will love us now and forever.[36]

Perseverance in Prayer

It has been said that the easiest thing, when it comes to prayer, is giving up. Persevering in prayer, when every indication is that nothing could possibly make less spiritual sense, comes only with the sustaining help of God's grace. Packer's realism is again in evidence as he reminds us of the countless forces in life that pull us away from time on our knees. Per-

---

[36] Ibid., 204.

haps after years of investing time and energy in some project, all along the way seeking God's blessing on it during extended seasons of prayer, we are faced with its abysmal collapse. Where was God? we ask. Doesn't he care? For others it is a long-lingering illness or some chronic pain that meets us at the beginning of each day. Prayer for healing has not yielded what we hoped, and it simply doesn't make sense to continue asking God for what he evidently has chosen not to give. Shattered relationships, whether in a marriage or among friends, can exhaust us both physically and emotionally and bring discouragement that discolors everything we do. Then there are those who suffer from a sort of clinical depression in which body chemistry joins forces with adverse circumstances to turn our whole world gray. Hopelessness sets in, and prayer seems so trivial.

These are the realities of life to which Packer draws our attention. Yet, at the same time, he encourages us to persevere in prayer and never to quit. Why? He supplies three brief but poignant answers. First,

> by compelling us to wait patiently for him to act, *God purges our motives*. Often our first formulation of a request is more self-centered and self-serving than it ought to be, just because of the many layers of egocentricity that encase our sinful selves, like the successive skins that encase the heart of an onion. As we wait on God, repeatedly renewing our requests, he leads us to see that the initial motivations of our asking, heartfelt as it doubtless was, were more concerned with comfort, convenience and glory for ourselves, and less with his honor, praise and glory than was right.[37]

Then, second, God orchestrates delay in responding to us so that we are compelled to wait as he providentially provides in ways more natural than miraculous. In other words, "though arresting answers to prayer, quick and spectacular, are sometimes given, it is not God's way to multiply miracles indiscriminately."[38]

Finally, the infinitely wise God, who always knows what is of greatest good for us, will often delay his answers in order that we might learn the difference between childishness and maturity. By this Packer is reminding us of the way of children. They demand instantaneous response. They cannot envision life without whatever they are convinced they must have.

---

[37] Ibid., 222.
[38] Ibid., 223.

They grow frustrated when their requests are not heeded. The concept of waiting, of patience and ever-increasing trust in the goodness and wisdom of God, simply doesn't register deeply in their hearts. By calling us to persevere, God weans us from unhealthy and childish reliance on the thrill of always getting our way, how we want it, and when we want it.

In conclusion, as noted at the beginning of this chapter, *prayer is all about knowing God*: his power to provide, his love in reforming our hearts to want what he wants us to want, his generosity in so often going far beyond what we could ever have imagined or asked in the first place (cf. Eph. 3:20–21), and his wisdom in determining what shape his answers will take in our lives, and when. The person who does not know God in this way, or lives in doubt as to his kindness and compassion, will forever find little of value in coming boldly to the throne of grace (cf. Heb. 4:16).

CHAPTER 9

GUIDANCE IN
CHRISTIAN LIVING

Discerning the Will of God

One would be hard-pressed to identify an issue of greater practical significance for Christian living than finding and following God's will. It may well be the most oft-asked question that people pose: how can I know God's will for ____? The anxiety that often accompanies this query and the self-condemnation and despair that follow the perception that one has "missed" God's perfect will create massively complex pastoral problems. The body of Christ should be thankful that someone with J. I. Packer's biblical and pastoral insight has spoken to this issue.[1]

Before we examine Packer's theology of guidance, we would do well to consider two particular points of emphasis in his overall theological perspective: the doctrines of adoption and divine sovereignty. The connection between these two truths and God's guidance of his children is obvious.

In the first place, God guides only his "children." Although Packer believes God's providential control to be pervasive and meticulous, only those who have by faith in Christ become the children of God can look confidently to divine guidance as a loving expression of how a father relates to his sons and daughters. Our confidence in the goodness of God's guidance, together with our ability to trust God with all of life, flows immediately out

---

[1] J. I. Packer and Carolyn Nystrom, *Guard Us, Guide Us: Divine Leading in Life's Decisions* (Grand Rapids: Baker, 2008).

of this filial relationship. Similarly, Packer insists that guidance is itself possible only on the assumption that God exerts pervasive control over all human affairs, a control that is simultaneously both exhaustive and perfectly compatible with human moral responsibility. A brief word about each of these emphases in Packer's theology is therefore in order.

Adoption: "The Highest Privilege That the Gospel Offers"

Is Packer exaggerating when he speaks of spiritual adoption as the highest privilege? To argue that adoption is a privilege "higher even than justification"[2] calls for some explanation and defense. Packer feels warrant for speaking this way because of the depth and wealth of relational intimacy that adoption brings to its recipients. Whereas it is a glorious reality to be declared righteous through faith in Christ, it is better still to stand in such close and loving fellowship with God and to rest in the joy of being called his "child." Packer goes so far as to say that "*the entire Christian life has to be understood in terms of it* [adoption]. Sonship must be the controlling thought—the normative category, if you like—at every point."[3]

For example, adoption appears in the Sermon on the Mount as the basis of Christian conduct. We are called to imitate the Father (Matt. 5:44–45, 48) and glorify the Father (Matt. 5:16) and to live so as to please the Father (Matt. 6:1–18). It is also to the Father that we are to direct our intercessory prayers (Matt. 6:9). Thus being a justified child of God is "the basis of *the life of faith*—that is, the life of trusting God for one's material needs as one seeks his kingdom and righteousness."[4]

Adoption is not restricted to our relationship with the Father. The Holy Spirit, says Packer, "makes and keeps us conscious—sometimes vividly conscious, always conscious to some extent, even when the perverse part of us prompts us to deny this consciousness—that we are God's children by free grace through Jesus Christ. This is his work of giving faith, assurance and joy."[5] Thus it is because of the saving work of the Son that the Spirit of adoption can bring us into experiential awareness of this marvelous privilege. Not only that, but the Spirit "moves us to look to God as to a father, showing toward him the respectful boldness and unlimited trust that is natural to children secure in an adored father's love." The Spirit also "im-

[2] J. I. Packer, *Knowing God* (Downers Grove, IL: InterVarsity, 1973), 206.
[3] Ibid., 209.
[4] Ibid., 212–13.
[5] Ibid., 220.

pels us to act up to our position as royal children by manifesting the family likeness (conforming to Christ), furthering the family welfare (loving the brethren) and maintaining the family honor (seeking God's glory)."[6] Adoption, then, is a thoroughly Trinitarian reality in its inception, in its nature, and in terms of how we subsequently relate to Father, Son, and Holy Spirit.

Adoption also shows us the meaning and motives of Christian living. As to the essential nature of holiness, it is fundamentally living out of the joy and love of a filial relationship with God into which the gospel of grace has brought us. Being a child of God, therefore, is more than status; it is a catalyst that enables the child of God to remain true to type, that is to say, faithful to and consistent with one's true Father. Knowing we stand in such intimate relationship to the Father is itself a strong, if not the strongest, motivation for authentic obedience and a life in which the believer shows himself or herself to be the spiritual progeny of God.

Thus when we read that our "Father knows" all the things we need (Matt. 6:32) and that his provision will never fail, the reality of his guidance over us in all things strikes deeply to heart. And when we are assured that, notwithstanding vicious persecution from the enemies of God, we may confidently know that not even a sparrow plummets to the earth "apart from" our "Father" (Matt. 10:29), our resolve to stand firm as he leads us even through the valley of the shadow of death is strengthened. If no other text solidifies the connection between adoption and guidance, Romans 8:14 surely does: "All who are led by the Spirit of God are sons of God." What this "leading" entails, we shall shortly see. But of this we can be certain: God lovingly guides and promises to provide only for those who are his sons and daughters through faith in Jesus Christ.

The Sovereignty of Our Heavenly Father

But can the Christian be confident that what our heavenly Father desires and pursues on our behalf he is capable of bringing to fruition? Yes, by all means, insists Packer. God, after all, is sovereign over everything that transpires; he is the one "who works all things according to the counsel of his will" (Eph. 1:11).

Many things come to mind when people refer to the "sovereignty" of God. Here is what Packer understands by it. As you read and reflect upon it,

---

[6] Ibid.

observe the beautiful harmony between God's causal priority in all things (as stated in the first paragraph) and human responsibility and moral accountability (as found in the second). They are gloriously compatible! The sovereignty of God, explains Packer, means that

> the living God, who created the entire universe and actively upholds it in being (otherwise it would vanish away, and so would we as part of it), knows everything that has been and now is and foreknows everything that will be just because, in a way that totally passes our understanding, he plans and decides and controls everything that takes place. From inside (and we are all insiders at this point) the cosmos appears as a huge interlocking system of cause and effect, the working of which scientists can examine, map out, and within limits predict because the processes all operate with what appears as built-in regularity. But Christians know what science can never find out, namely, that all the processes of nature are willed and sustained directly by the Creator, every moment, down to the smallest detail, as also are the free-flowing thoughts that run through our minds, and the dreams that befuddle us while we sleep, and the self-determined, accountable decisions about what we will and will not do that we make in a steady stream throughout our waking hours. Let us say it clearly: all the regularities of nature, including the functioning of our own minds and bodies, are as they are because God wills and keeps them so. Nothing would be as it is—nothing, indeed, would exist at all—were it not for the active will of God. . . .
>
> To affirm God's sovereignty over everything around us, within us, happening to us, and issuing from us takes nothing from our certainty (which Scripture confirms) that all our thoughts, words, and deeds, including all our motives, purposes, attitudes, and reactions, are truly our own, not forced upon us from outside but coming out from within us, so that we are in truth responsible subjects, open to assessment both by other people and by our own consciences, and finally by God himself. Rather it adds to our certainty that, as our continued existence and all our living really involve God, so God really involves himself in an overruling way, somehow (just how, no creature can conceive), in all our circumstances, motives, actions, relationships, experiences, joys, pains, pleasures, griefs, and ventures, which form the situational reality of our daily lives.[7]

---

[7] Packer and Nystrom, *Guard Us, Guide Us*, 199–200.

Thus we see that when it comes to his grand and all-encompassing oversight and guidance of his people, God "plans and decides and controls everything that takes place." All that Packer will subsequently say with regard to divine guidance must be seen in the light of this unflinching commitment to God's sovereign and providential oversight of human affairs, choices, and even our eternal destiny.

Guidance from God

Packer believes that the emotional paralysis so often tethered to uncertainty about God's will for one's life is of comparatively recent vintage. It is, he suggests,

> the fruit of a particular belief about God that blossomed in the world of pietistic experientialism in mid-nineteenth-century America that followed two generations of Wesleyan mission work and the Second Great Awakening. The belief was that immediate guidance from God in the form of voicelike thoughts and strongly inclined imaginings and inner urges was regularly given to Bible-believers who really needed it and humbly sought it.[8]

Packer would also lay considerable blame for this unfortunate development on the rise and influential spread of Pentecostalism. The latter has all too often promoted the expectation that when God leads and guides his people, he will communicate this internally to the mind of the believer or by some revelatory message, most often through the exercise of the spiritual gift of prophecy.

In response, Packer acknowledges

> that God on occasion in Bible times communicated with some people in the manner described above, and that he has not said he will never do so again, and that some at least of the glowing stories about guidance of this kind that are told can hardly be doubted. Some see reason to deny that God ever did, or will, communicate this way now that the canon of Scripture is complete, but that view seems to us to go beyond what is written and to fly in the face of credible testimony. It is not for us to place restrictions on God that he has not placed on himself![9]

---

[8] Ibid., 14.
[9] Ibid., 16.

Whereas God does not reveal things that bear canonical authority, this

> is not to deny that "private revelations," as the Puritans used to call
> them, ever take place nowadays. On that question we keep an open mind.
> Though we know that self-deception here is very easy, we would not
> short-circuit claims to have received words from God; we would instead
> test them, as objectively and open mindedly as we can, in light of the
> teaching of Scripture itself.[10]

That being said, Packer is clear that personal messages from heaven
are not and never were God's normal way of leading and guiding his
people or disclosing some specific dimension of his will for their lives.
Rather, God's usual way of showing us his desires and designs for our
earthly sojourn is through the appropriate application of what has been
inscripturated once and for all in the revelatory and infallible truths of
the Bible.

> This means that we shall have no time for any version of *fortune-telling*
> (the appeal to arbitrary signs and humanly designed "fleeces" to tell us
> what to do); nor for primary reliance on something best termed *"feeling-
> itis"* (the appeal to strong feelings and hunches, however sudden and
> sustained, to tell us what to do); nor for any form of *fear* lest a guidance
> mistake irrevocably ruin God's plan for our life.[11]

How, then, does God guide us primarily?

> The answer is, God's own instruction from and through his written Word.
> Direct guidance as to things we should and should not do is found in
> the Ten Commandments and the case-law based on them, in the oracle-
> sermons of the prophets recalling Israel to God's standards, in the wis-
> dom books of Proverbs and Ecclesiastes, in the teaching of Jesus, and in
> the many treatments of Christian behavior in the Epistles. And through
> the Word, via honest commitment to live by the Word and humble experi-
> ence of the Word's transforming power, God gives wisdom to discern his
> will in all situations that call for reflective thought.[12]

---

[10] Ibid., 17.
[11] Ibid., 29. As for those supernatural nudges from the Spirit, "it is not for us to make rules for God or to
deny that he made his will known this way when someone testifies that he did. We recognize that God
sovereignly may renew today any of the modes of communication that he used in Bible times—visions,
dreams, voices, inner promptings, whatever" (ibid., 229).
[12] Ibid., 33–34.

What Packer has in mind when he speaks of "direct guidance" from such biblical texts is not so much that these statements address us personally, as if they were written *to* us, by name. Rather, we trust that they were written *for* us, in the sense that unchanging principles of truth and wisdom are to be mined for how they might provide direction and counsel for the daily decisions all God's people face.

Thus, for example, when Paul speaks of being "led" by the Holy Spirit (Rom. 8:14; Gal. 5:18), he is not promising Christians an unending supply of exotic revelatory experiences, whether in dreams, trances, visions, or even inward and highly charged impressions upon the soul. Paul means, rather, the Spirit's sustaining strength as we take note of what the Bible teaches, as we seek out the counsel of friends wiser than we, followed by the exercise of what Packer calls "sanctified common sense." There are, of course, a variety of modes and forms in which God's guidance may come to us, but the bottom line

> in the guided life is always discernment and acceptance of the will of God so that our attitudes and reactions express joyful submission and faithful obedience to his leading. . . . Discernment comes through listening to Scripture and to those means of grace that relay biblical teaching to us in digestible form—sermons, instruction talks, hymns, books, Christian conversations, and so forth.[13]

In keeping with his determination never to confine God's ways to human dictates, Packer doesn't dismiss the possibility that God might lead someone to do the undeniably bizarre things asked of Old Testament prophets, but he insists these are exceptions, not rules.

> The regular shape of guidance is that God teaches us to apply revealed principles of action, both positive and negative; to observe parameters and limits of behavior that the Bible lays down; and thus to follow the path of faithful obedience and true wisdom, in fellowship with the Lord our shepherd who by his Spirit leads us so to do.[14]

In one particularly insightful place, Packer sums up the principal elements in a biblically informed approach to seeking God's will in matters on which the Bible is not as explicit as we might wish:

---

[13] Ibid., 36.
[14] Ibid., 37.

As we collect and survey all the available facts that are relevant princi- ples and parameters of decision and action; as we ask fellow Christians for words of wisdom and advice on the matter in hand; as we come to terms with the limitations and non-negotiable alternatives, working out the likely consequences of each possibility open to us so as to make sure we will not unwittingly choose the merely good in place of the best, we should constantly ask God to judge, correct, and direct our thinking— heading us off from deciding badly and granting us the Spirit-wrought reality of his peace in our hearts as we move into what we see to be the wise way into which he is leading us. We should be willing, and (like the psalmists) tell God we are willing, to wait on him patiently till the desired discernment comes.[15]

Signs and Fleeces?

What about "signs"? Might God on occasion lead us by means of particular signs or events or an unusual turn of circumstance? Certainly the possi- bility cannot be ruled out. The issue isn't whether or not God can do again what he often did in biblical times. The issue is whether such ought to be *expected* as the normative manner in which God guides his people into the experience of his so-called perfect will. Packer thinks not.

He does not believe, for example, that Gideon (in Judg. 6:36–40) pro- vides us with a paradigm for our individual decision making. The unusual manner in which God disclosed his will for Gideon was in the context of the latter's role as leader in Israel. But we should not, as a matter of course, expect God to speak to us today through some "fleece" that we propose or compose for him. Packer believes that with the completion of God's inspired and written revelation in the Bible, something people such as Gideon didn't have, it is only natural that

> outward signs should be fewer, as no longer needed in the same way. The apostles never tell Christians to seek signs of God's will for their deci- sions, as though the gospel and its ethical corollaries are not in them- selves sufficient to guide our steps, and Jesus warned the Pharisees explicitly against the irresponsibility of seeking after signs when they should be facing up to his words.[16]

---

[15] Ibid., 38.
[16] Ibid., 42. I must take slight exception to this latter statement by Packer. We must remember that the Pharisees, nonbelievers in the messianic identity of Jesus as they were, demanded a supernatural sign before committing themselves to him as Lord and Savior. If it were the case that a disciple of Jesus prayed

Thus Packer, citing Bruce Waltke, thinks that "'laying out a fleece' is generally the lazy man's way to discern the will of God. It requires no work, little discipline, and almost no character development."[17] He comes, then, to this summary:

> It thus appears that the quest for guiding signs, which is at best a blind alley and an obstacle to spiritual maturity, can be at worst setting one-self up to be deceived by Satan, the archetypical specialist in lying and deception, who is only too ready to foul up our decisions and commitments by setting false signs before us and leading us to misinterpret our circumstances and make ruinous decisions. And if bad does not in this way come to worst, the mindset that seeks signs and hesitates to act without them is bound to paralyze us morally and keep us from making commitments that we ought to make, and that in all conscience is something that truly limits what God will do in and through us. From no standpoint whatever, then, are we to expect signs to litter a properly God-guided path. If God gives signs, as he sometimes does, they are to be received as a bonus and an encouragement, but we should be seeking guidance via the specifics noted earlier and not by any form of a quest for signs.[18]

It may well be that the hankering after some supernatural sign to confirm guidance from above is the result of the misguided assumption that if we could only follow God's guidance perfectly, everything else in life would fall into place. Knowing God's will in this way, so some think (but not Packer), would serve to eliminate or at least greatly reduce the struggles and disappointments in life with which only unbelievers are thought to be saddled. But the realism of Packer is again in evidence when he reminds us that nothing in Scripture promises God's children that they will be guarded and shielded from the hardships and confusion that typically characterize all of life this side of the consummation.

Inward Impressions?

If not external and unmistakable signs of some sort, what about those inward impressions or sensations of the spirit that many equate with the

---

for some sign in order better to follow God's lead and honor his glory, a different assessment of the relative value of the sign might be warranted.
[17] Ibid., 43.
[18] Ibid., 43–44.

disclosure of God's will for us? Packer again demurs. The expression "I feel,"
he argues,

> is a red-flag phrase in this matter of guidance; self-proclaimed holy
> hunches can be a source of real danger. True, our Lord does indeed *some-*
> *times* gently nudge his sheep in one direction or the other—particularly
> those who know him well and are used to recognizing his voice within.
> But this is less the norm than many people assume, and it is not the place
> to start when seeking guidance from God.[19]

Wise, biblically informed Christians do not look first to impressions or
what Packer calls "subjective fantasies." Rather they begin and end with the
written Word of God, which they embrace confidently as their guidebook.
As we soak our hearts and minds in the Scriptures, God's living and active
truth seeps in and recalibrates our thinking and transforms our values. We
begin to think as Christ would think and desire as he would desire. In the
process our paths are lit up by the infallible counsel that forever remains
unchanged.

Sadly, far too many of God's people remain persuaded that the primary
means of divine guidance is the activity of the Holy Spirit speaking immediately into the heart, thereby transcending and bypassing the ordinary
mental disciplines entailed by the prayerful study of God's Word. Packer
believes that we must first and foremost analyze the alternatives before
us, making careful application of whatever relevant biblical principles we
discover in Scripture, all the while calculating the consequences of our
choices. To this, one must add a careful assessment of the pros and cons
of each volitional option we face, taking into account the advice of those
wiser than we, and being, at every point, honest about our own strengths
and weaknesses. Says Packer:

> We emphatically agree that leading us to the best decision is a min-
> istry of the Holy Spirit, first to last, but with equal emphasis we deny
> that under ordinary circumstances his ministry short-circuits or cir-
> cumvents any of these sometimes laborious intellectual procedures.
> On the contrary, they are precisely the means by which the Holy Spirit
> of God leads us into seeing clearly what it is right and good to decide
> and do in each situation.[20]

---

[19] Ibid., 59.
[20] Ibid., 136–37.

Neither Super-Spiritual nor Sub-Spiritual

Packer is ever diligent to direct us away from what he perceives to be un-healthy extremes when it comes to guidance from God. Two in particular he identifies as the "super-spiritual," on the one hand, and the "sub-spiritual," on the other. The former takes place when the Christian waits and waits and waits on the assumption that it is God's standard practice to provide some identifiable nudge from the Holy Spirit. Such promptings allegedly bring an overwhelming sense of assurance that, in a sense, baptizes the decision in virtual certainty. The result is that many remain inert and inac-tive until such nudges are forthcoming. And, once they are thought to have been granted, virtually nothing can dissuade the recipient of the alleged divine endorsement from acting upon it. Conversely, the "sub-spiritual" mind-set "has been described in para-trinitarian terms as faith in the Father, the Son, and the Holy Scriptures."[21] In this case, some Christians lose sight altogether of the powerful indwelling presence of the Holy Spirit and his role in guidance and provision.

Such extremes often come into play when one is seeking God's will for one's life vocation. Short of that distinctive internal feeling or vision or voice, many make no decision, which is itself a decision (and oftentimes a disastrous one). This isn't to say, notes Packer, that God cannot or never will supply us with some settled state of soul, that internal conviction of rightness and transcendent peace that may well accompany the right de-cision as over against the wrong one. His point, rather, "is simply that in many decisions of great consequence it is still unwarranted to expect, and in effect demand, some form of direct, informative encounter with God. That is what 'supernatural' refers to here."[22]

The destructive fallout from the super-spiritual expectations many have is that when such nudges, promptings, impressions, or voices and the like are not readily recognizable, one can easily fall into confusion about God's character, and depression over one's lot in life. It isn't unusual for some to experience the extremes of either inaction, on the one hand, or random and ill-advised decisions, on the other. Packer is convinced that the root of the mistake is twofold: "(1) an underlying mistrust of Christian reasoning, as not in itself a sufficiently spiritual activity, and (2) an undue reliance on significant gusts of emotion, whether euphoric or gloomy, to

---

[21] Ibid., 219.
[22] Ibid., 183.

show how one stood with God in relation to this or that particular problem." What was needed is

> a recognition that this almost superstitious preoccupation with how or what one felt, so far from being a sign of deep spirituality, was an eccentricity, a somewhat zany spin-off from the romantic movement in Western culture; and what was also needed was a recovery of confidence in Christian reason, even without the icing of supernatural signs on the cake of cogent, biblically based thinking.[23]

What may then be said in summary? Simply this: "God guides us by means of the Bible's teaching, the exercise of wisdom, and the counsel of fellow believers, plus insights and ideals sparked within us by the examples of faithful folk past and present, and supremely by the virtues shown in the way that the Lord Jesus lived."[24]

---

[23] Ibid.
[24] Ibid., 212.

CHAPTER 10

THE CAULDRON OF CHRISTIAN LIVING

The Inevitability of Suffering

If I've learned anything about J. I. Packer, it is that he is an unrelenting realist when it comes to the Christian life. "Unreality in religion," he writes, "is an accursed thing. . . . Unreality toward God is the wasting disease of much modern Christianity. We need God to make us realists about both ourselves and him."[1] We've seen this repeatedly when it comes to the ongoing struggle with indwelling sin. Packer will not tolerate any idealized notion of the Christian life in which the believer, whether through a second blessing or a passive yielding in faith, is assured of deliverance, this side of heaven, from the daily battle with the world, the flesh, and the Devil.

His honest, realistic, and rigorously biblical approach to Christian living is also evident when it comes to the issue of suffering. Whatever form our pain, frustration, and disappointment may take, says Packer, the New Testament is consistent and emphatic in viewing such experiences as "the natural condition of Christians and churches as long as they are in this world."[2] Suffering, he says, is "the Christian's road home." There are no detours around the anguish and heartache of living in a fallen and corrupt world. A life free from pain and trouble is portrayed by some in the

---

[1] J. I. Packer, *Knowing God* (Downers Grove, IL: InterVarsity, 1973), 251.
[2] J. I. Packer, "On Being Serious about the Holy Spirit," in *Celebrating the Saving Work of God*, vol. 1 of *The Collected Shorter Writings of J. I. Packer* (Carlisle, UK: Paternoster, 1998), 208–9.

West "as virtually a natural human right, and Christian minds have been so swamped by this thinking that nowadays any pain and loss in a Christian's life is felt to cast doubt on God's goodness."[3]

We must therefore stand firmly against any idea that if God genuinely loves us, he will guard us and insulate us or at least very quickly deliver us out of all the troubles and trials that threaten us on a daily basis. Tragically, many have been led to expect an unbroken series of triumphs over poor health and family disputes and financial shortages and the hostility of unbelievers. That isn't to say that faithful Christians won't experience divine sustenance and deliverance in times of trouble. "But our lives will not be ease, comfort, and pleasure all the way. Burrs under the saddle and thorns in our bed will abound. Woe betide the adherent of hot tub religion who overlooks this fact!"[4] It is a grievous mistake to imagine that

> the good for which God works is our unbroken ease and comfort. God's goal is, rather, our sanctification and Christlikeness, the true holiness that is the highway to happiness. Constant ease and comfort, therefore, are not to be expected. Yet Christians may nonetheless derive constant contentment from their knowledge that God is making everything that happens to them a means of furthering and realizing the glorious destiny that is theirs.[5]

Some today are given to a type of ministry that focuses so intently on the blessings and triumphs of the Christian life that it fails to do justice to what Packer calls "the rougher side of the Christian life."[6] Such folk give

> the impression that normal Christian living is a perfect bed of roses, a state of affairs in which everything in the garden is lovely all the time, and problems no longer exist—or, if they come, they have only to be taken to the throne of grace, and they will melt away at once. This is to suggest that the world, the flesh and the devil will give us no serious trouble once we are Christians; nor will our circumstances and personal relationships ever be a problem to us; nor will we ever be a problem to ourselves. Such suggestions are mischievous, however, because they are false.[7]

---

[3] Ibid.
[4] J. I. Packer, *Hot Tub Religion* (Wheaton, IL: Tyndale House, 1987), 81.
[5] Ibid., 151.
[6] Packer, *Knowing God*, 244.
[7] Ibid., 245.

But we mustn't think that Packer's realism is a grim perspective that breeds only gloom and grief. He has consistently spoken of our earthly sojourn as one filled with joy inexpressible and transcendent peace that flows freely from the love of God and the grace of the cross. The believer's joy is in the assurance that no matter how battered and beaten he may be in this life, nothing can separate him from the love of God in Christ Jesus. The believer's triumph isn't *around* trials or by way of escaping them, but in the promise of God's abiding presence through them, as the Lord leads and loves us even when we walk through the valley of the shadow of death.

The Destructive Triumphalism of the "Health and Wealth Gospel"

No one has spoken with greater force and clarity concerning the destructive errors of the health and wealth gospel than has J. I. Packer. To give the believer hope that some day in some way God will alleviate all burdens and elevate the faithful to a higher plane of both physical and financial triumph is to set people up for a disillusioning and painful fall. Packer's grasp on God's ways in regard to our trials and tribulations is far more biblically sound and pastorally sensitive.

Packer's contention is that God is typically more gentle with newborn Christians than with those who have walked in the faith for a considerable period of time. Early in the life of discipleship they are subject to frequent emotional exhilaration, are the recipients of surprising providential graces, and discover that their prayers are remarkably answered often in ways beyond what they have asked. When they share their faith they often reap remarkable spiritual fruit. God's purpose early on is to encourage them and establish in them a solid foundation for their future life in Christ. "But as they grow stronger," observes Packer,

and are able to bear more, he exercises them in a tougher school. He exposes them to as much testing by the pressure of opposed and discouraging influences as they are able to bear—not more (see the promise, 1 Cor 10:13), but equally not less (see the admonition, Acts 14:22). Thus he builds our character, strengthens our faith, and prepares us to help others. Thus he crystallizes our sense of values. Thus he glorifies himself in our lives, making his strength perfect in our weakness. There is nothing unnatural, therefore, in an increase of temptations, conflicts and pressures as the Christian goes on with God—indeed, something would be wrong if it did not happen. But the Christian who has been told that the normal Christian life is unshadowed and trouble-free can only conclude, as experiences of inadequacy and imperfection pile in upon him, that he must have lapsed from normal.[8]

Eventually each child of God will realize that he is being challenged and refined and led through unforeseen difficulties in order that his faith might be purged of its spurious and hypocritical dross. It is God's way to expose us to attacks from our enemies, both human and demonic, as well as to worldly temptations so that our dependence on him might deepen and our character be refined. God's aim isn't that we might fall, but that we might find his strength ever more adequate and his presence ever more precious. None of this is odd or reserved only for selected saints. Far less is it a punitive reaction to our lack of faith or disobedience. It is the routine chastening that God brings to bear on all whom he loves. To live largely devoid of such discipline is to cast doubt on our spiritual legitimacy as God's children (see Heb. 12:5–11).

And what becomes of that Christian who is not prepared for this, who is promised ease and comfort and consistent triumph? Packer believes that it

> sentences devoted Christians to a treadmill life of hunting each day for nonexistent failures in consecration, in the belief that if only they could find some such failures to confess and forsake they could recover an ex- perience of spiritual infancy which God means them now to leave behind. Thus it not only produces spiritual regression and unreality; it sets them at cross-purposes with their God, who has taken from them the carefree glow of spiritual babyhood, with its huge chuckles and contented passiv- ity, precisely in order that he may lead them into an experience that is more adult and mature.[9]

The bottom line is that such folk suffer from arrested spiritual devel- opment. Their growth in Christ remains forever stunted. They begin to develop a childish and irresponsible vision of life that typically revolves around self rather than the supremacy of Jesus Christ. Thus we learn how God draws us closer to himself. It is not, explains Packer,

> by shielding us from assault by the world, the flesh and the devil, nor by protecting us from burdensome and frustrating circumstances, nor

---

[8] Ibid., 246.
[9] Ibid., 248.

yet by shielding us from troubles created by our own temperament and psychology; but rather by exposing us to all these things, so as to overwhelm us with a sense of our own inadequacy, and to drive us to cling to him more closely.[10]

The Suffering That Sanctifies

The notion of redemptive suffering, or the idea that there is a spiritually positive benefit from suffering that is embraced under the oversight of God's loving discipline of his children, is not widely accepted in some circles today. Yet Packer helps us understand how God utilizes and orchestrates all our suffering as an instrument for the shaping of our character ever more after the image of Christ himself. The pains we endure are never wholly retributive or penal. Our frustrations and disappointments must be embraced as the tools by which God chisels away those dimensions of life and behavior that disfigure the image of Christ in us. All trial and opposition serve God's higher and sovereign purpose of remaking us into what we were created to be. They should not be resented or used as grounds for doubting his goodness. They are nothing less, says Packer, than the true tokens of his wisdom, designed to inculcate Christlike habits of action and reaction, all with a view to the ultimate praise of Christ.

Packer's point is that sanctification entails multiple paths down which God leads us in his loving efforts to change us from what we are by nature and choice into what Jesus is and ever will be. Along the way we will encounter physical and emotional discomfort, distress, frustration, and wounds of a wide variety, all of which are designed

> to activate the supernatural power that is at work in believers (2 Cor. 4:7–11); to replace self-reliance with total trust in the Lord who gives strength (1:8f., 12:9f.); and to carry on his holy work of changing us from what we naturally are into Jesus' moral likeness "with ever-increasing glory" (2 Cor. 3:18).[11]

This is just another way of saying that love, joy, peace, patience, kindness, and so on—the fruit of the Spirit—are ingrained in us most deeply "as we learn to maintain them through experiences of pain and unpleasantness, which in retrospect appear as God's chisel for sculpting our souls."[12]

---

[10] Ibid., 250.
[11] Packer, *Hot Tub Religion*, 80.
[12] Ibid., 81.

Did anyone have opportunity to see this more directly than Joseph in Genesis 37 and 39–46? During his time of undeserved incarceration he was tested and refined and taught to rely wholly upon God and the certainty of his promises. If anyone learned what it means to "wait" on the Lord, it was Joseph, as God used his experience of sustained hardship to teach those spiritual lessons that might otherwise never have been learned. We should not, therefore, be too surprised or offended

> when unexpected and upsetting and discouraging things happen to us now. What do they mean? Simply that God in his wisdom means to make something of us which we have not attained yet, and he is dealing with us accordingly. Perhaps he means to strengthen us in patience, good humor, compassion, humility or meekness, by giving us some extra practice in exercising these graces under especially difficult conditions. Perhaps he has new lessons in self-denial and self-distrust to teach us. Perhaps he wishes to break us of complacency, or unreality, or undetected forms of pride and conceit. Perhaps his purpose is simply to draw us closer to himself in conscious communion with him; for it is often the case, as all the saints know, that fellowship with the Father and the Son is most vivid and sweet, and Christian joy is greatest, even when the cross is heaviest. . . . Or perhaps God is preparing us for forms of service of which at present we have no inkling.[13]

Packer also reminds us that only rarely will we actually see and understand how God's wisdom is sculpting our souls through suffering. More often than not, we will walk in the dark. This is where our faith plays its part. God does not ask or expect us to track with his mysterious providential dealings. He only asks us to trust him enough to yield to whatever he brings our way and to rest in the unchanging promise of his love. The truth is that God is infinitely wiser than we are and has determined that the most effective way to inculcate and sustain humility in our hearts, as he simultaneously instructs us to walk by faith, is to keep hidden from our eyes virtually everything we otherwise might prefer to know about his providential purposes both in our individual lives and in the corporate experience of the church.

Weakness Is the Way

As we explore Packer's theology of suffering in relation to the Christian life, we can do no better than to take note of his comparatively short book *Weak-*

---

[13] Packer, *Knowing God*, 97.

ness Is the Way.[14] This straightforward volume delivers a powerful blow to the rampant triumphalism that has infected much of the Bible-believing world. Using Paul's second epistle to the Corinthians as his principal resource, Packer has once again provided us with both the theological depth and practical wisdom necessary to live in a way that pleases and honors Christ.

The reader should not draw false conclusions from the title. Whereas Packer advocates a form of weakness as the only way in which to live to the glory of God, he does not deny the proper place of being spiritually strong. The subtitle reminds us that it is in and through our weakness that Christ's powerful presence is made known. Packer's decision to take his cues from 2 Corinthians is a wise and helpful one, as it is here that the apostle bares his soul and honestly embraces his own weaknesses. This letter

> exhibits Paul to us at his weakest situationally—consumed with a pastor's anxiety, put under pressure, remorselessly censured, opposed outright and by some given the brush-off, and living in distress because of what he knew, feared, and imagined was being said about him by this rambunctious church at Corinth. We might have expected his sense of weakness in his relationship with the Corinthians to sour him and make him distant and defensive in addressing them. But no, there is no crumpling under criticism, no cooling of pastoral affection; and hope for the future, both here and hereafter, pours out of everything he says at every level.[15]

Thus, such weaknesses, far from a hindrance to successful ministry, are the very means by which the strength and sufficiency of Christ in the life of every believer are made known. Indeed, as Packer notes, "the way of true spiritual strength, leading to real fruitfulness in Christian life and service, is the humble, self-distrustful way of consciously recognized weakness in spiritual things."[16]

But what does Packer mean by "weakness"? He defines it as "a state of inadequacy, or insufficiency, in relation to some standard or ideal to which we desire to conform."[17] In the case of Paul in particular, and even of Christians in general, it means a realistic acknowledgment in facing not only our fundamental human limitations (such as those we encounter in the

---

[14] J. I. Packer, *Weakness Is the Way: Life with Christ Our Strength* (Wheaton, IL: Crossway, 2013).
[15] Ibid., 96.
[16] Ibid., 16.
[17] Ibid., 49.

physical, intellectual, and relational realms of life), but more importantly our sinfulness, our transgressions, and the guilt that these entail. Paul's counsel to the Corinthians (and to us) is that the only proper response is to "look to Christ as your loving Sin-Bearer and living Lord,"[18] to "love Christ, in unending gratitude for his unending love to you,"[19] and to "lean on Christ and rely on him to supply through the Holy Spirit all the strength you need for his service, no matter how weak unhappy circumstances and unfriendly people may be making you feel at present."[20]

Clearly, then, Packer is no advocate of morbid defeatism in Christian living. Drawing directly and deeply from Paul's confession in chapter 12 ("when I am weak, then I am strong," v. 10), he encourages us all to "lean on Christ, the lover of your soul, as Paul did, and in all your ongoing weakness, real as it is, you too will be empowered to cope and will be established in comfort and joy."[21] In other words,

> For all that Paul is writing out of a situation of weakness and, without doubt, a sense of weakness more intense than we meet in any other of his letters, he is not lapsing into self-pity or voicing gloom and doom, but he is expressing his sense of ongoing triumph in Christ in face of all obstacles.[22]

As Packer reads Paul, the latter "demonstrates a sustained recognition that feeling weak in oneself is par for the course in the Christian life and therefore something one may properly boast about and be content with"[23] (on this see especially 2 Cor. 12:6, 9–10). It is here that we need to pay close attention to Packer's insightful conclusion:

> In this, Paul models the discipleship, spiritual maturity, and growth in grace that all believers are called to pursue. When the world tells us, as it does, that everyone has a right to a life that is easy, comfortable, and relatively pain-free, a life that enables us to discover, display, and deploy all the strengths that are latent within us, the world twists the truth right out of shape. That was not the quality of life to which Christ's call led him, nor was it Paul's calling, nor is it what we are called to in the twenty-first

---

[18] Ibid., 50.
[19] Ibid., 51.
[20] Ibid.
[21] Ibid., 52.
[22] Ibid., 99.
[23] Ibid., 53.

century. For all Christians, the likelihood is rather that as our discipleship continues, God will make us increasingly weakness-conscious and
pain-aware, so that we may learn with Paul that when we are conscious
of being weak, then—and only then—may we become truly strong in the
Lord. And should we want it any other way?[24]

In the remainder of this short but superb book, Packer walks us
through 2 Corinthians and demonstrates at every turn how our acknowl-
edged weakness must become the platform for the display of Christ's supreme and all-sufficient power for living. Christ, notes Packer,

> is the source of our strength in weakness and of our hope of heaven.
> He sustains us when our life and well-being are under threat, and his
> redemptive self-giving for us teaches us generosity in financial giving
> to relieve others' needs, one way in which we express our gratitude
> for grace. Such are the aspects of what is sometimes called the all-
> sufficiency of Christ that 2 Corinthians displays. For Paul, the Lord Jesus
> is the controlling center of life in every respect, being both example and
> enabler throughout.[25]

Once again I find myself overwhelmingly grateful for a pastorally informed strategy for living in biblically grounded, Christ-exalting confidence that our weakness, far from serving as an insurmountable obstacle
to genuine Christian growth and triumph, is the very means through which
our risen Lord manifests the energizing and sustaining wonder of his grace
and power.

Overcoming Grief

Yet another dimension to the suffering through which all Christians must
at some point walk is the experience of grief. It isn't something that the
child of God can avoid. If you have ever loved someone deeply, you will experience grief when he or she leaves this life. We have hope of life eternal,
but that does not preempt grieving at such loss. In fact, the pain felt upon
the departure of loved ones from this life will generally mirror the joy we
felt while they remained with us. As much as their presence invigorated
our spirits, the shock of their death will serve to drain and even depress us

---

[24] Ibid., 53–54.
[25] Ibid., 117.

for a considerable period of time. This is especially the case when an illness or death comes without warning.

Packer defines grief as "the inward desolation that follows the losing of something or someone we loved—a child, a relative, an actual or anticipated life partner, a pet, a job, one's home, one's hopes, one's health, or whatever."[26] There is a sense in which grief "is the human system reacting to the pain of loss, and as such it is an inescapable reaction. Our part as Christians is not to forbid grief or to pretend it is not there, but to maintain humility and practice doxology as we live through it."[27]

Packer's observations on this phenomenon not only provide us with practical guidance, but also serve to shine a light into his own heart and the pastoral compassion that characterizes the life of this career academic:

> All our attempts to put grief into words seem to us . . . inadequate. At the very time when grief and our verbalizings of it bring us to tears, we find ourselves feeling that our grief is really too deep for tears and too agonizing for words. As we struggle with the ache of loss, the grip of our grief imposes a kind of relational paralysis. It hurts like hell, we say; perhaps it is a true reflection of hell, where the ache of losing God and all good, including the good of community, will be endless; be that as it may, a most painful part of the pain of grief is the sense that no one, however sympathetic and supportive in intention, can share what we are feeling, and it would be a betrayal of our love for the lost one to pretend otherwise. So we grieve alone, and the agony is unbelievable.[28]

And the agony intensifies precisely when it strikes home that we may never move beyond it. Having entered into the pain, we find it extraordinarily distressing to think that we may never emerge. Will the grieving process ever end? At times, we simply don't know, and the uncertainty can be debilitating. That being said, Packer is right to remind us that grieving was never meant to be a permanent state. Although it is a natural process, it will run its course, and we may justifiably expect to recover from it.

So how does one deal with grief? How does one endure its pain and eventually move beyond its debilitating effects? Packer finds in the experience of the Puritan Richard Baxter (1615–1691) a model for moving for-

---

[26] J. I. Packer, *A Grief Sanctified: Passing through Grief to Peace and Joy* (Wheaton, IL: Crossway, 2002), 11.
[27] Ibid., 12.
[28] Ibid., 160.

ward. Baxter had to deal with the loss of his wife, Margaret (1636–1681), who passed into the Lord's presence at the age of forty-five. In the aftermath of her death he wrote what is known as the *Breviate* (meaning, "short account"), a memoir of her life and their marriage together.

How did Baxter survive, and what lessons does Packer find in his experience and the instruction he left to us? First, Baxter had developed a long-ingrained mental habit of viewing all of life, including death, *sub specie aeternitatis* (from the standpoint or perspective of eternity). He was diligent to see everything in what Packer calls "two-worldly terms, with this world seen as a path of pilgrimage to that world."[29] Baxter also believed "that as he had never deserved God's gift of Margaret during their years of life together, so God's withdrawal of the gift was no more than he deserved for his failures in discipleship and devotion."[30] This "humbling sense that Margaret was always more, and losing her was never more, than he deserved cut off at the root the anger at God for letting the loved one die which is so frequently an element in the grieving of religious people today."[31] Finally, Baxter lived in expectation of his own death very soon. He certainly never expected to face an additional decade in the absence of his beloved wife.

Packer endorses Baxter's approach to how God wishes us to sanctify grief or how we are to turn it for our ultimate good and God's glory. All of life, every activity and emotion, including grief, "must be performed, and all experiences received and responded to, in a way that honors God, benefits others as far as possible, and helps us forward in our knowledge and enjoyment of God here as we travel home to the glory of heaven hereafter."[32] And how is this done? Of what truths must we remind ourselves as we labor to sanctify grief?

Packer, leaning on other Puritans as well as Baxter, mentions three inescapable realities to which we must constantly return. The first is *the truth of God's sovereignty*. We must come to grips with the fact that we, like everyone else, are always in his loving hands and that nothing we face, not even severe bereavement, can occur apart from his overruling will. Second is *the reality of our own mortality*, by which Packer means "that we, like everyone else, are not in this world on a permanent basis and must sooner or later

---

[29] Ibid., 169.
[30] Ibid., 170.
[31] Ibid., 171.
[32] Ibid., 187–88.

leave it for another mode of existence under other conditions."[33] Finally, we must remind ourselves of *"the reality of heaven and hell,*—that we leave this world for one or the other, and that we should use the time God gives us here to ensure that as saved sinners we shall go to heaven, rather than as unsaved sinners go to hell."[34]

And to what exercises of mind and heart (attitudes and actions) should the bereavement experience lead us? Again, Packer points to three: the exercise of *thanksgiving* (for all we valued and enjoyed in the person we've lost); the exercise of *submission to God* (as we resign to his purposes, confessing that we had no claim on the person who is now gone and that we trust God for whatever else the future may hold for us); and the exercise of *patience*, which is a combination of both endurance and hope.

As Packer understands the Puritans, he believes they would counsel us in this way. Of course, he is careful to point out that they never answered the question of how to sanctify grief in precisely the terms he employs, but Packer is confident they would concur. Every pastor, indeed every Christian, should take careful note of his advice in helping others cope and eventually overcome this sad experience.

1. Starting from where you are, do what you can (it may not be much at first) to move toward the thanksgiving, submission, and patience of which we have just heard.
2. Do not let your grief loosen your grip on the goodness and grace of your loving Lord.
3. Cry (for there is nothing biblical or Christian, or indeed human, about the stiff upper lip).
4. Tell God your sadness (several of the psalms, though not written about bereavement, will supply words for the purpose).
5. Pray as you can, and don't try to pray as you can't. (That bit of wisdom is not original to me, nor was it distilled in a grief counseling context, but it is very apropos here.)
6. Avoid well-wishers who think they can cheer you up, but thank God for any who are content to be with you and do things for you without talking at you.
7. Talk to yourself . . . about the loved one you lost.
8. Do not try to hurry your way out of the inner weakness you feel; grieving takes time.

---

[33] Ibid., 188.
[34] Ibid. (emphasis mine).

9. Look to God as thankfully, submissively, and patiently as you can (and he will understand if you have to tell him that you cannot really do this yet).
10. Feel, acknowledge, and face, consciously and from your heart, all the feelings that you find in yourself at present, and the day will come when you find yourself able, consciously and from your heart, to live to God daily in thanksgiving, submission, and patient hope once again.[35]

---

[35] Ibid., 189–90.

CHAPTER II

THE HUB OF CHRISTIAN LIVING

Theocentricity

The sweep of Packer's thought on the nature of Christian living is simply breathtaking. There is hardly a topic of importance he does not cover, or a question he does not ask and seek to answer. Of course, one cannot expect Packer, or anyone else, to write a substantive book on literally all aspects of Christian living. But Packer comes close!

As we approach the end of our exploration of his perspective on the Christian life, it seems prudent to devote a chapter to what appears to be the hub of Christian living as he perceives it. I have in mind the thoroughly theocentric or God-centered perspective that permeates all that Packer says, a perspective, I might add, that he largely gained from having immersed himself in the Puritans from the outset of his own Christian life. We begin with that theme for which Packer is most widely known, the knowledge of God.

The Centrality of Knowing God

"What is the best thing in life," asks Packer, "bringing more joy, delight and contentment than anything else? Knowledge of God."[1] This should come as no surprise to those familiar with Packer. Knowing God is of central

---

[1] J. I. Packer, *Knowing God* (Downers Grove, IL: InterVarsity, 1973), 33.

importance in living a life that is both productive for oneself and pleasing to God. This is simply one expression of the emphasis Packer places on the intellectual grasp of doctrinal truth. One cannot authentically love and enjoy or even obey a God of whom one knows little or nothing, or a God about whom one entertains false and distorted beliefs. Thus a cognitive grasp of the truths about God as revealed in Scripture is the *sine qua non* of all genuine Christian living. Whatever emotional "heat" may be generated in the heart must be the fruit of biblical "light" imparted to the mind. Indeed,

> we are cruel to ourselves if we try to live in this world without knowing about the God whose world it is and who runs it. The world becomes a strange, mad, painful place, and life in it a disappointing and unpleasant business, for those who do not know about God. Disregard the study of God, and you sentence yourself to stumble and blunder through life blindfolded, as it were, with no sense of direction and no understanding of what surrounds you. This way you can waste your life and lose your soul.[2]

This doesn't preclude, sadly, those who may yet wonder, why study God? The person who thinks in this way probably assumes that a study of the nature and attributes of God is impractical and of little help in today's world. Packer counters with the assertion that it is by far the single most practical project in which anyone can engage. He points us to Psalm 139 as but one example. Here

> the psalmist's concern to get knowledge about God was not a theoretical but a practical concern. His supreme desire was to know and enjoy God himself, and he valued knowledge about God simply as a means to this end. He wanted to understand God's truth in order that his heart might respond to it and his life be conformed to it.

Again, "the psalmist was interested in truth and orthodoxy, in biblical teaching and theology, not as ends in themselves, but as means to the further ends of life and godliness."[3]

What, then, does the activity of knowing God involve? Packer directs us to no fewer than four elements. There is, first, the task of listening to

[2] Ibid., 19.
[3] Ibid., 22.

God's Word and being receptive to its teaching as the Holy Spirit sheds light upon each passage. This also entails the willing application of such truth to life in terms of reshaping both what we believe and how we behave. Here again we see that Packer operates with a *functional* view of biblical authority and not merely a theoretical one. The Word is always living and active and transformative when it is read with a receptive heart. A second critical dimension is taking careful note of how God himself is portrayed in Scripture, observing the complexity of his personality and the multifaceted nature of his many (indeed, infinite) attributes. But knowing God must not stop with either of the first two elements. There must follow from them a joyful acceptance of God's commandments and a pursuit, in the grace God himself supplies, of obedience to them. Finally, all this should awaken love for God, a deep and abiding joy in God, and a consequent intimacy of fellowship with God that overflows in worship. How, then, should we express this love for God?

> In a word, by seeking to please him. The best definition of love focuses on the purpose of making the loved one great in all appropriate ways. We cannot, of course, confer greatness on God, but we celebrate his greatness and so exalt him and render him homage by our praise, by our direct obedience, and by always trying to do that which, of all the options open to us, we calculate will please him most. Thus we glorify him. The three notions meld into one: loving God, pleasing God and glorifying God, the composite goal of the Christian's life.[4]

Packer would also contend that one has fallen short in the knowledge of God until such time as the glory of God becomes central in all areas of life and thought. Although this often strikes the unwary Christian as divine selfishness (a blatant contradiction in terms, as Packer will shortly explain), God's ultimate aim in all his dealings with us is his own glory. God "does not exist for our sake, but we for his."[5] As noted, some object to this. Such folk

> are sensitive to the sinfulness of continual self-seeking. They know that the desire to gratify self is at the root of moral weaknesses and shortcomings. They are themselves trying as best they can to face and fight this

---

[4]J. I. Packer and Carolyn Nystrom, *Praying: Finding Our Way through Duty to Delight* (Downers Grove, IL: InterVarsity, 2006), 20.
[5]J. I. Packer, *Hot Tub Religion* (Wheaton, IL: Tyndale House, 1987), 36.

desire. Hence they conclude that for God to be self-centered would be equally wrong.[6]

Is this conclusion valid? No. Here is Packer's response, as noted earlier, in chapter 1:

> If it is right for man to have the glory of God as his goal, can it be wrong for God to have the same goal? If man can have no higher purpose than God's glory, how can God? If it is wrong for man to seek a lesser end than this, it would be wrong for God, too. The reason it cannot be right for man to live for himself, as if he were God, is because he is not God. However, it cannot be wrong for God to seek his own glory, simply because he is God. Those who insist that God should not seek his glory in all things are really asking that he cease to be God. And there is no greater blasphemy than to will God out of existence.[7]

Although we must proceed with caution here, it is surely right to say that the only thing God is bound to do is the very thing he requires of us: to glorify himself. Thus Packer drives home his point by declaring that "the only answer that the Bible gives to questions that begin: 'Why did God . . . ?' is: 'For his own glory.' It was for this that God decreed to create, and for this he willed to permit sin."[8]

There can be no genuine or transformative holiness in life until a person has for his primary and ultimate aim the glory of God alone. This is not optional, as if some who claim to know him in a saving way might choose to move in a different direction, with a different goal or aim. Packer rightly insists that

> every Christian's life-purpose must be to glorify God. This is the believer's official calling. Everything we say and do, all our obedience to God's commands, all our relationships with others, all the use we make of the gifts, talents, and opportunities that God gives us, all our enduring of adverse situations and human hostility, must be so managed as to give God honor and praise for his goodness to those on whom he sets his love (1 Cor. 10:31; cf. Matt. 5:16; Eph. 3:10; Col. 3:17). Equally important is the truth that every Christian's full-time employment must be to

[6] Ibid., 37.
[7] Ibid., 38.
[8] Ibid., 42.

please God. . . . Pleasing God in everything must be our goal (2 Cor. 5:9; Col. 1:10; 1 Thess. 2:4; 4:1).[9]

There is a sense in which this is so foundational to everything Packer has to say about the Christian life that we should have begun this book with it rather than concluding with it. But in either case, the point is made: the chief end of man is to glorify God by enjoying him forever!

The Christian Life Is a Christocentric Life

One element that could easily be subsumed under the previous point is that all genuine Christian living must be Christ-centered. This theme reverberates throughout virtually every page of everything J. I. Packer has written and echoes in nearly every word he has spoken. It is not enough to affirm the existence of "God" or to be theocentric in one's overall perspective. The Christian life is one in which the revelation of God is centered in his Son, Jesus Christ. All true knowledge of God is first and foremost knowledge of Christ. This is surely what Jesus himself had in mind when he declared, "And this is eternal life, that they know you the only true God, and Jesus Christ whom you have sent" (John 17:3). We read again in 1 John 2:23 that "no one who denies the Son has the Father. Whoever confesses the Son has the Father also."

But what precisely does it mean to "know" Christ Jesus? It certainly begins, as we've noted repeatedly, with a solid and extensive grasp of the truths revealed in Scripture about the person and work of Christ. Yet, even non-Christians can study the Bible. Even Satan and his demons possess accurate understanding of the identity of Christ. Thus, at the center of Christian living for Packer is a very real, vital, personal engagement with Jesus himself, not as a distant figure of ancient history but as the living Lord who loves and gives and guides and encounters us in Scripture. I should let him unpack this for us himself:

> More particularly, Christianity (so it is affirmed) is a prolonging and universalizing for all disciples of that one-to-one relationship with Jesus which his first followers enjoyed in Palestine in his earthly ministry. There are, indeed, two differences. First we know more of who and what

---

[9] J. I. Packer, *Concise Theology: A Guide to Historic Christian Beliefs* (Carol Stream, IL: Tyndale House, 1993), 185.

Jesus is than anyone knew before his passion. Secondly, once Jesus is now physically absent from us, our connection with him is not via our physical senses, but through his own inward application of biblical material to mind and heart in a way which is as familiar to believers as it is mysterious to others. But the actual sense of being confronted, claimed, taught, restored, upheld and empowered by the Jesus of the gospels has been the essence of Christian experience over nineteen centuries, just as it is demonstrably of the essence of what New Testament writers knew, promised and expected. To assume, however, that Jesus is alive, universally available, and able to give full attention simultaneously to every disciple everywhere (and this is the biblical and Christian assumption) is, in effect, to declare his divinity.[10]

For Packer, and rightly so, Christian faith means far more than merely acknowledging Jesus's deity. One must also seek out and find a personal relationship with him "in which we receive of his fulness and respond to his love in the devotion of discipleship."[11] What the Christian is claiming is that Jesus Christ,

the risen and enthroned Lord, is, though physically withdrawn from us, none the less "there," indeed "here," by his Spirit, in terms of personal presence for personal encounter. From such encounter (so the claim runs) trust in him, and love and loyalty to him, derive. . . . Fellowship with Jesus is not a metaphor or parable or myth of something else, but is a basic ingredient of distinctively Christian experience.[12]

In the following we find Packer at his best, making the point with unmistakable clarity and force:

Whatever cultural shifts take place around us, whatever socio-political concerns claim our attention, whatever anxieties we may feel about the church as an institution, Jesus Christ crucified, risen, reigning, and now in the power of his atonement, calling, drawing, welcoming, pardoning, renewing, strengthening, preserving, and bringing joy, remains the heart of the Christian message, the focus of Christian

---

[10] J. I. Packer, "Jesus Christ the Lord," in *Celebrating the Saving Work of God*, vol. 1 of *The Collected Shorter Writings of J. I. Packer* (Carlisle, UK: Paternoster, 1998), 26.
[11] Ibid., 27.
[12] Ibid., 35. We must remember, of course, that "though Jesus' *personal* presence is now available through the Holy Spirit to all who call on him everywhere, his *bodily* presence is gone" (J. I. Packer, "The Lamb upon His Throne," in *Celebrating the Saving Work of God*, 63).

worship, and the fountain of Christian life. Other things may change; this does not.[13]

Reading Packer is a wake-up call to anyone who may erroneously conclude that Christianity is little more than a worldview or religious philosophy or a commitment to embrace the ethics of Jesus in daily life. The essence of Christianity is neither a set of beliefs nor a pattern of behavior. It is "the communion here and now with Christianity's living founder, the Mediator, Jesus Christ."[14] And what does Packer mean by the word "communion"? In what sense do men and women on this earth experience that sort of relationship with someone who is in heaven? Says Packer:

> Invisibly present to uphold us as we trust, love, honor and obey him, he supernaturalizes our natural existence, re-making our characters on the model of his own, constantly energizing us to serve and succor others for his sake. When life ends, whether through the coming of our own heartstop day or through his public reappearance to end history with judgment, he will take us to be with him. Then we shall see his face, share his life, do his will, and praise his name, with a joy that will exceed any ecstasy of which we are now capable and that will go on literally forever.[15]

Being a Christian, therefore, is a matter of constantly reaching out to the invisibly present Savior by words and actions that express three things:

> faith in him as the one who secured, and now bestows, forgiveness of our sins, so setting us right with the God who is his Father by essence and becomes ours by adoption; love for him as the one who loved us enough to endure an unimaginably dreadful death in order to save us; and hope in him as the sovereign Lord through whose grace our life here, with all its pains, is experienced as infinitely rich and our life hereafter will be experienced as infinitely richer. It thus appears that Christianity is Christ relationally. Being a Christian is knowing Christ, which is more than just knowing about him. Real faith involves real fellowship.[16]

---

[13] J. I. Packer, "Jesus Christ, the Only Saviour," in *Celebrating the Saving Work of God*, 46.
[14] J. I. Packer, "A Modern View of Jesus," in *Celebrating the Saving Work of God*, 65.
[15] Ibid., 65–66.
[16] Ibid., 66.

Again, Christianity is Christ relationally. If there is a center or hub to all of Packer's thought on the Christian life, it is here. Christian living is living in conscious, joyful, trusting relationship with Jesus of Nazareth.

The Puritans

What an odd place in our narrative to talk about the Puritans! Or so it would seem. But there is good reason for this, insofar as the Puritans were thoroughly theocentric not only in their thinking but also in their approach to Christian living. Packer believes that few in the history of the church more clearly embodied a biblical understanding of a relationship with Christ than did those whose very name provokes scorn and ridicule in the modern world. Who the Puritans were, by name and place, is of less importance to us than what they believed and how they lived. Here is Packer's most helpful summation:

> The Puritanism of history was not the barbarous, sourpuss mentality of time-honored caricature, still less the heretical Manicheism (denial of the goodness and worth of created things and everyday pleasures) with which some scholars have identified it. It was, rather, a holistic renewal movement within English-speaking Protestantism, which aimed to bring all life—personal, ecclesiastical, political, social, commercial; family life, business life, professional life—under the didactic authority and the purging and regenerating power of God in the gospel to the fullest extent possible. This meant praying and campaigning for thorough personal conversion, consecration, repentance, self-knowledge, and self-discipline; for more truth and life in the preaching, worship, fellowship, pastoral care, and disciplinary practices of the churches; for dignity, equity, and high moral standards in society; for philanthropy, generosity, and a good-Samaritan spirit in face of the needs of others; and for the honoring of God in home life through shared prayer and learning of God's truth, maintaining decency, order, and love, and practising "family government" (a Puritan tag phrase) according to the Scriptures.[17]

All that was central to the Puritan practice of piety—whether self-examination, a piercing sense of the Spirit's conviction of our sin, motivation for holiness, self-dedication to the purposes of God, or above all else,

---

[17] J. I. Packer, *A Grief Sanctified: Passing through Grief to Peace and Joy* (Wheaton, IL: Crossway, 2002), 23–24.

perseverance in faith, hope, and love that have the person of Christ as their principal focus—was neither morbid nor self-absorbed, as has often been said, but was simply the inner reality of the Puritan's disciplined devotion.

If asked to identify those from church history who exerted the most formative influence on his theology and piety, Packer would without hesitation point to the Puritans. Several facets of life and thought must be noted in this regard. For example, we have already had occasion to observe the influence of John Owen on Packer's understanding of the Christian's battle with indwelling sin. Soon after his conversion Packer was momentarily captivated by an idealistic vision of consistent victory over the power of sin. Owen brought a healthy dose of realism to Packer's view of Christian living and put him on a path of honest self-suspicion regarding his lingering sinfulness and the importance of "mortification" to which all Christians are called.

The Puritans also taught Packer "to see and feel the transitoriness of this life, to think of it, with all its richness, as essentially the gymnasium and dressing-room where we are prepared for heaven, and to regard readiness to die as the first step in learning to live."[18] In other words,

> the Puritans' awareness that in the midst of life we are in death, just one step from eternity, gave them a deep seriousness, calm yet passionate, with regard to the business of living that Christians in today's opulent, mollycoddled, earth-bound Western world rarely manage to match. . . . For the extraordinary vivacity, even hilarity . . . with which the Puritans lived stemmed directly, I believe, from the unflinching, matter-of-fact realism with which they prepared themselves for death, so as always to be found, as it were, packed up and ready to go.[19]

A consistent thread through Packer's thought on the Christian life is that "all theology is spirituality." By this he means, as did the Puritans, that everything we think and believe about God will shape us either for good or for evil and will govern our relationship with God. Theology is for more than theoretical reflection. It must quicken the conscience and soften the heart. Depending on its degree of fidelity to the inspired Word, theology will either encourage our commitment to faith or harden the heart and

---

[18] J. I. Packer, *A Quest for Godliness: The Puritan Vision of the Christian Life* (Wheaton, IL: Crossway, 1990), 13.
[19] Ibid., 14.

detach us from robust belief. Says Packer, "If it fails to promote humility, it inevitably feeds pride."[20]

An especially vital focus of Puritan life was its holistic reach. The Puritans were diligent to bring everything under the lordship of Christ. "Their living," writes Packer,

> was all of a piece. . . . All awareness, activity, and enjoyment, all "use of the creatures" and development of personal powers and creativity, was integrated in the single purpose of honouring God by appreciating all his gifts and making everything "holiness to the Lord." There was for them no disjunction between sacred and secular; all creation, so far as they were concerned, was sacred, and all activities, of whatever kind, must be sanctified, that is, done to the glory of God.[21]

Insofar as the Puritans believed that God makes his way into the human heart (or will) through the head (or mind), they were consistently given to meditation on the Scriptures.[22] Whatever they could determine was applicable to their lives became the target of their mental attention. One thing they couldn't (and wouldn't) avoid in Scripture was the forthright way in which the dishonesty and deceitfulness of the sinful human heart was portrayed. Packer often uses the term "self-suspicion" to describe their approach to the inner life. Without yielding to morbid introspection, they were constantly on the lookout for "spiritual blind spots and lurking inward evils."[23]

Packer's classic work on the Puritans, *A Quest for Godliness: The Puritan Vision of the Christian Life*, is more than a descriptive historical analysis. With only an occasional exception, Packer's portrait of them is by way of personal endorsement. In other words, unless otherwise noted we are justified in taking the Puritan vision for Christian living as Packer's own. Knowing this to be true, we can learn much of Packer by looking closely at how he describes the Puritan diagnosis of the contemporary Christian soul. But it is more than diagnosis: there is in it a thoroughly biblical prescription for

---

[20] Ibid., 15.
[21] Ibid., 23–24.
[22] "All the Puritans regarded religious feeling and pious emotion without knowledge as worse than useless. Only when the truth was being felt was emotion in any way desirable. When men felt and obeyed the truth they knew, it was the work of the Spirit of God, but when they were swayed by feeling without knowledge, it was a sure sign that the devil was at work, for feeling divorced from knowledge and urgings to action in darkness of mind were both as ruinous to the soul as was knowledge without obedience" (ibid., 70).
[23] Ibid., 24.

spiritual healing. Packer does this by singling out three groups who have gone astray and then asking how the Puritans might be of help to them.

He begins with those he calls *restless experientialists*. Although somewhat lengthy, this statement of Packer's Puritan perspective warrants a close reading:

> Those whom I call restless experientialists are a familiar breed, so much so that observers are sometimes tempted to define evangelicalism in terms of them. Their outlook is one of casual haphazardness and fretful impatience, of grasping after novelties, entertainments, and "highs," and of valuing strong feelings above deep thoughts. They have little taste for solid study, humble self-examination, disciplined meditation, and unspectacular hard work in their callings and their prayers. They conceive the Christian life as one of exciting extraordinary experiences rather than of resolute rational righteousness. They dwell continually on the themes of joy, peace, happiness, satisfaction and rest of soul with no balancing reference to the divine discontent of Romans 7, the fight of faith of Psalm 73, or the "lows" of Psalms 42, 88 and 102. Through their influence the spontaneous jollity of the simple extrovert comes to be equated with healthy Christian living, while saints of less sanguine and more complex temperament get driven almost to distraction because they cannot bubble over in the prescribed manner. In their restlessness these exuberant ones become uncritically credulous, reasoning that the more odd and striking an experience the more divine, supernatural, and spiritual it must be, and they scarcely give the scriptural virtue of steadiness a thought.[24]

These folk have fallen victim to a form of worldliness that is man-centered, anti-rational, and largely individualistic. The result is a religious life that reduces to a thrill-seeking ego trip. Such folk desperately need the mature wisdom the Puritan tradition has bequeathed to us. And what might they say?

> First, the stress on God-centredness as a divine requirement that is central to the discipline of self-denial. Second, the insistence on the primacy of the mind, and on the impossibility of obeying biblical truth that one has not yet understood. Third, the demand for humility, patience, and steadiness at all times, and for an acknowledgment that the Holy Spirit's main ministry is not to give thrills but to create in us Christlike character.

---

[24] Ibid., 30.

Fourth, the recognition that feelings go up and down, and that God frequently tries us by leading us through wastes of emotional flatness. Fifth, the singling out of worship as life's primary activity. Sixth, the stress on our need of regular self-examination by Scripture, in terms set by Psalm 139:23–24. Seventh, the realisation that sanctified suffering bulks large in God's plan for his children's growth in grace.[25]

Packer labels the second group in need of the Puritan perspective as *entrenched intellectualists*. These are professing believers who consistently appear

> as rigid, argumentative . . . champions of God's truth for whom orthodoxy is all. Upholding and defending their own view of that truth, whether Calvinist or Arminian, dispensational or Pentecostal, national church reformist or Free Church separatist, or whatever it might be, is their leading interest, and they invest themselves unstintingly in this task. There is little warmth about them; relationally they are remote; experiences do not mean much to them; winning the battle for mental correctness is their one great purpose. . . . They understand the priority of the intellect well; the trouble is that intellectualism, expressing itself in endless campaigns for their own brand of right thinking, is almost if not quite all that they can offer, for it is almost if not quite all that they have.[26]

What might Puritanism offer as an antidote to this sort of arid intellectualism? Packer directs us to seven short but substantive solutions:

> First, true religion claims the affections as well as the intellect; . . . Second, theological truth is for practice. . . . Third, conceptual knowledge kills if one does not move on from knowing notions to knowing the realities to which they refer—in this case, from knowing about God to a relational acquaintance with God himself. Fourth, faith and repentance, issuing in a life of love and holiness, that is, of gratitude expressed in goodwill and good works, are explicitly called for in the gospel. Fifth, the Spirit is given to lead us into close companionship with others in Christ. Sixth, the discipline of discursive meditation is meant to keep us ardent and adoring in our love affair with God. Seventh, it is ungodly and scandalous to become a firebrand and cause division in the church, and it is ordinarily nothing more reputable

---

[25] Ibid., 31.
[26] Ibid., 31–32.

than spiritual pride in its intellectual form that leads men to create parties and splits.[27]

We come finally to the *disaffected deviationists*, by which Packer has in mind those who used to view themselves as evangelicals,

> but who have become disillusioned about the evangelical point of view and have turned their back on it, feeling that it let them down. Some leave it for intellectual reasons, judging that what was taught them was so simplistic as to stifle their minds and so unrealistic and out of touch with facts as to be really if unintentionally dishonest. Others leave because they were led to expect that as Christians they would enjoy health, wealth, trouble-free circumstances, immunity from relational hurts, betrayals, and failures, and from making mistakes and bad decisions; in short, a flowery bed of ease on which they would be carried happily to heaven— and these great expectations were in due course refuted by events. Hurt and angry, feeling themselves victims of a confidence trick, they now accuse the evangelicalism they knew of having failed and fooled them, and resentfully give it up; it is a mercy if they do not therewith similarly accuse and abandon God himself.[28]

The Puritans would remind them of the mystery of God, that he can never be fully comprehended or placed in our conceptual box, that his dealings are inscrutable. They remind us also of the love of God, as seen in the cross of Calvary. They point to the salvation of God, which began with our new life in Christ and will lead us through this world into eternal glory. They tell us about spiritual conflict with the world, the flesh, and the Devil, and also about the protection of God whereby he overrules and sanctifies the conflict; and about the glory of God, which becomes our privilege to make known by proving his sufficiency in all things and at all times.

Evangelism and the Sovereignty of God

Although some may think that evangelism is a responsibility of only those who bear the spiritual gift by that name, Packer rightly disagrees. To make known in personal witness our faith in Christ and to pray for the

---

[27] Ibid., 32.
[28] Ibid., 32–33.

conversion of those with whom we share are certainly essential to Christian life. We see this most clearly in Packer's now classic work *Evangelism and the Sovereignty of God*.[29]

Before we go any further, it may prove helpful to remind ourselves, from the chapter on divine guidance, precisely what Packer means by divine sovereignty. If I may be allowed to paraphrase, Packer argues that the consistent portrayal of God in Scripture is that he not only created all things out of nothing but also upholds everything in being, such that, were he to withdraw this preserving power that causes all things to cohere, everything would vaporize and vanish. Furthermore, he not only foreknows all things whatsoever that come to pass, but he also planned, decided, and decreed that such things should be. Although science may provide us with observable cause and effect explanations of the multitude of physical phenomena in our world, the Christian knows that the so-called laws of nature are but the expression of the divine will consistently imposed upon the material universe. This sovereign sway also extends to the spiritual realm of human souls, holy angels, and fallen demonic spirits. Quite simply put, there is no place, person, or power that falls outside the parameters of God's sovereign rule.

But Packer will not allow such a truth to detract from the very real and altogether genuine moral accountability of human beings. Whatever we think, say, feel, determine, and ultimately do is truly our own, for which we are responsible and shall give an account to God on the final day. In some way mysterious to all human probing, God is intimately involved in such willing, present to guide and overrule and prompt without thereby undermining the moral integrity of the human will or diminishing each person's accountability to God. This view, typically referred to as *compatibilism*, is at the very heart of Packer's understanding of divine sovereignty and human free moral agency. It is also the key to making sense of how we must eagerly and energetically bear witness to the gospel in evangelistic outreach, all the while trusting that God will accomplish his eternal purpose through us.

Some may be inclined to think that belief in this sort of divine sovereignty is something of an option. Some cherish the truth, while others despise it. But Packer insists that everyone believes in God's sovereignty, at least to some extent. He finds justification for this in the nature of prayer

---

[29] J. I. Packer, *Evangelism and the Sovereignty of God* (Downers Grove, IL: InterVarsity, 1971).

and thanksgiving. How does the fact that all Christians pray reflect a belief in divine sovereignty? His answer is that the recognition of God's sovereignty is the *basis* of all prayer.

> In prayer, you ask for things and give thanks for things. Why? Because you recognize that God is the author and source of all the good that you have had already, and all the good that you hope for in the future. . . . When we are on our knees, we know that it is not we who control the world; it is not in our power, therefore, to supply our needs by our independent efforts; every good thing that we desire for ourselves and for others must be sought from God, and will come, if it comes at all, as a gift from His hands.[30]

The same principle applies to the issue of thanksgiving, especially when it comes to expressing gratitude to God for our conversion. Now why do you say thanks to God for salvation? It is because

> you know in your heart that God was entirely responsible for it. You did not save yourself; He saved you. Your thanksgiving is itself an acknowledgment that your conversion was not your own work, but His work. You do not put it down to chance or accident that you came under Christian influence when you did. You do not put it down to chance or accident that you attended a Christian church, that you heard the Christian gospel, that you had Christian friends and, perhaps, a Christian home, that the Bible fell into your hands, that you saw your need of Christ and came to trust Him as your Saviour. You do not attribute your repenting and believing to your own wisdom, or prudence, or sound judgment, or good sense.[31]

Whereas all genuine believers take blame for their past sins, no one pats himself on the back for having at last been mastered by a persistent Christ. No one would ever dream of parceling out credit for salvation between God and himself. Surely no thinking Christian would suppose that the ultimate and decisive cause of his conversion is his own power of will and choice and not God's effectual grace. Says Packer:

> You have never told God that, while you are grateful for the means and opportunities of grace that He gave you, you realize that you have to thank,

---

[30] Ibid., 11.
[31] Ibid., 12.

not Him, but yourself for the fact that you responded to His call. Your heart revolts at the very thought of talking to God in such terms. In fact, you thank Him no less sincerely for the gift of faith and repentance than for the gift of a Christ to trust and turn to. . . . You give God all the glory for all that your salvation involved, and you know that it would be blasphemy if you refused to thank Him for bringing you to faith. Thus, in the way that you think of your conversion and give thanks for your conversion, you acknowledge the sovereignty of divine grace.[32]

One's belief in the sovereignty of God is also seen in that we ask him to save other souls. We do not ask merely that God would bring them to a point where they can save themselves. Our prayer is that God would graciously act so as to bring sight to their spiritual eyes and decisively save them! We do not pray that God would bring them to a place where they will soften their own hearts and create understanding in their own minds. No, we pray, "God, soften their hearts and give them understanding!" Packer explains:

You ask God to work in them everything necessary for their salvation. You would not dream of making it a point in your prayer that you are not asking God actually to bring them to faith, because you recognize that that is something He cannot do. Nothing of the sort! When you pray for unconverted people, you do so on the assumption that it is in God's power to bring them to faith. . . . In prayer, then (and the Christian is at his sanest and wisest when he prays), you know that it is God who saves men; you know that what makes men turn to God is God's own gracious work of drawing them to Himself; and the content of your prayers is determined by this knowledge.[33]

The sovereignty of God greatly affects not only our responsibility to evangelize but also the method or approach by which we share the gospel. While it is always our task to proclaim salvation, we must never forget that it is God alone who saves. If we considered it our task to actually produce converts to Christ, our methods would eventually turn manipulative, calculating, and sinfully pragmatic. The only relevant question in our minds would be, What method is most effective in securing results, irrespective of whether it in principle is consistent with

---

[32] Ibid., 13.
[33] Ibid., 15.

God's Word and the nature and cause of conversion itself? This isn't to deny that we are seeking conversions when we bear witness to the saving work of Christ. "But the way to tell whether in fact you are evangelizing is not to ask whether conversions are known to have resulted from your witness. It is to ask whether you are faithfully making known the gospel message."[34]

Some protest, arguing that if God is ultimately sovereign over who is saved in response to the gospel, we lose our incentive for preaching. After all, if it is his "will" to save a soul, he will save a soul. But Packer reminds us that the rule or standard of our duty is God's revealed will of precept, not his hidden or secret will of decree. We must not order our lives or pursue our tasks based on what we speculate may or may not be God's ultimate decree regarding any individual. Such knowledge has not been given to us, and it is nothing short of sinful irresponsibility, as well as arrogance, for us to conduct our lives as if we knew what God has chosen not to reveal.

The practical effect of this understanding of divine sovereignty in the sharing of our faith in Jesus is, for Packer, fourfold. First, the sovereignty of God's grace does not affect or in any way diminish the necessity of evangelism. Evangelism is necessary because Scripture teaches that no one can be saved without hearing the gospel and consciously believing it. Second, God's sovereignty in no way undermines the urgency of evangelism. We must never grow slack or indifferent when it comes to the state of lost souls, or think that we can delay our communication to them of the gospel message. Third, God's sovereign grace does not affect the genuineness of the gospel invitation or the sincerity of those who proclaim it. We can sincerely and genuinely promise all mankind that if they will repent and believe the gospel, they will be saved. Finally, God's sovereignty does not affect the moral responsibility of the individual sinner to believe the gospel. Says Packer:

> Whatever we may believe about election, the fact remains that a man who rejects Christ becomes the cause of his own condemnation. Unbelief in the Bible is a guilty thing, and unbelievers cannot excuse themselves on the grounds that they were not elect. The unbeliever was really offered life in the gospel, and could have had it if he would; he, and no-one but

---

[34] Ibid., 41.

he, is responsible for the fact that he rejected it, and must now endure the consequences of rejecting it. [35]

This brief survey was simply designed to highlight the God-centeredness of Packer's overall theological framework. If there is, then, a single biblical passage that summarizes how Packer conceives Christianity and the life to which we are called, it is found in the doxological outburst of the apostle Paul at the close of Romans 11: "For from him and through him and to him are all things. To him be glory forever. Amen" (Rom. 11:36).

---

[35] Ibid., 105.

CHAPTER 12

THE CONCLUSION OF CHRISTIAN LIVING

How to End Well

So when can we quit? Is there a point in the Christian life when we can take our foot off the pedal, throw our lives into neutral, and happily coast into heaven? After all, isn't that what the world counsels? Retire. Relax. Amuse yourself. Indulge in whatever pleasures you were denied in your working years. You're on the shelf, so take it easy. The end is in sight.

At the time of the writing of this concluding chapter, J. I. Packer is still very much alive and active. I hope and pray he still is when the book is published (and for years beyond that as well). He's eighty-eight, increasingly weak in body, but amazingly sharp and clearheaded. Might he not, after such a long and productive ministry, ease up a bit, back off, and patiently wait for either death or the Lord's return? Not on your (Christian) life!

Packer's stated aim, which he hopes will be imitated by all, is to make his remaining years an all-out sprint for the finish line. The call to obedience, fruitfulness, holiness, witness, learning, leading, prayer, and worship is lifelong. It ends only when life does. The body may well suffer progressive deterioration, whether in some form of dementia or organic disease. Energy wanes. Pains increase. The mind is less focused. But the call of Scripture, which Packer now echoes, is to live as fully as possible for God's glory until one's dying breath.

Finishing Our Course with Joy

The timing couldn't have been better. On the day I sat down to write this final chapter, a package arrived in the mail. Crossway had graciously sent me a copy of Packer's most recent (but I hope not last) book, *Finishing Our Course with Joy: Guidance from God for Engaging with Our Aging* (Wheaton, IL: Crossway, 2014). It is a short (106-page) but powerful appeal that we not conform to the self-indulgent and lazy ways of the world that beckon us to the golf course, the beach, the rocking chair, or wherever we might choose to squander our remaining years on earth. Packer's countercultural counsel comes from Psalm 71:5, 9, 14–18:

> You, O Lord, are my hope,
>   my trust, O LORD, from my youth. . . .
> Do not cast me off in the time of old age;
>   forsake me not when my strength is spent. . . .
> But I will hope continually
>   and will praise you yet more and more.
> My mouth will tell of your righteous acts,
>   of your deeds of salvation all the day,
>   for their number is past my knowledge.
> With the mighty deeds of the Lord GOD I will come;
>   I will remind them of your righteousness, yours alone.
> O God, from my youth you have taught me,
>   and I still proclaim your wondrous deeds.
> So even to old age and gray hairs,
>   O God, do not forsake me,
> until I proclaim your might to another generation,
>   your power to all those to come.

To what are we being called in this passage? What is the biblical expectation for all God's people in their latter years, after a lifetime of devoted service and love and pursuit of that holiness without which no man shall see God? Packer's contention is that "so far as our bodily health allows, we should aim to be found running the last lap of our Christian life, as we would say, flat out. The final sprint, so I urge, should be a sprint indeed."[1]

The urgency in this call is partly due to the never-ending onslaught of our enemy, the Devil. Many mistakenly, and dangerously, think that the

---

[1] J. I. Packer, *Finishing Our Course with Joy: Guidance from God for Engaging with Our Aging* (Wheaton, IL: Crossway, 2014), 21–22.

older one gets, the less attention Satan will pay us, turning his insidious efforts instead to the young and inexperienced. No. As Packer rightly notes, "Satan's war against each of us will end only with the end of this present life."[2] And Satan's strategy in this conflict is to persuade us that as we grow older, as "our outer self is wasting away" (2 Cor. 4:16), we should humbly acknowledge that life is "winding down" and so should we. "By moving us to think this way," says Packer, "Satan undermines, diminishes, and deflates our discipleship, reducing us from laborers in Christ's kingdom to sympathetic spectators."[3] Sadly, and all too often, local churches contribute to this mind-set and "behave as though spiritual gifts and ministry skills wither with age. But they don't; what happens, rather, is that they atrophy with disuse."[4]

Anyone who has read this book, or better still has read Packer himself (and I hope if this book accomplishes nothing else, it will spur many to take up his works and read the originals!), will recognize that the Christian life described by Scripture and this latter-day Puritan is the furthest thing imaginable from passivity. It is a race to be run, a fight to be fought, and a war to wage. But there is nothing grim and onerous in such a life, for it is energized by the power of God, permeated by intimacy with the Son, and filled with the joy of the Holy Spirit. Still, it is a life that tempts some to wonder when we might slow down, disengage, and drift. As far as J. I. Packer is concerned, the answer is never, this side of heaven.

Conclusion

So, whether you are young in years and new to the Christian faith, or, like James Innell Packer, older and spiritually ripe, the call to everyone who knows Christ, at every age, is the same: energetically engage, breathlessly run, relentlessly repent, passionately believe, fervently worship, and zealously seek after God and his holiness.

> Therefore, my beloved, as you have always obeyed, so now, not only in my presence but much more in my absence, work out your own salvation with fear and trembling, for it is God who works in you, both to will and to work for his good pleasure. (Phil. 2:12–13)

---

[2] Ibid., 59.
[3] Ibid., 63.
[4] Ibid., 64.

APPENDIX

Additional Exegetical and Theological Evidence for Seeing the Man of Romans 7 as a Christian

In addition to what Packer himself has written, several observations provide even greater support for the notion that Paul has in view the regenerate, born-again Christian in Romans 7.

We begin with the fact that Romans 7:7–25 is not parenthetical to Paul's main argument but is in the context of his discussion of the *Christian* life that covers all of Romans 6–8. If 7:7–25 is Paul's description of the unbeliever's struggle with the law, it "becomes an unnecessary interruption and digression in Paul's train of thought, much more suited to the context of Rom. 2–3 than that of 6–8."[1]

The most natural way to take the "I" in the disputed paragraph is as an autobiographical reference to Paul. The sustained and vivid use of this first person singular is not easily explained any other way (especially when taken in conjunction with the intensely personal cry of v. 24).

In addition, Paul shifts from the *past tense* in verses 7–13 to the *present tense* in verses 14–25. In other words, what sounds like past, non-Christian, testimony in verses 7–13 becomes current, Christian, testimony in verses 14–25. Also, if the struggle in verses 14–25 is Paul's preconversion experience, it would conflict with what he says elsewhere about his life as a Pharisee, especially in Philippians 3:6 and Galatians 1:13ff. Whatever else Romans 7 might be saying,

---

[1] James D. G. Dunn, "Rom. 7,14–25 in the Theology of Paul," in *Theologische Zeitschrift* 31 (September/ October 1975): 260.

there is no hint that Paul, before his conversion, was the victim of such an inward conflict as he describes here [vv. 14–25]; on the contrary, all the evidence is against it. . . . If Paul's conversion was preceded by a period of subconscious incubation, this has left no trace in our surviving records.[2]

Advocates of the view held by Packer also point out that Paul's description of the "I" in Romans 7 is inconsistent with what he says elsewhere of the natural or non-regenerate man. Note what Paul attributes to the man or the "I" of Romans 7:

- "I joyfully concur with the law of God in the inner man" (v. 22).[3]
- The "I" of Romans 7 hates evil and wishes to do good (v. 15).
- He concurs with the law of God, acknowledging it to be good (v. 16).
- According to verse 17, "the apostle identifies his ego, his person, with that determinate will which is in agreement with the law of God, and he appears to dissociate his own self from the sin committed. He distinguishes between his self and the sin that dwells in him and places the responsibility for the sin committed upon the indwelling sin."[4] Is this kind of self-analysis possible for the unregenerate person?
- He acknowledges his innate depravity (v. 18).
- He wants to do good (vv. 18, 21).
- He does not wish to do evil (v. 19).
- He joyfully concurs with the law of God (v. 22; cf. Ps. 119:97).
- He feels imprisoned by and in bondage to his sin (v. 23).
- He confesses his wretchedness (v. 24).

In summary, the man of verses 14–25 does bad things, but he hates them. They violate the prevailing bent of his will to do the good. In his inner man, the deepest and most fundamental seat of his personality, he loves God's law, delights in the good, hates evil and dissociates his will from it. Can this be said of the unregenerate? In the unregenerate there may well be a conflict between mind or conscience and the will. The conscience is convicted of sin and recognizes right from wrong. But the will resists and does not want to do what the conscience says

---

[2] F. F. Bruce, *Paul: Apostle of the Heart Set Free* (Grand Rapids: Eerdmans, 1977), 196.

[3] According to John Murray, "Whatever its precise import, it must refer to that which is most determinative in his personality. In his inmost being, in that which is central in will and affection, he delights in the law of God. This cannot be said of the unregenerate man still under law and in the flesh. It would be totally contrary to Paul's own teaching. 'The mind of the flesh,' he says, 'is enmity against God; for it is not subject to the law of God, neither indeed can it be' (8:7)" (*The Epistle to the Romans* [Grand Rapids: Eerdmans, 1968], 257).

[4] Ibid., 263.

is right. But in verses 14–25 the will of the man in view *does want* to do good.

Along the same line of thought, Paul's description of the man in verses 14–25 *is* consistent with what he elsewhere says of the Christian. According to verse 25b, this man is "serving" the law of God with his mind. Likewise, in Romans 6:18 Christians are those who have become "servants/slaves" to righteousness. All admit that Galatians 5:17 is describing the Christian, and yet the struggle between "flesh" and "Spirit" in that passage is seemingly parallel to the struggle in Romans 7. Would we not say that a struggle as serious as the one in Romans 7 can *only* take place where the Spirit of God is present and active? Otherwise would not an unregenerate person simply acquiesce altogether to the promptings of sin and the flesh?

Another argument in favor of taking the man of Romans 7 as a believer is verse 25b, which says that the struggle persists beyond the declaration of victory found in verse 25a. If verses 14–23 refer to a non-Christian who becomes a Christian in verses 24–25a, why does Paul say that the struggle is still a reality? As James Dunn notes:

> The antithesis between the inward man and the flesh is not overcome and left behind, it continues through and beyond the shout of thanksgiving— as a continuing antithesis between mind and flesh. The "I" is still divided. In other words, the struggle so vividly depicted in 7:14–25 does not end when the Spirit comes; on the contrary, that is when it really begins.[5]

Cranfield agrees:

> Verse 25b is an embarrassment to those who see in v. 24 the cry of an unconverted man or of a Christian living on a low level of Christian life and in v. 25a an indication that the desired deliverance has actually arrived, since, coming after the thanksgiving, it appears to imply that the condition of the speaker after deliverance is just the same as it was before it.[6]

We should also note that although Paul moves smoothly from a description of himself in verses 7–13 to that in verses 14–25, there is a notable difference between the two paragraphs, a difference which seems to demand that in the former he was unregenerate and in the latter regenerate.

---

[5] Dunn, "Rom. 7,14–25 in the Theology of Paul," 263.
[6] C. E. B. Cranfield, *A Critical and Exegetical Commentary on the Epistle to the Romans*, vol. 1, International Critical Commentary (Edinburgh: T&T Clark, 1975), 345.

In verses 7–13 we don't see a struggle. Sin assaulted him and left him for dead. But beginning with verse 14 a war is waged. It is not a consistently victorious fight for Paul, but at least he fights (presumably through the power of the Spirit, as described in Rom. 8:2ff.).

Furthermore, in verse 22 the "inner being" would appear to be a Christian, especially in light of what we see in 2 Corinthians 4:16; Ephesians 3:16; 4:22ff.; and Colossians 3:9ff. Also, is not the "inner being" identical with the "mind" of verses 23 and 25 in Romans 7? Note further the contrast between the man of 7:16, 21–22, 25 and the man of 8:7. The former man confesses the law of God as good, wishes to obey that law, joyfully concurs with it, and serves it with his mind. The unbelieving man, however, as described in 8:7, does not subject his mind to the law of God, being hostile to God and his law, and thus unable to sustain any attitude other than one of enmity.

Observe the intensity of language, the unusually strong feeling that is found in verse 24. If this is not the cry of Paul the believer, even as he writes Romans 7, it would be unduly dramatic and overplayed. To the objection that such a cry is inconsistent with the joy of salvation, Cranfield reminds us:

> The farther men advance in the Christian life, and the more mature their discipleship, the clearer becomes their perception of the heights to which God calls them, and the more painfully sharp their consciousness of the distance between what they ought, and want, to be, and what they are. . . . The man, whose cry this is, is one who, knowing himself to be righteous by faith, desires from the depths of his being to respond to the claims which the gospel makes upon him (cf. v. 22). It is the very clarity of his understanding of the gospel and the very sincerity of his love to God, which make his pain at this continuing sinfulness so sharp. But, be it noted, v. 24, while it is a cry of real and deep anguish, is not at all a cry of despair.[7]

Dunn likewise argues that this "is not the cry of the non-Christian for the freedom of the Christian; rather it is the cry of the Christian for the full freedom of Christ."[8] A. W. Pink has an especially forceful comment on this point:

> This moan, "O wretched man that I am," expresses the normal experience of the Christian, and any Christian who does not so moan is in an

---

[7] Ibid., 366.
[8] Dunn, "Rom. 7,14–25 in the Theology of Paul," 268.

abnormal and unhealthy state spiritually. The man who does not utter this cry daily is either so out of communion with Christ, or so ignorant of the teachings of Scripture, or so deceived about his actual condition, that he knows not the corruptions of his own heart and the abject failure of his own life. . . .

Nor is it only the "back-slidden" Christian, now convicted, who will mourn thus. The one who is truly *in communion* with Christ, will also emit this groan, and emit it daily and hourly. Yea, the closer he draws to Christ, the more will he discover the corruptions of his old nature, and the more earnestly will he long to be delivered from it.[9]

Finally, that Paul should qualify his statement in verse 18 that "nothing good dwells in me" with "that is, in my flesh," seems to indicate that there is more to Paul than "flesh," namely, Spirit. In the unregenerate there is *only* flesh.

---

[9] A. W. Pink, *The Christian in Romans 7*, http://www.pbministries.org/books/pink/Miscellaneous/romans _7.htm. The excerpts come from paragraphs 8 and 10.

A BRIEF, SELECTED BIBLIOGRAPHY OF THE WRITINGS OF J. I. PACKER

J. I. Packer's written productivity is legendary. Even more impressive than the number of his publications is the remarkable extent of the topics he addresses. The biblical and theological scope of his insights and the resultant written contributions are quite simply breathtaking. Don J. Payne's book *The Theology of the Christian Life in J. I. Packer's Thought: Theological Anthropology, Theological Method, and the Doctrine of Sanctification* (Colorado Springs: Paternoster, 2006), lists no fewer than 388 books, journal articles, book reviews, and entries in biblical and theological dictionaries, as well as a staggering array of forewords to other books. I have no intention of reproducing or expanding upon Payne's list, but rather wish to mention the primary resources I used in writing this theology of Packer on the Christian life.

(Note that there are ninety-one theologically substantive and often lengthy articles in the four volumes of Packer's *Collected Shorter Writings*.)

Primary Sources

The following are listed chronologically, according to their original publication dates.

"Fundamentalism" and the Word of God: Some Evangelical Principles. Grand Rapids: Eerdmans, 1958. 191 pp.

Evangelism and the Sovereignty of God. Downers Grove, IL: InterVarsity, 1971. 126 pp.

Knowing God. Downers Grove, IL: InterVarsity, 1973. 316 pp.

Keep in Step with the Spirit. Old Tappan, NJ: Fleming H. Revell, 1984. 301 pp.

Meeting God. Downers Grove, IL: InterVarsity, 1986. 64 pp.

Hot Tub Religion. Wheaton, IL: Tyndale House, 1987. 230 pp.

A Quest for Godliness: The Puritan Vision of the Christian Life. Wheaton, IL: Crossway, 1990. 367 pp.

Rediscovering Holiness. Ann Arbor, MI: Servant, 1992. 276 pp.

Concise Theology: A Guide to Historic Christian Beliefs. Carol Stream, IL: Tyndale House, 1993. 267 pp.

"The Empowered Christian Life." In *The Kingdom and the Power: Are Healing and the Spiritual Gifts Used by Jesus and the Early Church Meant for the Church Today?*, edited by J. I. Packer, Gary S. Greig, and Kevin N. Springer, 207–15. Ventura, CA: Regal, 1993.

Growing in Christ. Wheaton, IL: Crossway, 1994. 288 pp. Crossway has also published this book in three small volumes: *Affirming the Apostle's Creed, Keeping the Ten Commandments,* and *Praying the Lord's Prayer.*

Truth and Power: The Place of Scripture in the Christian Life. Wheaton, IL: Harold Shaw, 1996. 251 pp.

Celebrating the Saving Work of God. Vol. 1 of *The Collected Shorter Writings of J. I. Packer.* Carlisle, UK: Paternoster, 1998. 235 pp.

God Has Spoken: Revelation and the Bible, 3rd ed. Grand Rapids: Baker, 1998. 174 pp.

Serving the People of God. Vol. 2 of *The Collected Shorter Writings of J. I. Packer.* Carlisle, UK: Paternoster, 1998. 392 pp.

Honouring the Written Word of God. Vol. 3 of *The Collected Shorter Writings of J. I. Packer.* Carlisle, UK: Paternoster, 1999. 336 pp.

Honouring the People of God. Vol. 4 of *The Collected Shorter Writings of J. I. Packer.* Carlisle, UK: Paternoster, 1999. 338 pp.

"The 'Wretched Man' Revisited: Another Look at Romans 7:14–25." In *Romans and the People of God: Essays in Honor of Gordon D. Fee on the Occasion of His 65th Birthday,* edited by Sven K. Soderlund and N. T. Wright, 70–81. Grand Rapids: Eerdmans, 1999.

"Why I Walked: Sometimes Loving a Denomination Requires You to Fight." *Christianity Today* (January 1, 2003): 46–50.

"The Atonement in the Life of the Christian." In *The Glory of the Atonement: Biblical, Historical, and Practical Perspectives: Essays in Honor of Roger Nicole,* edited by Charles E. Hill and Frank A. James III, 409–25. Downers Grove, IL: InterVarsity, 2004.

Puritan Portraits: J. I. Packer on Selected Classic Pastors and Pastoral Classics. Fearn Ross-shire, UK: Christian Focus, 2012. 188 pp.

Taking God Seriously: Vital Things We Need to Know. Wheaton, IL: Crossway, 2013. 175 pp.

Weakness Is the Way: Life with Christ Our Strength. Wheaton, IL: Crossway, 2013. 125 pp.

Packer, J. I. "The Lost Interview." By Joel Belz. www.worldmag.org. December 7, 2013.

Finishing Our Course with Joy: Guidance from God for Engaging with Our Aging. Wheaton, IL: Crossway, 2014. 106 pp.

Coauthored Books

Packer, J. I., and Carolyn Nystrom. *Never beyond Hope: How God Touches and Uses Imperfect People.* Downers Grove, IL: InterVarsity, 2000. 178 pp.

Packer, J. I., and Thomas C. Oden. *One Faith: The Evangelical Consensus.* Downers Grove, IL: InterVarsity, 2004. 223 pp.

Packer, J. I., and Carolyn Nystrom. *Praying: Finding Our Way through Duty to Delight.* Downers Grove, IL: InterVarsity, 2006. 319 pp.

Packer, J. I., and Mark Dever. *In My Place Condemned He Stood: Celebrating the Glory of the Atonement.* Wheaton, IL: Crossway, 2007. 188 pp.

Packer, J. I., and Carolyn Nystrom. *Guard Us, Guide Us: Divine Leading in Life's Decisions.* Grand Rapids: Baker, 2008. 270 pp.

Packer, J. I., and Gary A. Parrett. *Grounded in the Gospel: Building Believers the Old-Fashioned Way.* Grand Rapids: Baker, 2010. 238 pp.

Secondary Sources

Lewis, Donald, and Alister McGrath, eds. *Doing Theology for the People of God: Studies in Honor of J. I. Packer.* Downers Grove, IL: InterVarsity, 1996. 280 pp.

McGrath, Alister. *J. I. Packer: A Biography.* Grand Rapids: Baker, 1997. 340 pp.

Payne, Don J. *The Theology of the Christian Life in J. I. Packer's Thought: Theological Anthropology, Theological Method, and the Doctrine of Sanctification.* Colorado Springs: Paternoster, 2006. 321 pp.

George, Timothy, ed. *J. I. Packer and the Evangelical Future: The Impact of His Life and Thought.* Grand Rapids: Baker Academic, 2009. 253 pp.

Ryken, Leland. *J. I. Packer: An Evangelical Life.* Wheaton, IL: Crossway, forthcoming.

GENERAL INDEX

good works, 64, 188
gospel invitation, 193
Graham, Billy, 52
gratititude to God, 191
great tradition, 21
grief, 171–75
Grills, Andrew, 19n12
growth. *See* spiritual growth
guidance, 151–62
Gundry, Robert, 111

habits, 104
happiness, 26
healing, 124, 187
heaven and hell, reality of, 174
higher life, 69, 110
Hoekema, Anthony, 112
holiness, 24, 28, 31, 63–89, 153, 180,
   188
   as communal, 81
   as happy business, 107
Holy Spirit, 121
   empowerment from, 123–24,
      126–27
   and holiness, 75
   indwelling of, 161
   internal witness of, 51, 58–59, 124,
      131
   leading of, 157
   ministry of, 119
   reveals presence of Christ, 129–30
   and sanctification, 132–34
homosexual behavior, 48–49
hope, 174
hot tub image, 25–26
human responsibility, 190, 193
humility, 66, 78, 80–81, 186, 187

image of Christ, 64–65, 132
imitation of God, 64
inaugurated eschatology, 116
individualism, 52, 81–82
indwelling sin, 16, 66, 69–70, 76, 94,
   117–18, 133, 163, 185

intellectualism, 188
introspection, 79–80, 186

Jesus Christ
   crucifixion of, 30–31
   deity of, 15, 59
   presence of, 129
   as substitute, 34
   sufficiency in our weakness, 169
Johnston, Raymond, 17
joy, 26, 106–7, 179

Keswick theology, 15–16, 69–73, 104,
   134
Knowing God (Packer), 119, 136
knowledge of God, 136–37, 150,
   177–81

Langston, Earl, 15
Latimer House, Oxford, 18
law
   and human sin, 113–14
   and love, 65
   as standard, 67
lectio divina, 144–45
legalism, 16, 64, 73, 128, 138
"let go and let God," 72, 93, 94, 95
Lewis, C. S., 13, 15, 138, 145
Lloyd-Jones, Martyn, 17, 18–20, 112
Longenecker, Richard, 112
Lord's Supper, 83, 85, 87–89
love
   for God, 26, 27, 179
   as hallmark of Christian life, 27
   for neighbor, 27
Luther, Martin, 22, 45–46, 50, 110

Manicheism, 184
maturity, 117
McCheyne, Murray, 135
McGrath, Alister, 16, 17, 18, 19
means of grace, 60, 82, 84, 127, 157
meditation, 143–45, 188
miracles, 124

SCRIPTURE INDEX

WISDOM FROM THE PAST
FOR LIFE IN THE PRESENT

Other volumes in the Theologians on the Christian Life series

AUGUSTINE

BAVINCK

BONHOEFFER

CALVIN

EDWARDS

LUTHER

NEWTON

OWEN

SCHAEFFER

WARFIELD

WESLEY

Visit
crossway.org/TOCL
for more
information.